MISSIONARY PRIESTS IN THE HOMELAND

OUR CALL TO RECEIVE

DR. SEBASTIAN MAHFOOD, OP
BISHOP RICHARD HENNING

En Route Books and Media, LLC

St. Louis, MO

✸ENROUTE
Make the time

En Route Books and Media, LLC

5705 Rhodes Avenue

St. Louis, MO 63109

Cover credit: TJ Burdick

Library of Congress Control Number: 2018908474

ISBN-13: 978-1-7325949-0-6

ISBN-10: 1-7325949-0-2

ACKNOWLEDGMENTS

The authors would like to acknowledge all participants in the work of the Parresia Project since its inception, thanks to a generous grant from a Catholic organization in 2009 to strengthen the reception process between missionary priests and seminarians and the U.S. dioceses they were invited to serve and the schools they were invited to attend.

Special thanks goes out to each of the contributing authors and to Christina Pride, an alumna of Holy Apostles College & Seminary, who researched and wrote all of the Country Reports that comprise the third segment of this book.

Visit the project's continued progress online at
https://www.catholicculturemap.org

DEDICATION

To the more than 10,000 missionary priests and seminarians
currently serving in US Dioceses and studying in US Seminaries,
Universities and Theological Schools

TABLE OF CONTENTS

Segment Two: One Missionary's Story

Segment Three: Representative Country Reports

INTRODUCTION

Missionary priests have served in the Catholic Church in North America since the colonial era. They have assisted in the evangelization and pastoral care of the Catholic people with personal sacrifice and witness to the universality of the Catholic faith. In the last fifty years, many Catholic dioceses in the United States have seen a rapid increase in the number of priests arriving from around the world to serve in ministry. Some of these priests came to the US as immigrants with their families and entered formation in the US setting. Others have come directly from seminary formation or ministry in other countries. From every continent but Antarctica, they bring with them a wealth of language and cultural identity. The transition from home culture to ministry in the US context has also presented challenges. Some struggle to be understood in a new language. Others experience loneliness or experience rejection in the new culture. Helping these priests to be better prepared and better welcomed has become an urgent need in the Catholic Church in the United States.

The Parresia Project was a grant-funded project conceived by Dr. Sebastian Mahfood, OP, and Bishop Richard Henning while both served as professors in the major seminary. The name, Parresia, was taken from the Greek New Testament where it is employed to describe the character of early Christian preaching: "open, bold, forthright." The initial idea was to adapt distance learning techniques to cultural orientation efforts for international priests arriving to serve in the US. Over the course of two years of meetings and interviews with those involved in the formation and ongoing formation of clergy it became clear that programs of orientation for arriving priests needed a larger context. The project broadened its approach to consider the preparation of the receiving communities and clergy as we all resources for the international priests themselves.

The Parresia Project hosted several gatherings of those concerned with these questions: clergy personnel directors, ongoing formation directors, seminary formators, and international priests themselves. These conferences considered the pitfalls and opportunities inherent in intercultural encounter, the role of cultural viewpoints in matters such as psychological testing and academic pedagogy, and the stresses placed upon missionary priests in the transition to a new culture. Such stresses were made all the more complex by the fact that the missionary priests were arriving to a setting that was and is itself multicultural.

In providing opportunities to conduct such conversations and explore strategies for improved intercultural understanding, the Parresia Project participated in the USCCB consultation process to revise and update the Guidelines for Receiving International Ministers in the United States (Third Edition, 2014). That document provided a broad approach to the reception process – one that included the concern for the receiving communities and that recommended the use of distance learning techniques. While that document now offers guidance to dioceses and religious communities across the US, it does not conclude the need for continued conversation regarding the power of culture in human communities.

There are ongoing opportunities for grace and new challenges as clergy and people strive to reach across cultural and linguistic boundaries. For example, Dr. Sebastian Mahfood, OP, advanced the work of the USCCB's "Building Intercultural Competencies for Ministers" program in various dioceses and in the programs of study at Holy Apostles College & Seminary in Cromwell, CT. That program trains both priests and laity to help establish the groundwork for a fruitful reception process that offers firm foundations for the ministry of the arriving minister.

This book is intended to contribute to that ongoing conversation. It includes a number of voices, approaches, and resources.

First Segment

The first segment of the book includes eight chapters. In the first chapter entitled "Communion across Culture: The Wisdom of the Sacred Scriptures for the Challenges and Gifts of Cultural Diversity," Bishop Richard Henning discusses the power of the Word of God in its concern for "the stranger and the alien." The Scriptures challenge boundaries between people and offer the grace of encounter and new understanding.

In the second chapter entitled "How Cultural Competence Develops," Dr. Len Sperry defines cultural competence as "the capacity and capability to recognize, respect, and respond with appropriate action to the needs and concerns of individuals from different ethnicities, social classes, genders, generations or religions" and provides a handful of cultural situations from the film *Gran Torino* to illustrate the point.

In the third chapter entitled "International Priests in the United States," Fr. Aniedi Okure draws from a 2006 study with Dean Hoge in addressing the following questions that have remained relevant over the past decade and a half: What ministry are international priests engaged in? Are they here solely to serve immigrant communities? Are they here as a pastoral response to the decreasing number of American-born priests? What is the effectiveness of this response? How are international priests received by the presbyterate and the laity? What are the pastoral implications of this new presence? What current practices need improvement?

In the fourth chapter entitled "Opening the Reception Process: Distance Learning and the International Priest," Bishop Richard Henning and Dr. Sebastian Mahfood, OP, outline practical uses of distance learning technology and techniques in the reception process.

In the fifth chapter entitled "Intercultural Competency and the Priestly Vocation," Fr. Allan Figueroa Deck, author of the "Building Intercultural Competencies for Ministers" project, explains the importance of our focus on intercultural competencies as "one of the more necessary means by which the Church will form priests more capable of fulfilling their magnificent calling."

In the sixth chapter entitled "The 'Missionary Option' *Evangelii Gaudium,* Cultural Competency and Foreign Priests," Paul Turnley, alumnus of Holy Apostles College & Seminary, proposes that the incursion of foreign priests is a blessing from the Holy Spirit as they bring with them the charism of missionary engagement in a Church that seeks to actively embrace the "missionary option."

In the seventh chapter entitled "St. Mary's Seminary's Program in Communication Skills Instruction," Dr. Elizabeth Carrow Woolfolk describes the development by St. Mary's Seminary of an inhouse model program for improving the accent and pronunciation of international seminarians who arrive from countries where English may be spoken as a primary language.

In the eighth chapter entitled "Holy Apostles College and Seminary's English as a Second Language Program," Caitlin Seadale Celella, ESL instructor at Holy Apostles, discusses the development by Holy Apostles College and Seminary of an inhouse English as a Second Language program for international religious sisters, priests, and seminarians from countries where English is not spoken as a primary language.

Second Segment

The second segment of the book is devoted to one missionary priest's story, an excerpt from his memoir *Life and Lessons of a Priest from a Warzone*. Father Robert Obol's, The Life and Lessons from a Warzone: A Memoir of Dr. Robert Nyeko Obol, is a well-told, fast-paced read about a young man from the Acoli tribe of Uganda. Persevering in his priestly vocation as war rages around him, he spends three years in Pajule parish in the Archdiocese of Gulu, Uganda, a country riddled with internecine conflict and bloodshed.

Identified among his motives to write the book, Father Obol desired to "communicate to readers who have not had an actual experience of war in their lives the feeling and nature of what daily life is like in politically unstable and volatile areas." What defines people living in warzones is the daily violence and uncertainty they experience as they come to learn that "the rules and norms that govern human conduct and human relations as we all know them do not apply." Warzones are places where questions of theodicy are framed, but they are also places, as Father Obol points out, where "family, faith, relationships, and the church community...provide meaning and strength" to the lives of the people who endure them.

The book begins in the middle of a gunfight: thirteen-year-old Robert Obol's father flees the compound to avoid capture by armed thugs who had attacked his home in the town of Buda in eastern Uganda. Over the next dozen pages, Father Obol races through his discernment process and seminary career to reach what will be the bulk of his focus in this 210-page biography: his years as a priest serving the people of Pajule while facing the Lord's Resistance Army of Joseph Kony. A significant part of the story is devoted to how

Father Obol survived a direct military attack on his parish, was briefly captured, escaped and nearly captured again.

Obol writes about the constant forgiveness that pours out from people who suffered greatly toward those who are the cause of their suffering. Speaking in terms of peace and reconciliation, Father Obol asks the question: "If a society has gone through so much violence, pain, and suffering, how will it ever put its past behind it and lead a normal life?" He answers by calling upon an Acoli practice in which "society as a whole embarks on a journey of reconciliation and forgiveness to restore harmony among its members through a ritual ceremony." Father Obol thinks this method will work not only because it has proven effective in the past, but also because it is "rooted in the spiritual value systems of the people, which are forgiveness, reconciliation, and love." True justice for the people of Northern Uganda, he writes, "is based on a restorative system of justice in which one comes face to face with the perpetrator of a crime against one, and after going through a cultural ritual process, forgiveness takes place." This process could be a model for how all conflict should be resolved, for it values everyone's humanity.

A number of things about this book are useful to our seminarians, most importantly the opportunity to expand their minds beyond the comparatively calm seminary walls in which they live to a developing understanding of global realities. Father Obol provides a missiological vision that understands the role of Providence in each of our lives and how it moves us to evangelize our worlds, even when we are at our most desperate.

The book also demonstrates a living ecclesiology: the church is shown to be ever present in people's lives, both in their moments of joy and their long hours of suffering. When the diocesan authorities asked Father Obol to abandon his parish after an attack had killed two people in it, he refused to leave. He remained in the war zone precisely because he was convinced that as a shepherd he could not abandon his flock. One also experiences a church that cares for everyone irrespective of faith tradition, a church that is open to engage with the world around her.

We also learn something important about the international priest, about 5,000 of whom are already working as missionaries within the United States. The international priest who comes to serve in a U.S. diocese is often met by his parishioners as a problem—he is difficult to understand, his dietary needs are impossible to grasp and his motive for coming is often suspect—when in fact he is a real treasure who should be valued as a person whose life experience can teach us how to better love the Eucharist, the source and summit of all Christian life.

Third Segment

The third segment of the book contains eight country reports concerning those countries from which the United States draws the greatest number of missionary priests and seminarians, including Colombia, India, Ireland, Mexico, Nigeria, the Philippines, Poland, and Vietnam. Priests and seminarians pour into the United States from these countries, and others, for the singular purpose of evangelizing to us—filling a need we in the United States have for this kind of missionary activity, a need that should humble us.

We tend to receive these priests and seminaries in a somewhat less than humble manner, clumsily tripping over social and cultural taboos without any realization or intention on our part. As a result, these missionary priests and seminaries are often poorly received, poorly engaged, and poorly thanked. Representative of a poor reception include the stories that some would tell. One Polish priest on stepping off his late-night flight after 14 hours on planes and layovers was picked up from the airport by someone whose

American accent was hard for him to understand, driven to the rectory, handed a key, and informed that he was scheduled to offer mass at 6:00 am the next morning. One Ugandan priest on stepping off his flight in a major U.S. city was met at the airport with a letter informing him of the date he was scheduled to return home five years hence. This was actually the norm for that diocese. One Nigerian priest asked us to print his story. It reads in part as follows:

> I got this hate email from someone who didn't like the fact that I preached about the rejection many experience around us and we ourselves have to go through in life. The same rejection I preached about came back to me with the email asking me to return to my home country, Nigeria, and to go preach to the terrorist group (Boko Harram) who are raping and killing women.
>
> So, I was inspired the following weekend to encourage the congregation further, from the hate email I got, that the Gospel of Christ is a message that I cannot in conscience compromise as a priest, even in the face of rejection, persecution, hate and insults.
>
> Bottom line, I will very much stay and not be cajoled into leaving as the hate email desires. Neither would I stop preaching with love, compassion, respect and care the TRUTH of the gospel.

Whether or not the American author of that email intended for his words to be interpreted in the way the priest read them, such is the impression that was received. There are many more stories of our own incompetencies in welcoming and engaging missionary priests (all international priests are missionary priests) on their arrival in our communities and of the ignorance with which we treat them over the course of their ministries. And, again, much of it is unintentional, such as when we prefer an American priest to administer our baptisms, weddings, and funerals because "nobody can understand the new Father," or the result of unchallenged systemic biases. An observant pagan might ask if this is how we treat those who come to show their love for us, what do we have left to offer those who oppose us? So, this is part of the reason for our publication of this book at the start of the third decade of our third millennium, a book that was drafted across the lived experience of the past two decades since the millennium turned.

SEGMENT 1

Some Introductory Articles

Chapter 1

Communion across Culture: The Wisdom of the Sacred Scriptures for the Challenges and Gifts of Cultural Diversity

Bishop Richard Henning

"O Lord, thy Word is a lamp unto my feet and a guide unto my path." (Psalm 119:105)

American society has seen periodic eruptions of controversy and raucous conversation about identity, race, and justice. People are grappling with the question of how to relate to one another in private, work, and public spaces. Even if the conversation may be difficult and sometimes painful, there is a moment of opportunity to try and understand a little more clearly the experience of neighbors and friends. How do we respect the uniqueness of each identity while recognizing the shared dignity of each human being? How do we move from debate to concrete efforts for a more just society? How do we overcome the temptations of mistrust, hatred, and violence and find new hope for solidarity and compassion?

Much of the conversation about these matters has taken place from the perspective of the social sciences. Indeed, the social sciences have contributed much to our understanding of the role of culture in human life and the tools and strategies for moving past cultural conflict to mutual understanding. Even so, these tools of modernity are not the first or last word on the matter. For those who know and revere Sacred Scripture, the questions of inter-cultural conflict and understanding have been a part of the human experience from the beginning. While the social sciences have important tools for the analysis of human conflict, they are weaker in addressing the "why" of the search for mutual understanding and reconciliation. The Scriptures, by contrast, are very focused on the "why" and offer powerful motivation for the hard work of intercultural engagement.

The Sacred Scriptures offer profound wisdom about the limits and the glories of what it means to be human. They reveal God's love for humanity and the summons to participate in that love. In the characters and stories of Holy Scripture, the reader encounters men and women struggling with many of the same temptations and questions - and finds valuable insights for the conversion of the heart.

What follows is a selection of moments from the Scriptures that touch upon the relationship between people or persons and "the other," "the stranger." It is not a comprehensive accounting of all the passages that offer wisdom in this regard. There are always more treasures to be found in reflection upon the Word of God. Nonetheless, may these examples, and the guidance of the Holy

Spirit assist us in reflecting upon God's summons to genuine communion with the Lord and with one another.

Imago Dei

"Then God said: Let us make human beings in our image, after our likeness." (Genesis 1:26)

"When God created human beings, he made them in the likeness of God; he created them male and female." (Genesis 5:1b-2a)

If we are looking at the ways in which the Holy Scriptures help us to relate to the "stranger," "the other," we must first acknowledge that the Bible asserts the fundamental unity of humanity – a unity founded upon relationship with God. As we will see, the Scriptures recognize the diversity of human culture, language, and experience, but never fail to remind us of our universal shared identity made in the *imago dei*, the image and likeness of God.

In the contemporary setting, conversations frequently focus on and use the language of race. The language and concepts of the debate are largely modern phenomena. Early science began applying this language some 300 years ago. Ironically, the origins of this perspective saw a hardening of divisions among people and unjust social hierarchies established on unfounded claims of superiority or inferiority for one "race" or another. Those socially constructed notions have been disproven by contemporary biological research. Biologically speaking, race does not exist. If we consider the differences in human DNA, they are miniscule and concern surface traits. While individuals may have varying characteristics as a result of their genetic inheritance, there is no such thing as racial superiority or inferiority. All human beings are just that – human. Human varieties and the tensions that come with differences of cultural perspective and language are driven by behavior rather than biology.

The Scriptures acknowledge the tensions that arise among human groups, but never understand human diversity and any attendant conflict as driven by biology or DNA, but by familial, tribal, ethnic and cultural differences. This biblical insight is critical. If race were merely a matter of biology, it would reduce the possibility of mutual understanding and solidarity. If it is really a matter of culture and behavior, then human beings have a choice – they can repent of fear, hatred, and division. And from that repentance flows the opportunity to build solidarity and an appreciation of the richness of the human experience.

So even as we consider the question of human diversity, we do so upon a foundational conviction that every human person possesses a profound dignity conferred by the Creator. As children of the One God, the God of Love, people of every race and nation are brothers and sisters called to love as we have been loved.

The Gift of Babel

"Come, let us build ourselves a city and a tower with its top in the sky and so make a name for ourselves..." (Genesis 11:4a)

They were astounded, and in amazement they asked, "Are not all these people who are speaking Galileans? Then how does each of us hear them in his own native language? (Acts 2:7-8)

The first eleven chapters of the Book of Genesis constitute a sort of human "pre-history" before the narrative shifts to the accounts of Abraham and his family. As we saw above, the pre-history begins with creation and that beautiful assertion that human beings are made in the image and likeness of God. By the third chapter, at the outset of the story of the human family, the text reveals a different aspect of human identity – the original sin. Made by love and for love, the first humans fail to trust the Creator and prefer the exercise of their own will. Sin, suffering, and death ensue. The remainder of this first part of Genesis is a tale of human violence and cruelty contrasted with the forbearance and fidelity of the Lord.

The pre-history concludes with the famous tale of Babel. In that account, human beings strive to construct a great tower that will reach the heavens. God punishes their hubris by confusing their language and scattering them. On the surface, this story appears to suggest that the differences in human language are somehow a punishment for human arrogance. In fact, this story is more complex than that.

The chapter is concluding this first section of Genesis by returning to the effects of the Fall introduced at the outset of the human story. This brief chapter points to the truth that human beings continue to desire to be the masters of their own fate – to be gods. The chapter also points to another chilling truth – when some would be gods, others must be slaves. We are told in this chapter that the people all speak one language and that they are yoked to one great task – the tower. On one level, it is the world's first totalitarian state. From this perspective, God's intervention is really a liberation of the people from the false promise of the tower and their slavery to leaders who would lord it over them. This perspective also places the "punishment" in a new light. Creation is characterized by enormous variety. In this moment, the Lord restores the people to their natural diversity. It is more than liberation from slavery to the tower, it is liberation from sameness.

In the Acts of the Apostles, the account of Pentecost in Chapter Two relates the miracle of Pentecost. That account, sometimes called the "reversal of Babel," has a very curious aspect. It does not reverse the existence of multiple human languages – of the variety so characteristic of creation. Rather, the listeners each hear the Apostles speaking in *their own language*. This is not sameness. It is a moment of encounter and communion that preserves the gift of human diversity.

A Chosen People

"I will make of you a great nation, and I will bless you; I will make your name great, so that you will be a blessing. I will bless those who bless you and curse those who curse you. All the families of the earth will find blessing in you." (Genesis 12:2-3)

"There is no partiality with God." (Romans 2:11)

The book of Genesis has a distinct element of tragedy in that it opens with the beauty and wonder of creation marred by the Fall. The human failure to trust God and to pursue our own will results in an alienation between God and man. From that follows the alienation of human beings from one another, from themselves, and from creation itself. Genesis grapples with this tragic development and the sad contrast between the fidelity of God and the continuing and increasing infidelity of humankind.

In the pre-history of humanity found in the first eleven chapters, the situation appears hopeless. In chapter twelve, though, there is a shift in the narrative and the mood. God appears to embark upon a new tactic in the Divine plan to reconcile a rebellious creation – the Lord chooses Abram and establishes a special relationship with him – now Abraham – and his family. This decision to choose one man, one family, one nation for this relationship makes no sense by the standards of the world. This man and his family will never be one of the great empires with wealth and conquering armies. By contrast, Abraham's family will live in a vulnerable state, always on the edge of oblivion – pressed on every side by those very empires. By the logic of love, though, the choice is a wonder to behold. God is love. And love is personal. How could anyone claim that they know love if not by loving at least one other person. We can only love in general by loving in particular. And so the Lord and Creator of the Universe speaks to the heart of one man – a man who returns the gift by his faithfulness. He trusts, leaves behind the familiar, and follows the will of the Lord.

Nonetheless, this particular choice is not the abandonment of the other nations. It is God working from the particular to the universal. For as the Lord promises Abraham – this fragile family so dependent upon the providence of God will be the "blessing to the nations." Here the book of Genesis prophetically and cryptically points us forward to the life and ministry of the Lord Jesus which will at last resolve the unfinished tragedy of Genesis. In that deeply personal relationship between Father and Son, the fidelity of the Father will find its match in the trusting self-gift of the Son and the alienation of creation will find its reconciliation. In that moment too, the gift of the chosen people will expand and multiply that gift to the nations as they too will be drawn into that intimate communion of love. That son of Abraham, Paul, deeply aware of his origins in the chosen people, will come to understand the magnitude of God's plan and the wideness of His mercy. Paul will acclaim that this God shows no favoritism – His grace and His love have always and ever been meant for any and all who would hear His word and respond with trust and love.

A Fearful Enemy

"Now I know that there is no God in all the earth, except in Israel. Please accept a gift from your servant..."(2 Kings 5:15b)

"I tell you, not even in Israel have I found such faith."(Luke 7:9)

Differences in culture, language, and way of life often provoke suspicion, misunderstanding, and hatred among human communities. In cases where communities reach violence or go to war, the fear and division intensifies all the more. For the Israelites, the Arameans were a constant threat – a terrible and feared enemy. You can imagine the confusion and suspicion of the King when the commander of the enemy hoard arrives on his doorstep. Naaman suffered from leprosy and his captive Israelite slave girl had told him of the prophet Elisha. While the king quailed, the prophet spoke with the boldness of one who knows the power of the Living God. Elisha rebuked the king for his fear and commanded the enemy general with authority. The miraculous healing of leprosy that followed brought an even greater surprise – the enemy general who renounced his pagan ways and turned to the worship of the Lord.

In Jesus' day, the Romans were the hated enemy. With their wealth and military might, the Romans had conquered broad swaths of the Mediterranean world. Galilee and Judea suffered under their crushing taxes and brutal enforcement of their rule. It is shocking that the Centurion, a leader from the feared and oppressive enemy, has shown compassion and generosity to the local Jewish community. This same man expresses understanding and faith to Jesus so that the Lord exclaims that his faith exceeds even that of His own people.

It is fascinating that the Sacred Scriptures offer us figures like these two military men and enemies of the people. Their transformation by encounter with God calls into question our own view of the world and the people we might think our enemies. We also see that in God even fearsome enemies become friends for our God is a God of reconciliation and healing.

A Change in Perspective

"The people of Nineveh believed God; they proclaimed a fast and all of them, great and small,- put on sackcloth." (Jonah 3:5)
"What God has made clean, you are not to call profane." (Acts 10:15b)

The Book of the Prophet Jonah presents a very different kind of prophet when compared to the other great prophets of the Old Testament such as Isaiah, Jeremiah, Elijah, and Ezekiel. They were men who responded with courage and fidelity to the call of the Lord even in the face of opposition and persecution. Jonah, by contrast appears a rather hapless prophet who attempts to flee the Lord's command, complains bitterly over mere discomfort, and questions the Lord's judgement when it differs from Jonah's own opinion of matters. This book is so different because it presents the prophet in rather comic terms. It's hard not to laugh when you read this book with its fantastical elements and ironies. Consider that even as Jonah tries to escape his destiny, the great fish spits him out upon the very shore he feared. He is convinced that the evil Ninevites will kill him and yet they sincerely repent at his preaching. When they repent, Jonah does not feel satisfaction that they responded to his prophecy, he complains about God's merciful treatment.

The genius of this little book is that it uses its comedy to shift the perspective of the listener. Nineveh was a great and terrible enemy to Israel – a stand-in for any people that is despised. The chosen people must hear this tale and learn with the hapless Jonah that God has a larger perspective. Even the Ninevites are a part of creation and have a place in His plan. As the listener chuckles at the foolishness of Jonah and his narrow perspective, the grace of the book is that its humor challenges the listener to consider his or her own narrow perspective and see with the broader, compassionate view of the Lord.

In the Gospels and the Acts, Peter the Apostle is not a comic figure. However, he does offer the reader an example of an Apostle whose heart is in the right place while needing to be taught by the Lord. In a number of passages, we see that his desire to follow the Lord contrasts with his stubbornness. He can be too quick to judge. The Lord who sees his heart corrects and guides him. For any reader, Peter becomes a model of one who is flawed but finds transformation by the grace of the Lord. In this, he is a sign of encouragement for any and all who might feel the weight of their flaws before the goodness of the Lord.

In Chapter Ten of Acts, we have one of those moments when Peter requires schooling. By a vision, the Lord prepares Peter for a visit to the household of a Gentile, Cornelius. It is ironic that Peter happened to be staying at the house of a Jewish Tanner – this was an unclean profession and yet Peter seems undisturbed. Yet, he speaks of the "unlawfulness" of associating with a Gentile. The vision rebukes Peter for deciding for placing a boundary that the Lord has already overcome. Peter is changed by the vision and by the visit to the household of Cornelius where he encounters fervent faith and welcomes new believers to the sacrament of baptism. Peter's prior assumptions about who belonged and who was "outside" have been upended and now he relates to the other in a whole new way – the way revealed to him by the Lord Who refuses to place any person "beyond the pale."

These two very different figures, the hapless prophet and the headstrong Apostle must embrace humility. In humble submission to the vision and will of God, new perspectives, and new relationships become possible.

The Whole Story

"You shall not oppress a resident alien; you well know how it feels to be an alien, since you were once aliens yourselves in the land of Egypt."(Exodus 23:9)

Stories are powerful things. They are the most common and most effective means of communicating truth available to us. In addition to being memorable, they allow for a breadth and depth of meaning difficult to offer in other settings. Any parent knows that children will hear a story where they might ignore an explanation. If you wanted to communicate your identity to another, would you offer a catalog of your achievements and opinions, or would you rather tell your "story?"

Human groups typically have stories that establish and build a shared identity. Sometimes such stories are benign, at other times they can be contemptuous of others – ignoring or devaluing them.

The Sacred Scriptures utilize narrative or story throughout. In a sense, the Scriptures tell the story of the people of God in relationship to the Lord. Understandably then, the text is most often focused on Israel's story.

If these narratives are meant to establish and build Israel's identity then there is a very strange aspect of the Biblical narrative. In numerous places the Old Testament requires the people to treat outsiders with justice and compassion. The narrative continuously reminds Israel of its own failings and the parts played in its history by men and women from the outside. It is a history where the Lord protects both Isaac and Ishmael. It is a history where the great liberator Moses is raised among Egyptians and helped in the desert by Midianites. It is a history where Joseph, betrayed by his own brothers, can rise to high office in a foreign land. It is a history where the foreigner Ruth offers one of the more beautiful examples of family and where the Canaanite prostitute Rahab plays a role in the conquest of the land. It is a history where the foreign emperor Cyrus is called to deliver the people from exile. It is a history where Uriah the Hittite is faithful while the great King David behaves faithlessly.

If the Old Testament is the national story, it appears devoid of nationalism. Instead, it does not fear to tell the whole story – a story that acknowledges the place and the value of the "other."

Stranger and alien

"The woman said to Elijah, 'Now indeed I know that you are a man of God, and it is truly the word of the LORD that you speak.'" (1 Kings 17:24)

"She replied and said to him, 'Lord, even the dogs under the table eat the children's scraps.'" (Mark 7:28)

It is curious that the tensest relationships can occur between peoples who live near each other. In some cases, the two groups may even share cultural characteristics. Nevertheless, that very closeness over time may mean rivalry for resources and periods of conflict. Such was the relationship between Israel and Phoenicia which lay to the north of Galilee. The Phoenicians, as part of the Semitic "Sea-Peoples" were linked to the Philistines who caused such grief in the early days of the Israelites.

Perhaps we should be surprised then that the Lord sends the prophet Elijah to Sidon to stay with the Phoenician widow of Zerephath during a drought and famine (1 Kings 17). This woman, already on the cusp of death from famine, shares what little she has with the prophet. Elijah rewards her generosity with a miracle that sustains her and her son through the famine. Later, when her son falls ill, she calls upon the prophet and Elijah heals her dying son.

In the Gospel of Mark (7:24-30), another woman of the region, unnamed but described as "Syrophoenician," approaches Jesus seeking healing for her sick daughter. Jesus' response to her plea is troubling: "it is not right to take the food of the children and throw it to the dogs." At first glance, it appears that Jesus is insulting the woman on account of her identity as a foreigner. A deeper consideration of the encounter suggests something else at work. The passage relates to the prior teaching of Jesus concerning laws of ritual purity – the same laws that should have prevented Him from having anything to do with this woman. His disciples might well have cheered on the Lord's response to the woman. She belongs to a wealthy elite (her daughter is in bed – a sure sign of wealth in that time) who ruled over the Jewish peasants of the region and often called them "dogs," a terrible insult to people who considered dogs unclean animals. The Lord Jesus sees her heart and throws back the very kind of language she might have used on her peasants. Surprisingly, the woman does not defend her status or pride. Instead, she accepts the rebuke and humbles herself. The Lord Jesus heals her daughter and sends the woman home. Perhaps this was the surprise to the disciples – that Jesus would do this act of love and compassion for one who is alien.

These women should have been beyond the interest or compassion of Elijah and Jesus. By Jewish law and by long custom, they were strangers and aliens. But they were never aliens to God and God's compassion flows over them with healing, life restoring power. They are strangers and aliens no more.

Who Is My Neighbor?

"For my house will be called a house of prayer for all peoples." (Isaiah 56:7b)

"But a Samaritan traveler who came upon him was moved with compassion at the sight." (Luke 10:33)

The Scriptures which shaped and guided the Chosen People Israel reminded them repeatedly that the Gentiles too had a place in the plan of the Almighty. The Law demanded that the people treat strangers with justice and with compassion borne of a solidarity founded upon Israel's own experience of suffering and loss. The prophets, and Isaiah in particular, go further in reminding the people of their vocation to be that "blessing to the nations." Isaiah's witness on this account is made all the more powerful by the circumstances of his prophecy at times of threat and conquest by foreign enemies. This prophet who walked with his people in exile prophesies to them of God's plan to welcome the Gentiles at the very heart of Israel – in the worship of the temple. It is difficult to imagine that all of those receiving this message welcomed it. Many must have preferred language of judgement and God's plan to punish those who oppressed them. Yet Isaiah reveals the will of God to them – a will for reconciliation and mercy. This is more than sympathy for others in suffering – in some sense the very lines drawn by people between "us" and "them" are being shifted.

One of the more famous and beloved parables of Jesus is that of the "Good Samaritan" in Luke 10. The Jews and Samaritans of Jesus' day lived in close proximity. The hostility between these neighbors intensified on account of their competing claims to the heritage of the Israelites. When in the context of a question about the greatest commandment, Jesus is asked the question "who is my neighbor?" His answering parable challenges his listener with the tale of a hated rival who proves to be compassionate and righteous. Jesus compellingly reveals God's redrawn boundaries – boundaries that fall before the truth of divine compassion. In fact, this story is also a story about Jesus Himself. To perceive this aspect, we must place ourselves in the place of the man in the road. Human beings, by our rebellion and sin, were rendered strangers and aliens. We were helpless and lost, incapable of saving ourselves. It is the Lord Jesus who stoops to lift us, heal us, deliver us. He chooses us as neighbor and that grace is our salvation. As He has done, He commands us to do: "go and do likewise."

In these brilliant few verses the Lord redefines our hopes and our view of one another. The definition of neighbor here is not founded upon tribe, tribe, nation, or any other human identity marker. This is a summons to compassion and solidarity. Note that this story follows the summary commandment to love God and neighbor. The commandment is not a mere moral principle – it is a summons to restoration to the fullness of our humanity before the Fall. For we were made in love and for love. All the divisions we imagine must fall before this great summons to solidarity.

Conflict

"For all of you who were baptized into Christ have clothed yourselves with Christ. There is neither Jew nor Greek, there is neither slave nor free person, there is not male and female; for you are all one in Christ Jesus. And if you belong to Christ, then you are Abraham's descendant, heirs according to the promise." (Galatians 3:27-29)

The Acts of the Apostles depict an early Christian community which is prayerful, unselfish in sharing resources, and courageous in proclaiming the good news. We also see a new community facing its first major conflict concerning the place of Jewish ritual law in Christian life. In the Gospels, Jesus demonstrates His authority to set aside ritual prescriptions of the Law, especially when those prescriptions keep people from God's mercy. Consider for example, His interactions with lepers, tax collectors, and known sinners. On the other hand, Jesus' own biography indicates His family's observation of Jewish law. After all, He is a circumcised Savior, presented in the Temple with the offering prescribed in the law. It should not surprise us that some early Christians imagined that they should continue such practices and that Gentile converts should likewise be observant as disciples of the Jewish Messiah.

Conflict over the question erupted early on as the number of Gentile converts began to increase dramatically. That increase was due in large part to the work of Paul, the "Apostle to the Gentiles," who became a ferocious advocate of accepting Gentiles into the fold without demanding that they observe Jewish ritual law. While Paul's initial motivation might have been the practical obstacles to conversion raised by these laws, his argument rapidly became theological. Paul had belonged previously to the most zealous branch of the Pharisees, the Shammaites. All Pharisees believed that the long suffering of the Jewish people at the hands of their enemies was the result of the failure of the people to live in fidelity to the covenant. They introduced an innovation in that they called upon all the people to keep the stricter purity code previously required of Priests and Levites only. They believed that if the whole people became holy in this way, God would intervene to fulfill His promises of deliverance. While milder members of the sect attempted to persuade their fellow Jews, the Shammaites were so zealous as to use violence and coercion to require it. They were particularly incensed by Jews who engaged with the hated Gentiles. Here is the motivation behind Paul's (then Saul) persecution of the Church.

After encountering the Lord Jesus, the converted Paul came to understand the sinfulness of his violent ways and devoted himself to this new and renewed life as an Apostle of the Lord. With repentance, prayer, and reflection, Paul comes to understand that reconciliation with God comes not by the strict observance of the priestly code, but by the self-offering of Jesus Christ. Grace becomes his byword and he argues from the Old Testament that the plan of God, now fulfilled in Christ Jesus, is for the reconciliation of all humanity, Jew and Gentile. Rather than Gentiles needing to become Jews to follow Jesus, both Jew and Gentile must now look to relationship with the Lord. Paul challenged his fellow Christian leaders to understand this aspect of the Christ event and put aside their concerns for ritual purity. In some ways, Paul was the ideal man to make and win this argument. As he puts it, he was a "Hebrew of the Hebrews," educated in the Law. At the same time, he had been raised in a Gentile city and he was at ease in the language and the culture of the Greek speaking world. His intercultural competence helped transform that early Christian flock. He no longer used violence, but he was still willing to argue with great passion. His letters certainly give evidence of his passion in these disputes - "O stupid Galatians!" comes to mind. By the power of the Holy Spirit, this unique and determined man charged into that first great conflict and helped the Church understand God's plan for the nations.

This truth of the early Church should reassure us that conflict has been with us from the beginning – even on matters of the most profound importance. We might also want to note the inestimable value of leadership that can speak and understand the language and culture of the other.

Communion of Love

"God is love, and whoever remains in love remains in God and God in him." (1 John 4:16b)

The "why" of the drive for engagement across cultures flows from the truth of God. God is love itself. The Trinity is a communion of love. The Lord Jesus, the "Word made flesh" is the face of the God of love. Even as He reveals the fullness of God to human beings, we see in Him our own origins and highest destiny. He reveals to us also the face of a fully renewed human person.

The Sacred Scriptures grapple with the frequent and varied ways in which humans fail to love. The distrust, suspicions, prejudices, and foolish attempts to define ourselves apart from others are on full display. Alongside those failures, we also see the Lord's invitation to both reverence our differences and find our common humanity. The Scriptures offer the grace of interpersonal encounter to broaden our perspective and deepen our mutual understanding. They reveal the tender care of the Creator for all creation and the desire of the Creator that we should be reconciled to God and to one another. They show the grief and suffering inflicted by hatred and the liberating grace of compassion and solidarity. They teach us that our highest purpose and deepest meaning are found when we open our hearts to Divine Love.

In the particular case of understanding across cultures, the Sacred Scriptures give us the "why" and insights regarding the "how." They teach us to begin with the truth of our shared identity, made in the image and likeness of God. They point to the way in which story is among the best ways to communicate complex truth. They remind us that conflict need not be feared by those who commit to honest dialog. They challenge our view of the world and each other and demand that we "see" and "hear" from the perspective of the Lord. They invite us to see the hard work of understanding as grace and opportunity rather than rule and burden. They reveal that in respecting, understanding, and loving one another we find our truest selves.

"So then you are no longer strangers and sojourners, but you are fellow citizens with the holy ones and members of the household of God."(Ephesians 2:19)

Chapter 2

How Cultural Competence Develops

Len Sperry, M.D., Ph.D., D.Min.

Cultural competency (or intercultural competency) has traditionally been conceptualized in psychology as the development of awareness of the professional's cultural identity and belief systems, and the knowledge and skills necessary to work with diverse populations.[1] In this article, cultural competence is defined as the capacity and capability to recognize, respect and respond with appropriate action to the needs and concerns of individuals from different ethnicities, social classes, genders, generations or religions. It consists of four components: cultural knowledge, cultural awareness, cultural sensitivity and cultural action.[2] This definition emphasizes capacity, capability, appro-

---

[1] D.W. Sue, P. Arrendondo and R. McDavis, "Multicultural Counseling Competencies and Standards: A Call to the Profession," Journal of Counseling & Development, 70 (1992), 477–486.

[2] L. Sperry, "Culture, Personality, Health, and Family Dynamics: Cultural Competence in the Selection of Culturally-Sensitive Treatments," The Family Journal, 18 (2010), 316–320; L. Sperry, "Culturally, Clinically, and Ethically Competent Practice With

priate action, scope and components.

Capacity refers to ability, while capability is the attitude to strive to achieve more than the minimal level of competence. A full range of appropriate actions are emphasized including words, attitudes, decisions, policies and other behaviors that are informed by knowledge, awareness and sensitivity of a given cultural situation. Scope refers to all aspects of culture, including socioeconomic status, and religious and generational differences that are often overshadowed by a focus on ethnic differences. Finally, the definition includes the four components of cultural knowledge, cultural awareness, cultural sensitivity and cultural action.

Of these four, cultural sensitivity is the most critical component of cultural competence because it includes both the capacity for a welcoming attitude and a recognition and appreciation of the likely consequences of cultural actions. In my opinion, the absence of cultural sensitivity significantly limits the theoretical value and practical utility of the traditional conceptualization of cultural competency. However, it is conceptualized, there is some consensus that everyone possesses some level of cultural competence, although that level may range from very low to very high.

Most professionals, including ministry personnel, are concerned about levels of cultural competence and how cultural

---

Individuals and Families Dealing With Medical Conditions," The Family Journal, 19 (2011), 212–216; and L. Sperry, "Inner Life and Cultural Competence," in The Inner Life of Priests, eds. G. McGlone & L. Sperry (Collegeville, MN: Liturgical Press, 2012).

competence can be further developed and increased. It is commonly assumed that higher levels of cultural competence are associated with more effective ministry. This concern was evident in both panelists' remarks and the general discussion during the 2nd Biennial Joint Conference on Intercultural Competency held in June, 2012, in Conshohocken, Pennsylvania. Three themes from those discussions are the focus of this article: respect and tolerance, mutuality, and full-scale cultural sensitivity. Each theme is described and illustrated with a segment from the movie script of Gran Torino starring Clint Eastwood.[3] An analysis of the components and levels of cultural competence is provided for each scene.

Respect and Tolerance. A deep and abiding respect and tolerance for the attitudes, beliefs and behaviors of others is essential to developing higher levels of cultural competence. While it is true that cultural knowledge may be useful in this theme, cultural awareness—particularly awareness of one's own values, worldview and biases—is even more important. Furthermore, in this theme, capability (the 49 How Cultural Competence Develops attitude to strive to achieve more than the minimal level of competence) is as important as capacity for tolerance and respect.

Cultural Situation Number 1:

Let's begin with a situation from *Gran Torino* in which respect

---

[3] Robert Lorenz, Bill Gerber and Clint Eastwood. (2008). Gran Torino. [Motion picture]. United States: Village Roadshow Pictures.

and tolerance are absent in both parties. The scene involves Walt Kowalski, a retired, lower-middle-class Polish widower and Korean War veteran who lives in an ethnically changing neighborhood. He has tried to ignore a Hmong family that moved next door. The other individual is Phong, the grandmother of Sue and Tao and matriarch of the Hmong family. Phong does not speak English and has traditional Hmong values and worldviews. She immigrated to the United States about 20 years ago and has never forgiven U.S. soldiers for the way they treated those in her village in Southeast Asia. Her level of acculturation would be considered low.

Both are sitting on their porches; Walt is reading the newspaper and Phong is knitting. Under his breath he mutters that it used to be a nice neighborhood before the Hmong moved in. Phong looks over at Walt and gives him the "evil eye" and says to herself that he must be too dumb to realize that he is not welcome in the neighborhood and that he should just move out like the rest of the white people. Walt glances at her and spits and she glares back at him and spits a large amount of beetle juice.

The cultural parameters in this situation include ethnic, language and acculturation differences between Walt and Phong. Following are assessments of both Walt's and Phong's levels of cultural competence.

Walt's Cultural Competence. This situation suggests that Walt's level of cultural knowledge, cultural awareness and cultural sensitivity are relatively low. Thus, it is not surprising that his cultural actions are negative, as shown by his racist and prejudicial words along with his sneering and contempt-filled spitting. Overall, his level of cultural competence is very low.

Phong's Cultural Competence. Similarly, an assessment of Phong's cultural competence suggests she has minimal cultural knowledge, cultural awareness or cultural sensitivity. Thus, it is not surprising that her cultural actions are negative, as shown by her prejudicial words, evil eye glance and her contempt-filled spitting, which seems to make her the winner of this interchange.

Commentary on Respect and Tolerance. Respect and tolerance are essentially absent in both parties in this scene. Neither appears to demonstrate any positive or even neutral response, such as ignoring the other. Instead, they both openly demonstrate their negative evaluation of the other, with spitting serving as a marker of their mutual disdain.

Mutuality. Also essential in developing higher levels of cultural competence is the theme of relational mutuality and the willingness to learn from one another. Beyond being civil or even courteous to those who are culturally different, this theme requires that a relationship is developed and nurtured. Mutuality means that the relationship demonstrates some elements of sharing and caring. It also requires that both parties are open to learning and changing as a result of that relationship. When this theme is operative, increased cultural competence is possible.

Cultural Situation Number 2:

In this situation, Walt has just rescued Sue, Phong's granddaughter, and her Caucasian boyfriend from the harassment of an African-American gang. Walt offers to drive her home in his pickup truck. As they are driving Sue asks Walt if he has a "savior complex." He sarcastically comments that if Asian girls were so smart, why was she walking around in a neighborhood that was so unsafe? She agrees that it wasn't very smart and is not ruffled at all by Walt's gruffness and racism as they continue to drive. Walt then asks why she was hanging around with a white boyfriend, when she should be dating one of her own kind, a "Humung." She asks if he means "Hmong" to which he responds by asking who the Hmong are and where they are from. She gives him a brief culture and geography lesson, to which he asks why they are in his neighborhood and not back in Southeast Asia. She recounts how the Hmong had joined the American forces in fighting the Communists in Vietnam, and the aftermath in which the Hmong were killed after the American forces left Vietnam. This led to large numbers of Hmong immigrating to the U.S. Walt then quips about how the cold and snowy weather of the Midwest should have deterred the Hmong immigrants. Sue just laughs at his racist remark. Walt then asks about Sue's brother who appears to be retarded. Sue says that her brother, Tao, is actually quite smart but hasn't found a sense of direction in his life. As she gets out of Walt's truck she adds that Hmong girls find it easier to adjust to American culture than Hmong boys, and that while Hmong girls go to college Hmong boys go to jail.

The cultural parameters in this situation include ethnic, generational and language differences between Walt and Sue.

Walt's Cultural Competence. Walt's cultural competence in this situation is relatively low due to the low levels of cultural knowledge, cultural awareness and cultural sensitivity that he demonstrates in this interchange. Nevertheless, the cultural action of rescuing Sue from being harassed by the gang showed caring and concern despite his racial and stereotyped comments.

Sue's Cultural Competence. Sue's cultural competence in this situation is very high because she displays high levels of cultural knowledge, cultural awareness and cultural sensitivity. Accordingly, her cultural actions and responses suggest she is more amused than offended by Walt's racial remarks and attitude. In contrast to her grandmother, Sue is highly acculturated to lower-middle-class American values and way of life.

Commentary on Respect and Mutuality. What is remarkable about this scene is that despite Walt's lack of basic cultural knowledge, mispronunciations, disrespect and disparaging comments Sue does not take offense by withdrawing or reacting defensively. Instead, she is willing to engage with Walt in a relationship that will eventually become very close and life-giving for both of them. She is an effective teacher of Hmong culture. The reality is that Sue "passes" Walt's "rite of initiation" in which he is disrespectful and provocative. For his part, Walt shows a willingness to learn about Hmong culture and social mores from Sue. This scene shows the beginnings of mutuality, which will result in a relationship of increasing respect, sharing and caring as the story unfolds.

Cultural Situation Number 3:

In this situation, Father Janovich, the associate pastor of the local Catholic church, shows up at Walt's home a few weeks after the funeral for his wife. The two have never formally met, although the priest ministered to Dorothy regularly in the months before she died and preached the homily at her funeral mass.

The priest greets Walt by his first name, to which Walt makes it clear that he is to be addressed as "Mr. Kowalski." Then the priest describes how he had become close to Dorothy, Walt's wife, in the months before her death and that he promised her that he would "keep an extra sharp eye on you." Walt's response was to say he appreciated the priest's kindness toward his wife but asked that he leave. In response the priest says that Dorothy specifically said her wish was for Walt to go to confession. To that Walt responds that he never much liked church and only went because of his wife. He adds that he has no desire to confess to a boy who has just been ordained.

The cultural parameters in this situation involve both generational and socioeconomic differences between Walt and Father Janovich.

Walt's Cultural Competence. Walt's cultural competence is relatively low in this situation because of the low levels of cultural knowledge, cultural awareness and cultural sensitivity that he demonstrates in this interchange. This is especially reflected in his actions, harsh words and lack of hospitality in not inviting the priest inside his home.

Father Janovich's Cultural Competence. Father Janovich's cultural competence in this situation is also low, particularly because of his lack of cultural knowledge and awareness of generational and socioeconomic differences. Even though they both share the same ethnicity, Polish American, the two could not be more different. The priest is likely from an upper-middleclass background with a college education, including a graduate degree and ordination. Walt, by contrast, has a high school diploma, endured heavy combat in Korea, worked for 28 years on the Ford assembly line before retiring, and lived for 40 years in a blue-collar community in which he is the only remaining Caucasian. The sad irony is that the priest has a higher level of cultural competence with regard to the Hmong culture than he does with the elder Polish American. He knows Hmong values and is aware of their needs, economic and social pressures and acculturation issues; he even works with some Hmong gang members in the community.

Commentary on Respect and Mutuality. Father Janovich's assumption that he had permission to call a parishioner—more than twice his age—by his first name in his initial meeting reflects both disrespect and some degree of cultural insensitivity on the part of the priest. On three subsequent occasions with the priest, Walt also objects and demands to be addressed as Mr. Kowalski. Despite that, Father Janovich worked to engage Walt in a mutual relationship. These efforts paid off and both learned from each other and grew as the relationship developed. This mutuality and reciprocity is evidenced in the homily Father Janovich preaches at Walt's funeral, where he reports that "Walt Kowalski said that I didn't know anything about life or death because I was an overeducated, 27-year-old virgin who held the hands of superstitious old women and promised them eternity." The priest added that Walt had no problem calling things the way he saw them. The priest admitted that he knew little about life or death until he got to know Walt.

Full-Scale Cultural Sensitivity. As noted in the introduction to this article, cultural sensitivity is critical to developing high levels of cultural competence. That is because cultural sensitivity builds on cultural knowledge and cultural awareness, and is manifested in both the capacity for a welcoming attitude and a recognition and anticipation of the likely consequences of cultural actions. One might assume that ministers who are naturally empathic and easily demonstrate a welcoming attitude are high in cultural sensitivity. However, this assumption is incorrect unless these ministers also exhibit the second aspect of cultural sensitivity, the capacity for anticipating the likely consequences of cultural actions. Full-scale cultural sensitivity includes both aspects. The reality is that failures in cultural competency often result from failure to anticipate the negative consequences of what appeared, at first, to be appropriate cultural actions.

Cultural Situation Number 4:

In this situation, Walt is faced with his lack of anticipation of the dire consequences of his cultural action. Earlier in the story, when Walt began developing a relationship with his Hmong neighbors, Tao and Sue, a Hmong gang also began to intimidate Tao. When a fight breaks out that spills over onto Walt's property, Walt threatens to kill anyone that messes with Tao. When the gang continues to target Tao, Walt steps in and attacks one of the gang leaders, demanding that they leave Tao alone or deal with Walt directly. The gang's response is to shoot up Tao's house and kidnap Sue, who is beaten and raped. Walt is overcome with grief at the news and staggers across the yard to his house where he slumps into an easy chair and cries. It is the first time in fifty years that Walt has cried. He cries for Tao, Sue, his wife, his kids and himself.

Commentary on Respect, Mutuality and Cultural Sensitivity. Not only has Walt become more respectful and capable of mutually caring relationships, he has been able to demonstrate the first aspect of cultural sensitivity with his welcoming attitude toward Sue, Tao and their extended family. However, he did not demonstrate the second aspect, because he failed to anticipate the inevitable, and disproportionately intense, retaliatory response of the gang.

Cultural Situation Number 5:

The next scene follows immediately afterwards when Father Janovich appears at Walt's home. The front door is partly open and the priest, addressing Walt as Mr. Kowalski, asks if he can come in. Walt invites the priest to enter and sit down across from him. The priest asks if Walt is OK to which Walt nods. The priest comments that the police have left and that, out of fear, the Hmong neighbors were unwilling to identify the perpetrators. Walt suggests that neither Tao nor Sue are going to experience any peace until the gang members are no longer around, until they "go away forever." The priest asks Walt what he means, to which Walt says, "You heard what I said." He adds that he is not afraid of the gang. Walt asks the priest what he would do if he were Walt. The priest replies that he believes Walt would want vengeance. Walt next asks what the priest would do, to which Father Janovich says that he would come over and talk to Walt. He also acknowledges how close Walt has become with his Hmong neighbors. Pleased by this, Walt asks if the priest wants to share a beer, to which the priest says he'd love one. The priest grabs four beers out of the cooler next to the couch, two for each of them. After taking a big swig of Pabst, the priest says that it just isn't fair, to which Walt responds, "Nothing's fair, Father." They sit in silence for a while and the priest asks, "What are you going to do, Mr. Kowalski?" to which Walt responds "Call me Walt." The priest nods and asks what Walt is planning. Walt responds that he is not sure yet, but that "they don't have a goddamned chance."

Commentary on Respect, Mutuality and Cultural Sensitivity. Unlike previous meetings between Walt and Father Janovich, this dialogue exhibits much more respect and mutuality. It is the first time that Walt asks and permits the priest to call him Walt. In response to Walt's first query, the priest says what he imagines Walt will do, which is impulsive action. However, in response to Walt's second query, the priest says he would step back, talk about options and presumably consider the consequences of each. This makes a deep impression on Walt, as his final cultural action attests, when he draws the gang members into an ultimate showdown. Both want justice for Sue and Tao, and both pursue different options, while clearly aware of the consequences. In their respective ways, both Walt and Father Janovich manifest high levels of cultural sensitivity. This results in overall high levels of cultural competence for both.

Conclusion

The overriding assumption is that everyone has some level of cultural competence, although that level may range from very low to very high. The article began with the questions, how does cultural competence develop and how can it be increased? These questions can be answered with the following three-theme formula:

Respect and tolerance +

mutuality and a willingness to learn from one another +

full-scale cultural sensitivity =

cultural competence.

What the narrative suggests is that all three themes are essential to developing and increasing cultural competence. If even one theme is missing or weak, the level of cultural competence will be lower than if all three themes are present, strong and vibrant.

Chapter 3

International Priests in the United States

Rev. Aniedi Okure, O.P.

INTRODUCTION[4]

In 2004, the National Federation of Priests' Councils (NFPC) and the Office for Priestly Life and Ministry (PLM) of the United States Conference of Catholic Bishops (USCCB) commissioned a study to examine the increasing number of priests born abroad and now ministering in the United States and the implication for the

---

[4] This study was presented as a report to a combined meeting of the United States Conference of Catholic Bishops' committees for Clergy Consecrated Life and Vocations, Cultural Diversity in the Church, and Child and Youth Protection during the June 2011 meeting of the United States Conference of Catholic Bishops (USCCB) in Seattle. This study has been updated for inclusion into the present volume.

Church in the United States. The study, published in 2006,[5] addressed a number of questions: What ministry are international priests engaged in? Are they here solely to serve immigrant communities? Are they here as a pastoral response to the decreasing number of American-born priests? What is the effectiveness of this response? How are international priests received by the presbyterate and the laity? What are the pastoral implications of this new presence? What current practices need improvement? This article summarizes the results of the study.

PARTICIPANTS IN THE STUDY

The study included a broad range of people across dioceses, both lay and ordained, including clergy born in the United States and clergy from other countries currently working in the United States. Specifically, the study included U.S.-born bishops, vicars for clergy, pastors, diocesan officials, lay pastoral workers, and a stratified random sample of more than one thousand international priests from Africa, Asia, Europe, and Latin America – including Brazil and the Caribbean.

The study also gathered information from three focus groups of international priests. The first focus group was drawn from the Washington D.C. metropolitan area – namely, the Archdioceses of Washington and Baltimore and the Diocese of Arlington. The second focus group included priests from several dioceses in Texas

---

[5] Dean R. Hoge & Aniedi Okure, *International Priests in America: Challenges and Opportunities* (Collegeville, MN: Liturgical Press, 2006).

gathered in San Antonio at the Oblate School of Theology for a cultural orientation program. The third focus group was comprised of priests serving in the San Diego metropolitan area. The study limited its input from international priests to those who arrived in the United States in 1985 or thereafter.

THE UNITED STATES IN HISTORICAL AND GLOBAL CONTEXT

To provide a context for understanding the present situation, the study examined the history of priests in the United States from the 1800s to 2004, the ratio of priests per laity from 1900 to 2004, and the origins of international priests from 1985 and thereafter. It also examined the worldwide ratio of laity to priests and the increase or decrease of seminarians worldwide. The study found that earlier international priests came from Europe. Initially, Spanish priests came with Columbus. Before 1830, most priests were French. From 1830 to 1985, arriving priests were mainly Irish. From 1985, international priests came predominately from Africa, Asia, and Latin America, reflecting also the demographic composition of the new arrivals in the United States.

The study found that at the turn of the twentieth century there were about 1,000 laypeople per priest in the United States. The Church in the United States experienced a boom of priests in the 1940s and 1950s, such that there were 614 laypeople for every priest. These two decades enjoyed the lowest number of laypeople per priest. After these boom decades, the number of laypeople per priest began to rise, beginning in the 1960s. By the year 2000, there were 1,313 laypeople for every priest, double the ratio of the 1940s (see Table 1). The presbyterate experienced a more than 50% drop in the numbers of priests between the highpoint in 1980 (58,398) and 2012 (27,594).

The new wave of international priests in the United States beginning in the mid-1980s has not reversed the overall downward trend in the ratio of priests to laity. In 1980, although the number of priests was 58,398—much higher than the 1940s and 1950s—the number of laypeople per priest continued to rise to 856 laypeople per priest. By 2004, there were 1,478 laypeople for every priest. This shows an increase of 2.4 times the number of laypeople per priest over the boom decades, that is, a 71% increase of laypeople per priest compared to the 1940s.

The number of laypeople per priest doubled between 1980 and 2009, rising from 856 to 1,680, and more than tripled since the boom decades of the 1940s and 1950s. While the laity per priest ratio in the United States is relatively low compared to most countries, the reality of ecclesial arrangements and neighborhood parishes in the United States, especially in metropolitan areas, makes this change an acute one, and the "priest shortage" from that standpoint is a harsh reality. Despite parish mergers, closings, and clustering, American Catholics who were accustomed to priests' availability in the 1980s have experienced a sharp decrease in the number of priests who are available to celebrate the sacraments.

Official ecclesiastical statistics confirm this. Data from the USCCB website and from the *Official Catholic Directory* showed

40,788 priests in 2009,[6] a decrease of 17,610 from 1980 or a decline of 31%. In the same period, the number of Catholics rose from 48 million to 68 million, an increase of 20 million or 41%. The dual trend of increasing numbers of Catholics and decreasing numbers of priests continued in 2011.[7] Of the 36,128 priest listed in the 2011 *Official Catholic Directory*, 7,851 are classified as "retired, sick or absent," leaving 28,277 in active duty. The downward trend continues. Data from the 2012 OCD show a total of 35,460 priests of which 7,868 are classified as retired, sick or absent, leaving 27,594 in active service or one priest for 2,815 Catholics. Projections that take into account the age of American priests and the enrollment of seminarians indicate that the trend will definitely continue into the near future.

The figures for 2009–2012 on which calculations were generally based include significant numbers of priests who are retired and who are classified as "sick or absent" by their dioceses. The "sick or absent" are excluded from pastoral ministry, making the overall figure of active priests much less. The percentage of diocesan priests in this category varies from 8% to as much as 38% of the total priests in the diocese. Collectively, of the total number of priests in the United States listed as retired and "sick or absent" constituted 25% of the presbyterate in 2009, 21.4% in 2010, 21.7% in 2011 and 22.2% in 2012.

Additionally, some priests in the active workforce have other

---

[6] See *The Official Catholic Directory, Anno Domini 2009* (Berkeley Heights NJ: P. J. Kenedy & Sons 2009).

[7] *Id.*

full time assignments and can only provide part-time pastoral ministry. When all these factors are taken into consideration, the number of laypeople per priest is much higher than commonly supposed (see Table 1).

DATA ON INTERNATIONAL PRIESTS

Data collected from dioceses indicates that about 25% of priests in active service (8,500) in the United States were born outside of the country. About 300 new international priests are added to the American presbyterate each year, 80% of whom are diocesan. Of these, 30% received part of their seminary training in the United States. They are located mainly in the Pacific states, the Southwest, the South, the New York metropolitan area, and dioceses on the Atlantic coast of the United States. They come predominately from India, the Philippines, Vietnam, Nigeria, Mexico, Colombia, and Poland.[8]

ORIGINS OF INTERNATIONAL PRIESTS 2010

In 2010, most international priests came from Africa, Asia, and Latin America. European priests came mostly from Poland. About 300 continue to arrive every year. Compared to their American-born counterparts, foreign-born priests are much younger. They are located mostly along the eastern and western coasts of the United States and in dioceses in major metropolitan areas.

---

[8] See Segment 3 below for country reports relating to these.

Thirteen dioceses have more than one hundred priests who were born abroad: New York, Los Angeles, Newark, Galveston-Houston, the Archdiocese for Military Service, San Antonio, San José, Sacramento, San Bernardino, Atlanta, Orlando, Chicago, and Rockville Center. New York City and Los Angeles boast the largest numbers of international priests, 319 and 250 respectively. Not all are recent arrivals. Many have been here for some time and have naturalized as United States citizens. A majority of the more recent arrivals, especially those from Africa, Asia, and Latin America, feel that they are not fully accepted as equal partners in ministry. Some feel that their American counterparts do not trust them.

The average age of international priests in active ministry is 46, comparatively younger than the average age of U.S.-born priests.[9] Among the international priests are full-time students (11% diocesan, 16% religious) who provide pastoral services on a limited basis. The majority are full-time ministers who expect to be in the United States for a much longer period (73% diocesan and 77% religious). Some have naturalized as U.S. citizens (37% diocesan and 31% religious) and are incardinated into dioceses within the country.

---

[9] According to a 2009 CARA survey, one-third of American priests in active ministry are sixty-five years of age or older. One-third of the presently active priests will be retired or on limited service in ten years. The results of this survey are presented in Mary Gautier, Paul Perl, & Stephen Fichter, *Same Call, Different Men: The Evolution of the Priesthood Since Vatican II* (Collegeville, MN: Liturgical Press, 2012).

AMERICAN CATHOLICS' VIEWS OF INTERNATIONAL PRIESTS

A 2009 survey of the Center for Applied Research in the Apostolate (CARA) at Georgetown University indicates that about 34% of American Catholics have experienced international priests in their parishes. The responses to their presence vary. Some are wary of the practice of bringing international priests to serve in parishes. Others advocate bringing more international priests to fill the pastoral needs of the local church and to make up for the declining number of local vocations to the priesthood. Still there are others who are eager to see the diversity in American society reflected in the Catholic presbyterate. The CARA survey indicates that 53% of American Catholics say they are very satisfied with international priests, and about 34% say they are somewhat satisfied.

Those For More International Priests

American Catholics who favor bringing more international priests into the United States say that we need them to serve the growing immigrant populations in our parishes and to fill the gap opened by our shortage of priests. Many say that international priests help universalize the church and that the presence of international priests is a practical expression of our Catholicity.

In 2011, more voices from the pews echoed these sentiments, especially in culturally diverse communities and communities with recent immigrant populations. Catholics wanted to see the demographic diversity in the broader American society and the increasing diversity of faces in the parishes reflected in the Catholic presbyterate. Some indicated that even if the international priests do not minister directly in their parish communities, seeing these priests as part of the presbyterate in the United States makes them feel at home in the Catholic Church.

Those Against More International Priests

Those who oppose an increased presence of foreign priests in the United States point to language problems, cultural misunderstandings, and differences in ecclesiology.[10] They consider bringing foreign priests into the United States to be an irrational deployment of priests, a postponement of the restructuring of ecclesiastical leadership, and a limitation on lay involvement in such leadership. Others think that the presence of international priests hinders efforts to recruit local vocations, implying that augmenting the American presbyterate with international priests makes American-born Catholics lazy in promoting vocations to the priesthood.

While some feel that the presence of international priests delays the ascension of the laity in leadership roles within the local church, there is evidence to the contrary. The number of international priests added to the presbyterate between 1985 and 2010 is less than half the overall decline in the number of priests during that period, so the need for lay leadership has continued to

---

[10] These three problems—language, culture, and ecclesiology—were held against European priests 100 years earlier.

grow despite the arrival of international priests. More than ever, a growing number of women religious, deacons, and laypersons serve in ecclesiastical leadership across dioceses of the United States. They hold such positions as parish administrators, officers of ecclesiastical tribunals, and diocesan chancellors. Ruth Wallace has documented the rising trend of the laity who serve as parish administrators.[11] The number of laity in leadership positions within the church in the United States has risen regardless of the presence of priests from overseas.

According to a 2010 CARA survey, the number of laypeople (catechists, women religious, members of secular institutes, and lay missionaries) and deacons providing pastoral care increased from 3.2 million in 1998 to 3.8 million in 2002 to about 4.5 million in 2009. At the same time, the survey indicates that 56% of American Catholics prefer the presence of a priest in their local churches, given the sacramental orientation of Catholics. Forty-seven percent are comfortable with laypersons leading their local church communities.[12]

The role of international priests can be limited by the growth of lay leadership within the dioceses of the United States. With laity running parishes, international priests are often seen merely as dispensers of the sacraments. They serve as parochial vicars and

---

[11] Ruth Wallace, *They Call Her Pastor: A New Role for Catholic Women* (Albany, NY: State University of New York Press, 1992); *They Call Him Pastor: Married Men in Charge of Catholic Parishes* (Mahwah, NJ: Paulist Press, 2003).

[12] Gautier, Perl, & Fichter, *Same Call, Different Men.*

chaplains in hospitals, retirement communities and nursing homes. Few international priests are pastors.

EXPERIENCES OF INTERNATIONAL PRIESTS

International priests are generally appreciative of the opportunity to minister in a different country. Nonetheless, many feel that they are not treated fairly in placements and appointments and that they are not well appreciated. There is a general feeling that they are seen as second-class priests and that they are not fully accepted as equals by brother priests born in the United States. Some international priests feel that they are often made into scapegoats for whatever goes wrong in dioceses. Three main issues affect international priests deeply: (1) loneliness and isolation; (2) lack of acceptance, especially among other priests; and (3) lack of proper orientation.

Loneliness and Isolation

In February of 2010, Cardinal Roger Mahony called upon priests to cultivate "affective priestly fraternity." He emphasized that fraternity does not just happen; fraternity must be cultivated, among other means, through praying together and sharing meals. He noted that cultivating a habit of fraternity leads priests to see themselves as collaborators. The cardinal cautioned that a "creeping isolation" among priests poses a danger not only to the presbyterate, but also to the pastoral life of the church, since "no priest thrives spiritually or pastorally in isolation."[13] The "creeping isolation" observed by the cardinal among the general presbyterate, and confirmed by a CARA survey about the lack of genuine closeness among American priests, is exacerbated among international priests.[14]

There is an urgent need to address this issue. Many international priests feel they are alone in their ministry and disconnected from co-workers within the church. They feel that they are seen as religious contractors whose pastoral expertise is needed within the church but who are not welcomed as persons or as leaders. One international priest expressed this feeling as follows: "Our pastoral expertise is needed within the church but we are not invited to hang around."

Acceptance Issues

In addition to the challenges facing the general presbyterate, international priests struggle with issues of acceptance and acculturation in their new cultural and ecclesial environments, along with the trials of being far away from home. International

---

[13] Cardinal Roger Mahoney, "Affective Priestly Fraternity," *Origins* 39, no. 37 (25 Feb. 2010).

[14] The CARA survey shows that 70% of American priests believe, "what is lacking is that closeness among priests." Mary L. Gautier, "Emerging Trends in Priestly Life and Ministry: Findings from 40 Years of Research," a talk delivered at the NFPC Annual Priests' Conference (Albuquerque, NM, 2-5 May 2011). *See* Gautier, Perl, & Fichter, *Same Call, Different Men.*

priests feel they are not treated fairly and that their U.S.-born brother priests do not accept them as part of the local community or as equals. The issue of acceptance runs deep among many international priests. The issue is captured in some of the quotes that follow. "The attitude is that when they see you they think 'here comes one of them' and they ask you 'When did you come?' 'How long are you going to stay?' 'Are you going to go back?'" Another puts it this way: "When you come, it is like they are torn between seeing the necessity of your presence and the needs of the ministry here, and the fact that you are an intruder. They give you the idea that this is just by-the-way, and you are not going to be accepted on a permanent basis." One international priest in hospital chaplaincy observed: "The [c]hurch here does not welcome us fully, yet the most difficult part of ministry is usually pushed to us, like hospital chaplaincy where you have to carry the pager day and night even on holidays. The American-born priests in general do not like this kind of ministry yet they do not show appreciation for those of us who do it." While these may seem like sweeping generalizations, the feelings run deep, and many international priests express similar sentiments.

Another international priest noted: "Sometimes it feels as if there is a huge difference in the practice of Catholicism. I mean the attitude of the people and how it affects your spirit. We preach one church, one family yet the way you are treated tells you that the oneness does not include you." One priest expressed sorrow at being seen first and foremost as a foreigner rather than as a priest and member of the church he serves: "Many people see you as foreign no matter what, even if you are naturalized. They see the part of the world you come from rather than the fact that you are a priest of the Catholic Church. They equate the poverty of your country of origin with intellectual poverty and then you have to prove yourself." In the same vein, another priest observed: "The attitude of American superiority and constant questioning to validate your authenticity makes one doubt the universality of the Catholic faith. There is so much of having to prove yourself here and your validity as an ordained priest." Some international priests believe that Americans perceive their training, which took place abroad, as somewhat deficient. This perception might come from the fact that some international priests are technologically less savvy or lack the mastery of American-style parish administration.

International priests in special ministry, especially hospital chaplaincy, feel that they are made scapegoats by American Catholics for whatever is going wrong in the church and whatever they may consider to be unreasonable rules in parishes. One priest observed that, "the issues they (American Catholics) talk about took place before I came to the United States, not to mention that I was not even born at the time. Yet they blame me for it." One hospital chaplain reflected: "Those of us in hospital ministry attending to the sick and dying seem to bear the brunt of the misdeeds of pastors in their parishes. We seem to do the dirty job which I don't mind but I need to be appreciated." International priests feel strongly that fellow Catholics born in the United States are quick to publicize their shortcomings but slow to show appreciation for their ministry.

Orientation to American Society and the Church

The issue of orientation continues to challenge dioceses that invite the services of international priests. Many international priests indicate that they were not given adequate orientation, not shown how to "work the ropes," and not provided with time to adjust to life in the United States. Many indicate that they could have avoided one or another faux pas, "if someone told me about it." Some dioceses have adopted and used the USCCB's *Guidelines for Receiving Pastoral Ministers in the United States.*[15] But much remains to be done. The need to administer sacraments to the faithful often trumps the need for structured orientation and acculturation of international priests. Furthermore, dioceses incur financial costs for structured orientation. Yet the great benefit to international priests, their host pastors, and parishioners has proven that it is money well spent.

Orientation is vital to equip the newly arrived international priest with essential practical skills for living in the United States, including legal and civic requirements, getting a social security number, and cultural "dos" and "don'ts." A structured orientation program prepares the priest for ministry within the church in the United States and facilitates his ability to interact within the structure of the local parish. International priests who attended structured orientation programs in addition to continuous

---

[15] United States Conference of Catholic Bishops, *Guidelines for Receiving Pastoral Ministers in the United States*, rev. ed. (Washington, DC: USCCB, 2003).

mentoring found it very helpful (99%).

We can borrow a leaf from the medical profession. Every medical personnel employed in a new facility, regardless of qualifications and experience, undergoes a period of structured orientation. In some respects, every local church is different. Sometimes there are stark differences within the same diocese. Newly arrived international priests should be apprised of these differences and systematically oriented to their new field of ministry.

INCLUSION EFFORTS ON BOTH SIDES

The international priest and his host community need to work at inclusion. Inclusion does not spontaneously happen. Rather, inclusion demands calculated effort on both sides. The "new kid on the block" can be seen as a disruption to the circle of friends formed over many years, beginning in the seminary and enjoying common experiences and cultural understandings. Both international priests and American-born priests must take time to work at inclusion. Doing so is mutually beneficial.

VIEWS OF INTERNATIONAL PRIESTS FROM THE PEWS

Most Catholics in the United States are happy with the presence and ministry of international priests. They note that international priests manifest the universality of the Catholic Church. Their presence marks a difference between the Catholic Church and the many Christian denominations here. One recent convert observed that he was motivated to become a Catholic because of the demographic diversity within the Church: "In my former church it was just us. But in the Catholic Church, you see priests and people from all over the world. The Catholic Church is truly universal." The United States is very cosmopolitan, and the fact that the local church community reflects the country's ever-growing demographic diversity is a wonderful testimony to Catholic universality. The faces of American Catholics continue to change. In addition to a growing number of Catholics from recent immigrant populations, the 2010 U.S. census showed that 32% of Americans identified themselves as multiethnic. Interracial marriages grew by 28% between 2000 and 2010 and account for 10% of all marriages in the US.[16] Some laypeople note that international priests trained abroad bring diversity in their preaching style and tend to revive "lost" devotions in the church. One parishioner commented regarding the international priest in her parish: "He is a good storyteller and uses symbols in his homily that make us remember the homily long after."

PERCEPTIONS BY AMERICAN-BORN PRIESTS

American-born priests are aware of the challenges within the presbyterate in regard to international priests and of the call for open dialogue about the presence of international priests and

---

[16] *See* U.S. Census 2010 at http://www.census.gov/newsroom/releases/archives/2010_census/cb12-68.html (last visited Feb. 15, 2013).

multicultural issues within the Church. Some native priests, however, perceive that some international priests are more concerned with the pecuniary rewards of the ministry, are reluctant to adapt to their new cultural and ecclesial environment, see themselves as "nobility," and put on an air of superiority – especially if they have to "take orders" from the laity. These perceptions, while generalizations, are not entirely unfounded. Individual idiosyncrasies are brought to bear in the process. Some of these perceptions, however, result from cultural misunderstandings. Overall, the negative perceptions among some American-born priests of their international brothers highlight the need for open dialogue and for structured and continuous orientation, so that the church in the United States can fully benefit from the presence and invaluable services provided by international priests. In the 2009 CARA survey, 69% of American priests indicate that it is important to engage in open discussion about collaborating with international priests working in the United States.[17] Some individuals have even taken the initiative to create a forum for addressing this issue.[18]

---

[17] Gautier, Perl, & Fichter, *Same Call, Different Men.*

[18] An example of this is the Parresia Project initiated by Msgr. Richard Henning of the Seminary of the Immaculate Conception in Huntington, NY and Dr. Sebastian Mahfood, O.P. of Holy Apostles College and Seminary in Cromwell, CT..

CONCLUSION

The need for orientation cannot be overemphasized. International priests feel they could have avoided some mistakes if they had been given proper orientation. Some allegations of sexual misconduct against international priests are cases of the invasion of "boundaries," which could have been avoided with proper orientation to American culture. Nonetheless, not all international priests welcome the idea of orientation with enthusiasm. They are uncomfortable with structured orientation and consider it an attempt at "re-education." With a proper and culturally sensitive approach, however, these fears can be laid to rest. The directors and staff of orientation programs are developing such approaches.

The American-born presbyterate must work consciously at including international priests. Although this task is not simple, where it is achieved, the benefits include mutually enriching trust and friendship. The "creeping isolation" indicated by Cardinal Mahony can generate a feeling that affects the self-esteem of international priests. Many American priests have made great efforts to reach out to international priests. Sometimes they are at a loss at what to do, being cautious not to offend the international priests. Structured orientation is necessary not only for international priests, but also for the local pastors who will host them.

Table 1
Ratio of Priests to Laypeople 1900–2012[19]

Year	Number of Priests	Millions of Catholics	Ratio of Priests to Laypeople
1900	11,987	12	1:1,001
1910	16,550	16	1:967
1920	21,019	20	1:951
1930	27,864	20	1:718
1940	35,839	22	1:614*Lowest
1950	43,889	29	1:661
1960	54,682	42	1:768
1970	58,161	48	1:825
1980	58,398	50	1:856
1990	53,088	59	1:1,111
2000	45,699	60	1:1,313
2004	43,304	64	1:1,478
2009	**40,788 (ALL)**	**68**	**1:1,680**
2009	**32,223 (ACTIVE)**	**68**	**1:2,110 (ACTUAL)[20]**
2010	**28,653 (ACTIVE)**	**68.3**	**1:2,383 (ACTUAL)**

---

[19] *Hoge & Okure, International Priests in America; and Promise to Protect, Pledge to Heal: International Priests 2010, available at* http://www.usccb.org/issues-and-action/child-and-youth-protection/upload/2010-International-Priests.pdf *(last visited 29 Aug. 2015).*

2011	**28,277**	**68.5**	**1:2,422**
2012	**(ACTIVE)**	77.7	**(ACTUAL)**
	27,594		1:2,815
	(ACTIVE)		(ACTIVE)[21]

Table 1 shows a steady decline in the number of priests beginning in 1980 when the number peaked at 58,398. Between 1980 and 2009 the number had dropped by 17,610 for a loss of 30%, despite the increasing number of international priests. In the same period, the number of Catholics rose by approximately 18 million from 50 million to 68 million for a gain of 36%.

---

[20] The "actual" priest to layperson ratios for 2009, 2010, 2011 and 2012 are derived from the total number of priests listed as active in the Official Catholic Directory for those years. Previous years were calculated on the total number of priests, including those listed as "retired, sick or absent."

[21] Between 1980 and 2012 the priest per layperson ratio more than tripled, from 1:856 to 1:2,815.

Table 2
Dioceses with 50 - 99 International Priests (IP) in 2009[22]

Diocese	Total Number of Priests	Number of International Priests	Percentage of International Priests
Arlington, VA	222	56	25
Austin, TX	222	53	24
Boston, MA	1,338	76	6
Brooklyn, NY	699	91	13
Brownsville, TX	114	63	55
Corpus Christi, TX	177	91	51
Denver, CO	286	73	26
El Paso, TX	122	50	41
Honolulu, HI	128	51	40
Metuchen, NJ	233	82	35
Miami, FL	236	94	40
Oakland, CA	385	70	18
Palm Beach, FL	142	75	53
Patterson, NJ	384	70	13
Phoenix, AZ	238	90	38

[22] *Percentage calculated from the total number of priests in The Official Catholic Directory Anno Domini 2009 (Berkeley Heights NJ: P.J. Kenedy & Sons, 2009) and Promise to Protect, Pledge to Heal: International Priests 2009, available at http://www.usccb.org/issues-and-action/child-and-youth-protection/upload/international-priests-2009.pdf (last visited 29 Aug. 2015).*

Portland, OR	316	51	16
San Diego, CA	264	81	31
San Francisco, CA	386	69	18
Seattle, WA	253	70	28
St. Petersburg, FL	252	79	31
Stockton, CA	77	64	83
Tucson, AZ	180	83	46
Tyler, TX	81	57	70
Venice, FL	196	85	43
TOTAL	**6,931**	**1724**	**25%**

Table 3

Dioceses with More Than 100 International Priests (IP) in 2009[23]

Diocese	Total Number of Priests	Number of International Priests	Percentage of International Priests
Atlanta, GA	251	113	45
Chicago, IL	1,600	103	6
Galveston-Houston, TX	408	187	46
Los Angeles, CA	1,092	250	23
Military Service, DC	--*[24]	147	--
New York, NY	1,489	319	22
Newark, NJ	911	187	21
Orlando, FL	185	105	57
Rockville Center, NY	413	101	24
Sacramento, CA	270	132	49
San Antonio, TX	344	144	42
San Bernardino, CA	245	120	49
San José, CA	340	134	40
Total	**4,197**	**2042**	**27%**

---

[23] *Collated from The Official Catholic Directory Anno Domini 2009 and Promise to Protect, Pledge to Heal: International Priests 2009.*

[24] Priests in the Archdiocese for the Military Services are listed in their original dioceses of incardination and are therefore not listed here.

Table 4
Dioceses with 30–49 International Priests

Diocese	Total #Priests	Number of International Priests	Percentage of International Priests
Alexandria, LA	75	34	45
Biloxi, MS	73	40	55
Bridgeport, CT	296	44	15
Charleston, SC	118	33	28
Dallas, TX	171	48	28
Detroit, MI	618	41	7
Fort Worth, TX	115	43	37
Hartford, CT	426	39	9
Joliet, IL	287	41	14
La Crosse, WI	183	34	19
Lafayette, LA	202	37	18
Laredo, TX	52	35	67
Las Cruces, NM	70	32	46
Monterey, CA	127	41	32
New Orleans, LA	360	32	9
Pensacola/Tallahassee, FL	86	33	38
Philadelphia, PA	977	43	4
Richmond, VA	178	48	27
Santa Fe, NM	221	30	14
Santa Rosa, CA	86	34	40
Savannah, GA	100	34	34

St. Augustine, FL	121	41	34
St. Louis-Our Lady of Lebanon	50	40	80
Stamford Ukrainians, CT	48	36	75

Table 5
Profile of International Priests[25]

	Diocesan	Religious
Average age	47	45
Full time student	11%	16%
Attended orientation after arrival	33%	35%
Expect to be in the US 5 plus years	73%	77%
Program less than two weeks	49%	33%
Found program useful	96%	100%
Naturalized US Citizens	37%	31%

Issues Facing International Priests

	Diocesan	Religious
Loneliness	18%	29%[26]
Too much work	12%	17%[27]
Not accepted as equals	64%	43%
The way authority is exercised	8%	17%

---

[25] The Profile of International Priests is limited to those who arrived the United States in or after 1985.

[26] In the 2009 CARA survey, 70% of American priests indicated that genuine closeness is lacking among priests. *See* Gautier, Perl, & Fichter, *Same Call, Different Men.*

[27] Coincidentally, 17% of American priests in the 2009 CARA survey considered "too much work" to be a great problem for them personally. *See* Gautier, Perl, & Fichter, *Same Call, Different Men.*

Chapter 4

Opening the Reception Process: Distance Learning and the International Priest

Rev. Msgr. Richard Henning, S.T.D., and Dr. Sebastian Mahfood, O.P.

THE STATE OF THE QUESTION

International priests have served the Roman Catholic Church in the United States since its inception. With congregations consisting largely of immigrants or Spanish and French speaking Catholics absorbed by the expansion of U.S. territory, it was only natural that the clergy reflected the remarkable mixture of ethnicities in the Church.[28] New communities lacked the "home-grown" vocations of more established communities, and the nascent Church needed to recruit or welcome priests and religious

---

[28] At the first U.S. Church Synod in Baltimore in 1791, some 80% of the attending priests were born outside the U.S.

from other countries and cultures. Only in the 20th century did the Church in the U.S. begin to produce sufficient vocations to meet the needs of many dioceses and archdioceses. Especially in the years following World War II, Catholics in the U.S. saw the highest ratios of priests to lay faithful, large numbers of local vocations, and the prospect of sending U.S.-born clergy to serve in overseas missions. Yet even in those years of plentiful vocations, international priests and religious continued to form an important part of the life of the Catholic Church in the U.S.[29]

The 1970's saw the beginning of a rapid decline in the number of vocations in the United States. This decline has caused dioceses and religious communities to return to the earlier custom of recruiting priests and religious from other countries. While there is ample precedent for such recruitment in the history of the Church in the U.S., the contemporary situation presents some significant differences from past experiences.

The most significant difference concerns the composition of the lay faithful in the U.S. In 1920, the percentage of foreign-born Catholics in the country reached a historic high of 75% of the Catholic population. In the past, many foreign-born priests served communities composed largely of immigrants from their home countries. In those instances where an international priest served people from cultures other than his own, potential conflicts arose from inter-ethnic tensions rather from a divide between those born

---

[29] Many Catholics in the U.S. might be surprised to learn that even today, some 40% U.S. dioceses are considered "Mission" dioceses by the Congregation for the Propagation of the Faith.

in or outside of the U.S. The Catholic Church in the U.S. still benefits from a large and growing immigrant presence. Now, however, the Catholic population in the U.S. includes a substantial body of Catholics from various ethnicities born and raised in North American culture who might perceive a priest born elsewhere as "foreign."

Secondly, the culture gap between international priests and Catholic laity in the U.S. has widened. For the most part, past inter-ethnic tensions arose among various European groups within the Church. At present, the cultural mix is wider and more complex with international priests arriving from non-European cultures in Africa, Asia, the Pacific Islands, and South and Central America.

Two more factors distinguish the situation of foreign-born priests in the U.S. today from the situation of foreign-born priests in the past. The relative ease of international travel and increasingly sophisticated communications technologies allow international priests to remain connected to their own home countries and cultures to an unprecedented extent. Finally, in the contemporary setting, the faithful are more aware of the role of culture in the life of the Church, and more tools exist for assisting the process of dialog and mutual understanding.

Given some of the differences between the situations of foreign-born priests within the U.S. in the past and the present, this latter day recruitment of international priests to serve in the U.S. has engendered controversy. In response to that controversy, the Bishop's Committee on Migration issued *Guidelines for Receiving Pastoral Ministers in the United States* in 1999 and updated those guidelines in 2003.[30] The Committee called for orientation programs that would take place before the priest arrived in the U.S. (pre-departure orientation), time to adjust upon arrival in the U.S., pre-placement orientation, and ongoing orientation and spiritual direction for the first three years.

In 2006, Dean R. Hoge and Dominican Father Aniedi Okure authored a crucial study, *International Priests in America.*[31] Sponsored by the National Federation of Priests' Councils, the study surveyed the history of international priests in the U.S., reported on the arguments for and against the recruitment of such priests, provided an outline of reception efforts and programs, and made six specific recommendations for the reception process:[32]

1. that the 1999/2003 guidelines be observed and implemented;
2. that initial orientation take place in the country of origin before the arrival of the international priest;
3. that receiving pastors and communities be prepared for the arrival of an international priest;

---

[30] Committee on Migration of the United States Conference of Catholic Bishops, *Guidelines for Receiving Pastoral Ministers in the United States,* rev. ed. (Washington, D.C.: United States Conference of Catholic Bishops, 2003).

[31] Dean R. Hoge & Aniedi Okure, *International Priests in America: Challenges and Opportunities* (Collegeville, MN: Liturgical Press, 2006). This study is a unique and essential tool for any consideration of the reception of international priests in the U.S.

[32] *Id.,* 124.

4. that orientation programs be expanded;

5. that mentors be provided to international priests; and

6. that international priests themselves be consulted in the development of these programs.

Hoge and Okure supported their findings with statistics from a 1999 study conducted by the Center for Applied Research in the Apostolate (CARA). That study indicated that approximately 16% of priests serving in the U.S. were born outside the U.S. That number represents a national average, so the percentage of foreign-born priests varies from diocese to diocese. In some dioceses, the average is significantly higher than 16%. The same research indicated that an average of 28% of seminarians were born outside the U.S. This number includes seminarians who were studying in the U.S. and planning to return to their home countries. Nevertheless, 84% of foreign-born seminarians were training for ministry in the U.S.[33]

No national studies have been conducted since the 1999 CARA study. The fact that the number of international seminarians is higher than the national average for priests, however, indicates that the percentage of foreign-born priests active in the U.S. will rise with each ordination class. In addition, dioceses within the U.S. continue to recruit international priests. Informal estimates place the number at about 300 new international priests each year.[34] It is

---

[33] *Id.*, 11–12.

[34] John L. Allen, Jr., "American Catholic Demographics and the Future of Ministry," *National Catholic Reporter* (30 Apr. 2010).

clear that, barring some significant change in the policies of most dioceses, the CARA estimates of 1999 are now too low. The percentage of international priests in the U.S. is significant already, and it continues to grow.[35]

In the last several decades, many dioceses have responded to the arrival of international priests by establishing local programs to help them adjust to life in the U.S. These programs vary greatly. Some involve contracting with secular firms for services such as language instruction or accent reduction. In other cases, dioceses establish their own processes of receiving the priest in practical and ministerial matters. No full inventory of such efforts at present exists, but it is fair to observe that they are generally ad hoc efforts established to address the "problem" of cultural and linguistic boundaries.

Only three programs in the U.S. have national prominence and reach in their work with international priests: the Cultural Orien-

---

[35] This discussion begs the question of the identity of the "international priest." Here we indicate by that term any priest serving in the U.S. who was born outside the U.S. This would include those recruited to serve directly from their home dioceses or communities in other countries, those who come to the U.S. for post-graduate study and minister part or full time, those who are recruited by dioceses in the U.S. as seminarians and who complete their training at a U.S. seminary, and those who come to the U.S.as immigrants and who later pursue a vocation. Clearly, this is a broad range of individuals with different needs; however, all of these circumstances raise the possibility of cultural tension and misunderstanding on the part of the priest or the community in which he serves.

tation Program for International Ministers (COPIM) at Loyola Marymount in Los Angeles, California; the Oblate School of Theology in San Antonio, Texas; and the Vincentian Center for Church and Society in Queens, New York. All three of these institutions operate programs for international priests. COPIM and the Oblates also include components that address the pastors and communities who will welcome international priests. The Hoge-Okure study found that one-third or less of international priests undergo any sort of formal orientation program upon arrival in the U.S. About half attend local programs and half attend the three programs named above.[36] While these three institutions administer excellent and effective orientation programs on the national level, no programs exist to prepare international priests before they arrive in the U.S. No programs exist that devote their efforts specifically to the preparation of the receiving community. No programs exist that address the increasing number of international seminarians. COPIM and the Oblates use mentoring, but their programs do not continue for the three years recommended by the 1999 guidelines.

The local and national response to the increase in the number of international priests in the U.S. has been impressive. The question of whether to recruit international priests, raised by the Hoge-Okure study, has been answered by the de facto presence and continued arrival of international priests. The challenge in 2010 and beyond concerns the quality and comprehensiveness of the reception process for international priests and seminarians. How

---

[36] Hoge & Okure, 157–58.

may the Church in the U.S. expand efforts to address all of the stages recommended in the 1999 guidelines? How may these guidelines be revised over time to reflect the changing needs of the Church? How may the Church in the U.S. increase the mutuality of the process to include resources for receiving pastors and communities? How may all of these needs be addressed in light of limited resources and an ever-increasing number of international priests?

THE PARRESIA PROJECT

Beginning in the summer of 2009, the authors of this article received a planning grant to fund the Parresia Project.[37] In its original inception, we hoped to establish an institute to work with international seminarians. In that institute, we planned to employ distance-learning technologies to increase the reach and effectiveness of the program.

In February 2010, the Parresia Project hosted a gathering of 22 individuals from around the U.S. who work in seminaries or with international priests and seminarians. The group included two international priests and representatives from the three major

---

[37] *Parresia* is the Greek term used in the New Testament to describe the quality of early Christian preaching and witness. Difficult to capture with one English word, it may be translated as "openness," "boldness," "clear," etc. We chose this word because of our desire to increase the openness and mutuality of the reception process for international priests and seminarians.

programs mentioned above. Our original goal, seeking help to establish an institute, shifted quickly because the group expressed strong opposition to the idea of yet another institute – even one that would be directed primarily toward seminarians. Participants pointed out that the current national programs already experience difficulty in recruiting candidates. While the group expressed interest in the potential of distance learning technologies, participants explained that the infrastructure and faculty for the use of such technologies is not yet sufficient for the task. Participants also spoke about the urgent need for more data on the number and placement of international priests and some sense of the local programs that exist in various dioceses and communities. Finally, participants at the Parresia meeting expressed a desire to move together beyond the ad hoc nature of much of the current response to a more systematic and collaborative approach toward preparing foreign-born priests for ministry in the U.S.

Following the February consultation, we shifted the short-term goals of the Parresia Project. Abandoning the plan for a new institute, we incorporated the requests of the consultants into an implementation grant proposal for which we received $150,000 to establish a welcoming protocol and develop workshops and materials for diocesan use. With sponsorship from the Seminary Department of the National Catholic Educational Association and the Seminary of the Immaculate Conception in Huntington, N.Y., the Project engaged over the two-year grant period in four areas of work, namely: research, networking, advocacy, and resource development.

We hope to collaborate with other organizations in gathering data with regard to the presence of international priests and seminarians, the programs that assist their reception process, and the relative effectiveness of various approaches. We intend to publish the results of that research at the conclusion of the two-year process. We will continue the conversation begun in February 2010 by establishing working groups for research and conducting two further gatherings in 2011 and 2012. We intend to help raise the importance of this question with local and national ecclesiastical leadership. In particular, we will advocate increasing the percentage of international priests and seminarians who have the opportunity to attend programs like those run by COPIM, the Oblates, and the Vincentian Center. Finally, our project began with an interest in the use of distance learning technologies. This fourth component of our work is perhaps the most important contribution we may make. Distance learning offers significant potential in responding to the needs mentioned above with regard to the mutuality and comprehensiveness of the reception process.

THE POTENTIAL USE OF DISTANCE LEARNING TECHNOLOGY

Distance learning involves pedagogy and methods applied to the education of students who are not physically present in the traditional classroom. In a hybrid setting, such methods are used in concert with traditional classroom learning. Distance learning itself is not a new phenomenon. The 20th century saw the development of correspondence courses that educated students at a distance. The rise of digital technology and the increasing availability of high-speed Internet access have brought distance learning from the peripheries into the center. Many educational institutions conduct course components or entire courses in the online environment. While most theological seminaries and institutes still require residential components in their degree programs, an increasing number of schools conduct entire distance learning programs with developing communications technology.

Contemporary classroom settings frequently use technology as well. The primary distinction between transmissive learning (the predominant form of traditional learning) and transactive learning (the predominant form of distance learning) is the change in the style of interaction between instructor and student, student and student, and student and subject. The traditional classroom operating under a transmissive model presumes the interaction of students by physical proximity and the opportunity to discuss subject matter inside or outside the classroom. The primary interaction between student and professor takes the form of lessons or lectures in the classroom, although there may also be interaction outside of class meetings. The student interacts with subject material through lectures, readings, and research.

Distance learning must make interaction more intentional without the physical proximity of the classroom. Efforts to increase interactivity have brought transformational developments to the pedagogy of online and distance instruction. Whereas early attempts to use the Internet for education involved a replication of the transmissive format in the recording and posting of traditional classroom lectures, current pedagogy emphasizes the necessity of interaction in new and creative ways for the purpose of generating a viable community of learners who more fully employ the potential of the Internet and attendant technologies. Instructors use telephone, discussion boards, video conferencing, email, survey or form tools, Camtasia, PowerPoint, Word, electronic submission of assignments, and other technologies to provide students with content and to assess their learning. The same tools provide means for students to get to know one another and to begin to learn from one another. Good online pedagogy encourages cooperative projects among the students for these purposes. It likewise provides online "spaces" for informal interaction and for sharing insights or ideas. Distance learning remains controversial among many traditional faculties who raise questions about the loss of the "human" component to learning. While such objections are worthy of consideration, it might be observed that traditional classrooms also can lack in human interaction. Pedagogical methods matter at least as much as the setting in which education takes place.

In the case of the reception process for international clergy and seminarians, the traditional classroom setting has many drawbacks. Many priests who come to the U.S. understandably feel belittled by the implication that they must be sent "back to the classroom." More significantly, the traditional classroom is geographically bound and numerically limiting. Distance learning opens new possibilities for increasing the reach and breadth of orientation programs and the interactivity of reception processes. It also fulfills other goals articulated by Popes John Paul II and Benedict XVI—to cast the Church's nets into the deep of cyberspace, to insert media instruction into pastoral formation programs, and generally to "encourage the witness of faith in a digital world."[38]

The potential of employing distance learning technology in order to prepare foreign-born priests for ministry in the U.S. may best be explored according to the stages outlined by the 1999 guidelines.

STAGE 1: PRE-ARRIVAL ORIENTATION

To date, no programs have attempted to conduct orientation in the home country before the arrival of an international priest or seminarian as recommended by the *Guidelines for Receiving Pastoral Ministers*.[39] The reason is the practical difficulty inherent in mounting such an effort in many different countries. International priests arrive from dozens of countries and some of those countries have distinct cultural groups within their borders. How would it be possible for a local diocese or even an international

---

[38] Pope John Paul II, Encyclical On the Permanent Validity of the Church's Missionary Mandate *Redemptoris missio* (7 Dec. 1990); Pope John Paul II, Message for the 36th World Communications Day, "Internet: A New Forum for Proclaiming the Gospel" (12 May 2002); Pope John Paul II, Apostolic Letter, "The Rapid Development" (24 Jan. 2005); Pope Benedict XVI, Message for the 43rd World Communications Day, "New Technologies, New Relationships. Promoting a Culture of Respect, Dialogue and Friendship" (24 May 2009); Pope Benedict XVI, Message for the 44th World Communications Day, "The Priest and Pastoral Ministry in a Digital World: New Media at the Service of the Word" (16 May 2010).

[39] *Guidelines for Receiving Pastoral Ministers*, 23.

institution to create and maintain orientation programs in so many places?

While the Internet is not readily available in all rectories and homes throughout the world, Internet cafes have become common throughout the developing world. With that in mind, it is possible to deliver pre-arrival orientation through simple and/or more complex distance learning tools in many cases.

On the simple side, a receiving parish might begin by using a program such as Skype to have a videoconference between a group at the parish and the priest who will be arriving in a few months. This would build anticipation in advance of the new priest's arrival and begin to establish bonds between the priest and at least some select parishioners. The pastor or parish staff, likewise, might begin an email correspondence in advance of the priest's arrival in order to share some of the practicalities of life in that locale and learn something of the priest's home culture.

On the more complex level, culture-specific lessons could be developed and delivered online around the world to priests who are or might be coming to the U.S. Such lessons need not be formal lectures, but might be a mixture of video and text with interactive components such as an attendant discussion board or online seminars with live interaction.

These examples are the most obvious means of using distance learning technology to prepare foreign-born priests for their impending arrival in the U.S. With a little creative brainstorming, such technologies would make it possible for the first time to fulfill the 1999 guidelines' recommendation for pre-arrival orientation.

STAGE 2: PRE-ASSIGNMENT ORIENTATION

The *Guidelines for Receiving Pastoral Ministers* envision a period of adaptation to American culture of two or three months, including a formal orientation program.[40] This recommendation has not been implemented as envisioned. Most foreign-born priests arrive to informal and brief processes of welcome by personnel directors and pastors, and, as mentioned above, only about one third ever experience a formal orientation program at the local or national level.

It may be better to re-envision this stage as "immediate" orientation, encompassing the practical matters of settling into life in the U.S. as well as more particular issues of adjusting to new ministries. Current programs employ models more like the traditional classroom. The national orientation programs run by COPIM, the Oblates, and the Vincentian Center involve physical attendance at workshops of varying lengths that together total about fourteen days.

These face-to-face programs, together with various local orientation programs for newly arrived foreign-born priests, provide crucial opportunities for the international priest to interact with instructors and to discover a peer support system. We would recommend that such programs continue largely as they are, although they need more candidates to flourish and to allow for the establishment of additional programs. Distance learning should not replace these existing programs, but rather should supplement

---

[40] *Id.*, 23–24.

and amplify the effects of these orientation programs.

Here follow our recommendations for practical ways that distance learning can supplement programs already in existence for orienting foreign-born priests who have recently arrived in the U.S. First we will address programs aimed at the priests themselves, then we will address programs aimed at the communities that are receiving these priests. The greatest potential of distance learning in the immediate stage of reception lies in the possibility of providing orientation content to receiving communities.

Distance learning can supplement orientation programs already in existence even before those programs begin. Distance learning technology could be used to begin the process of introducing international priests to one another. For example, a blog or wiki would allow space where participants and faculty might create a profile of their history and interests, including the possibility of pictures or video. Participants might also receive readings or information in advance through a web page. With a little more effort, such pre-program content might be multimedia and interactive.

During the program, most of the interaction will be in-person. Even here, however, the creative application of distance learning technology has the potential to enrich the international priests' orientation. For example, video conferencing would allow alumni of the program to address participants, giving a human face to stories of integration into U.S. ministries and providing an opportunity to share struggles and victories in the process of bridging cultural boundaries. Similar interactions could also take place through discussion boards that introduce participants in the program to be their larger peer groups.

When the in-person workshops have concluded, distance learning technology could be used to continue to deliver content, thereby lengthening and amplifying the amount of material and the time for absorption. The participants can return to ministerial work but continue to learn on a part time basis. Such learning might incorporate multi-media tools. Some multi-media exercises might be available online and accessible according to the schedule of the individual, or there may be opportunities through the use of chat rooms or video conferencing for synchronous participation by several individuals. The same web environment provides many ways for participants to continue fostering peer relationships and support. It also provides a possible means for faculty or staff from the orientation program to remain available for advice and support in those first weeks after the participant's return to ministry.

In addition to enriching the orientation of newly arrived international priests, distance learning technology can also be employed to provide orientation programs for the communities receiving those priests. Multimedia lesson modules might be developed for delivery online to Pastors and parish staff. Similar modules might address core leadership in the parish such as parish councils or parish volunteers. The same kind of resources could be made available to the entire parish though the parish website. The lessons might be targeted to a review of the culture of the individual priest who is preparing for arrival in the parish. The lessons need not be long; they could be presented in several parts of 5-10 minutes each. The modules can be prepared by the contributors to an orientation program and adapted to local needs.

For instance, the local parish might provide a profile of the individual priest, including some message of his own.

The immediate purpose of such modules would be to help the receiving community gain some sense of the priest's home culture and avoid the misunderstandings that can occur in the process of encounter between persons of different cultures. In the longer term, the modules could facilitate bonding between the priest and the receiving community.

STAGE 3: ONGOING ORIENTATION

If the pre-assignment orientation is a form of "immediate" orientation that addresses the questions and stresses of the newly arrived foreign-born priests' first cultural encounters in the U.S., ongoing formation provides "remote" orientation that addresses the long-term stresses of life in a new culture. It must address issues like loneliness, homesickness, and the everyday stresses of life in ministry such as changes in assignment or conflicts in the rectory. For reasons such as this the 1999 guidelines and the Hoge-Okure study recommend ongoing orientation over the course of the first three years of an international priest's ministry in the U.S.[41] As part of that orientation process, Hoge and Okure stressed the importance of mentoring for the international priest.[42]

The current national programs do not provide for three years of orientation. Two of the three programs provide for some degree

---

[41] Hoge & Okure, *International Priests in America*, 8.

[42] *Id.*, 20.

of mentoring. While it is difficult to determine the extent of mentoring programs on the local level, some dioceses are using mentors as a way of receiving the international priest. This raises the related question of whether programs exist that prepare the mentors.

Many receiving communities have a strong interest in the question of accent reduction and the development of English language skills. While the current national programs do not extensively engage these issues, local programs often focus on language. Such language instruction is generally expensive and time consuming. Furthermore, the frustrating truth is that the effectiveness of language instruction and accent reduction varies widely.

In the case of ongoing formation, mentoring, and language and accent instruction, many potential uses exist for distance learning technologies and methodologies. Here follow practical suggestions for how distance learning can address each of these three needs of the international priest settling into a ministry in the U.S.

The first need is for ongoing orientation from peers and support groups. International priests serve in every part of the U.S. Some are in urban areas in easy reach of communities or other priests from their home culture. Others may serve in more isolated environments. All of them need peer relationships and support. The relationships established during immediate orientation can be extended by the use of web resources. In addition to informal email communication, discussion boards and websites could be used to maintain contact and provide mutual support. The same technology would provide the possibility of ongoing communication to international priests by national organizations such as offices of the USCCB or the National Federation of Priests' Councils. These organizations might prepare a brief overview of some topic of interest to priests from other cultures.

The second need is for mentoring. Like the immediate orientation workshops, mentoring is a task that requires in-person interaction. Distance learning technology cannot replace that crucial interaction, but it might still be employed to provide content to mentors, offering them insight into the culture of the individual priest and into the process of mentoring such a priest. The use of the Internet for this purpose would also allow for the combination of resources and the attendant improvement of the quality of the instruction.

The third need is for ongoing training in the English language. On this topic, it is interesting to note that Duke University recently converted all of its first and second year foreign language courses to online courses. Duke has found that the online environment provides the best results for beginning language students. Duke reserves classroom instruction in languages for the more advanced students where conversation and personal interaction become more important. In the case of international priests, it is difficult to imagine that an individual or a diocese would implement its own language and accent reduction program. In most cases, dioceses seem to rely upon other entities for such instruction. Those entities may already use web-based resources to supplement their classroom instruction. In cases where an ecclesiastical entity conducts a program of its own, nevertheless, distance learning allows for the delivery of additional content to the international priest. It also allows for that content to be delivered at the time convenient to the student choosing and without the need for travel.

CONCLUSIONS

On the national and local level, the Church in the U.S. has responded to the arrival of increasing numbers of international priests by developing processes of reception and orientation. At present, there are many excellent programs that assist such priests to minister more effectively in their new cultural context.

Nonetheless, important issues remain to be addressed in the longer term. Much of the response to the arrival of international priests has been ad hoc. The response addresses some local needs or parts of the need, but a comprehensive implementation of the recommendations of the 1999 guidelines or the recommendations of the Hoge-Okure study remains a desideratum. Furthermore, present efforts focus primarily on the arriving priest, leaving him with the burden of adjusting to U.S. culture and society. A great need exists for preparation of the communities receiving these priests and a more mutual process of encounter between cultures.

The Parresia Project has been formed to advocate for a more comprehensive and mutual reception process. Parresia advocates opening the process of integrating foreign-born priests into the U.S. to receiving communities and strengthening the resources available for orienting international priests. Parresia also hopes to open conversation on this topic of such great importance to the present and future of seminary formation and priestly ministry in the U.S. The Parresia Project also wishes to develop and promote the use of distance learning methods and technology in the reception process.

Distance learning will not be an easy solution to a complex and long term challenge, but it does offer significant potential for the increased effectiveness of current programs, the development of programs to meet the recommendations of the 1999 guidelines and the Hoge/Okure study, and an increased mutuality in the process by which international priests arrive in and serve in Catholic communities of the United States.

Chapter 5

Intercultural Competency
and the Priestly Vocation

Allan Figueroa Deck, S.J., Ph.D., S.T.D.[43]

PASTORAL REALITIES: DEMOGRAPHIC, SOCIAL AND CULTURAL

We live in a time of exhilarating and sometimes disturbing change. This is true from the perspectives of both civil society and the Church. Of the many factors that contribute to the pace of new developments in society and the Church, the movement of peoples, or migration, is a major one. For the Church in the United States this has meant a shift—demographic, social, cultural and economic—from the middleclass stability that it achieved in the middle of the twentieth century to a new period characterized by reorganization due to a rising Catholic immigrant population, a

---

[43] Allan Figueroa Deck is Executive Director of the USCCB's Secretariat of Cultural Diversity in the Church of the United States.

declining middleclass European American cohort, and a declining number of priests and religious.

The tragic scandals regarding the sexual abuse of minors by clergy had several consequences, one of them being the loss of hundreds of millions of dollars that could have been used to fund an emerging new configuration of parishes and Catholic institutions. The disappearance of more than 2,000 parishes over the past two decades as a result of closures and clustering of parishes together with migration and high natural birthrates for Hispanics dramatically affects church life. As the Center for Applied Research in the Apostolate's 2011 study titled *Emerging Models of Parish Leadership* reports, fully one third of today's parishes are multicultural, that is, shared among two or more distinct cultural and language groups.[44] Often several cultural groups share a parish, and the number of such multicultural parishes keeps rising. Perhaps equally significant, the social class status of today's U.S. Catholics is bifurcated between an upwardly mobile but aging European American cohort and a relatively youthful, struggling working class of immigrants and their children.

The disappearance of thousands of priests and religious due to retirement and death over the next ten to fifteen years will only intensify the changes taking place in parishes, schools and Catholic organizations of every kind. Fewer parishes, priests, and religious

---

[44] See U.S. Parish Life Study, Emerging Models of Parish Leadership, http://cara.georgetown.edu/CARAServices/emergingmodels.html   (last visited 29 Aug. 2015).

will be tending to more numerous diverse communities, while the rising number of deacons and laity who are taking up the slack will find themselves challenged as never before.

In this article I wish to put our feet on the ground and reflect on these dramatic new circumstances that demand adaptations in the way we think about ministerial formation, especially that of priests. The suggestions I make here are totally consistent with what the Magisterium has actually been saying for decades now as well as the vision proposed over the years through five successive editions of the *Program of Priestly Formation* (PPF).[45] Practical realities, however, are making it almost impossible to ignore the urgency. It is time to take a long, hard look at one of the central challenges facing priests and all pastoral agents today and certainly tomorrow: the integration of intercultural competencies into formation programs. Every ecclesial minister beginning with the priest must be prepared to work in and with today's bewildering cultural, linguistic, and social contexts. The growing cultural diversification of the Church in the U.S. is surely a hopeful reality as the Church becomes more *catholic* than ever. But this brings with it the urgent need for a more inclusive vision and appropriate knowledge, attitudes, and skills among ecclesiastical leaders, especially priests, for addressing these challenges.

Pope Benedict XVI has set the tone for the Church's efforts to

---

[45] The latest edition is United States Conference of Catholic Bishops, *Program of Priestly Formation*, 5th ed. (Washington, DC: USCCB, 2006), *available at* http://www.usccb.org/upload/program-priestly-formation-fifth-edition.pdf [hereinafter PPF].

reach out to others and promote inter-religious and intercultural communication. Speaking of the encounter with the "other," the Benedict XVI highlighted the biblical image of the Courtyard of the Gentiles, in which peoples from every land and nation engaged each other outside the Temple in Jerusalem. In a video message broadcast especially to youth and young adults on 25 March 2011 in support of the Pontifical Council on Culture's Courtyard of the Gentiles initiative, the Holy Father said:

> Dear friends, you are challenged to build bridges between one another.... Our first step, the first thing we can do together, is to respect, help and love each and every human being because he or she is a creature of God and in some way the road that leads to God. As you carry on the experience of this evening, work to break down the barriers of fear of others, of strangers, of those who are different; this fear is often born of mutual ignorance, skepticism and indifference. Work to create bonds with other young people without distinction and keeping in mind those who are poor or lonely, unemployed, ill or on the margins of society.[46]

---

[46] Pope Benedict XVI, Video Message, "In this Courtyard of the Unknown   God"   (25   Mar.   2011),   *available   at* http://chiesa.espresso.repubblica.it/articolo/1347271?eng=y&refresh_ce.

THE PRIESTLY MISSION TODAY: EVANGELIZATION

The framework for grounding this discussion about the vocation of the ordained priesthood in the context of diversity in today's world is given by the Magisterium in four groundbreaking documents: the Second Vatican Council's *Gaudium et spes* (especially sections 56 and following), Pope Paul VI's *Evangelii nuntiandi,* arguably the most influential ecclesial document to be issued since Vatican II, and Pope John Paul II's *Catechesi tradendae* and *Redemptoris missio.* In these normative documents, the Holy See clearly asserts the identity and mission of the Church in terms of the evangelization of cultures. Pope Benedict XVI has enhanced this vision of identity and mission with his insistence on the New Evangelization, which highlights the decline of Christianity in so-called Christian nations of Europe and North America and points to the particular challenges of the Church's encounter with modern culture, especially secularity and the ideology of secularism. Underlying the Church's understanding of its identity and therefore the role of its hierarchical leaders— bishops, priests, and deacons—is the contemporary encounter of the Incarnate Word Jesus Christ with the various ethnicities, races, and cultures, and especially with the highly influential secular, modern, and postmodern cultures.

The mindset of seminarians and priests may at times reflect the accommodation that they and the faithful in general have made with a given period and culture. In the middle of the twentieth century, the Church in the U.S. experienced a high point of stability and acceptance. A Catholic was elected president of the

U.S., while the number of students in Catholic grade and high schools reached its highest level in history, as did the number of parishes, priests, and religious men and women. Perhaps Catholics became accustomed to that expansive experience of a certain kind of success and came to honestly view the priestly life within the context of an accepted, prosperous, and rather middleclass institution. Those days have certainly come to an end, and a generation of U.S. Catholics now passing on may experience some difficulty in adjusting to the demise of the halcyon days of the "Ozzie and Harriet" suburban parish. Perceptive pastors have noted a sense of mourning among some European American Catholics who miss the church of the 1950s and 1960s. In the case of some clergy, there may also have been a tendency to imagine the life of a priest in an idealized manner, as fitting into a pleasant niche that corresponds to a world that is fading away. Today's seminarians and priests consequently need a certain grittiness that will serve them well in the face of new pastoral realities. An authentic priestly vocation means being called to serve real communities—the People of God not as one might imagine them to be, but as they truly are.

In addition, the fact that presbyterates are changing dramatically in cultural make-up is just dawning on us. The Summer 2011 issue of *The CARA Report* states that 39% of seminarians in the theologate today are not of European ancestry (White or Anglo Caucasian) and the majority of these were not born in the U.S.[47] The number of non-U.S.-born seminarians,

---

[47] *The CARA Report* 17, no. 1 (Summer 2011), 10.

moreover, increases every year. Intercultural competence, therefore, is clearly not just a matter relevant to parish, diocesan, or school life. It pertains as well to priestly fraternity itself now and in the years to come. There is an urgent need among priests and seminarians to develop the capacity for effective, appropriate intercultural relations if indeed presbyterates are to be sources of strength, unity, and mutual support for bishops and the priests. This is also urgently indicated by the rising number of international priests now distributed throughout the U.S. Frequently such priests find themselves working in neither their own native cultures nor in that of any they have previously experienced. So it needs to be said quite clearly: Intercultural competencies are not a requirement for only European American priests and seminarians, but for all of them. Today the possibilities for ongoing intercultural encounters are endless. For example, Hispanic priests find themselves serving European American, Vietnamese, and African American communities. Or Vietnamese priests are learning Spanish to serve Hispanics. Consequently, an approach toward the pastoral care of diverse groups characterized by creating distinctive territories or silos, such as the personal or national parish of the past, is necessarily giving way today to an approach that effectively gathers diverse communities into larger mixed groupings that Fr. Brett Hoover, C.S.P. has called "shared parishes." [48] Shared parishes arise through the creation of clustered parishes. Shared parishes also appear for other practical reasons,

---

[48] *See* Brett Hoover, *The Shared Parish: Latinos, Anglos, and the Future of U.S. Catholicism* (NY: New York University Press, 2014).

since so many diverse groups are in the same locations and their bishops are not able to find priests and other ministers from each of the pertinent groups. The countries of origin of today's Catholic immigrants and international priests are, moreover, extremely diverse; they literally come from every continent. Thus the need for intercultural skills on the part of ministers is higher than it has ever been before in the history of U.S. Catholicism.

In any case, the Magisterium's insistence on the Church's missionary nature requires a renewed mindset among priests and their *formatores*, a mindset that sees the priest as more than anything else as a man on a mission as distinct from someone filling a clearly defined niche. This means a minister who is reaching out, taking risks, willing to move and work with the ever-expanding mixture of the faithful that history is bringing to his doorstep. The focus of the diocesan priest on his local church community is altogether appropriate, but something has to be added to it: his local diocesan church is often no longer the stable, familiar place it used to be; it is undergoing change. To effectively minister in this emerging church demands becoming intercultural and even bilingual or multilingual, since that is what one's local reality demands. The missiological aspect of priestly life, therefore, must be stressed in view of the facts on the ground, such as the fact that six out of every ten Catholics under the age of 35 in the U.S. today are Hispanic. Moreover, if one adds the rising number of Asian and Pacific Islander and African Catholics together with the significant numbers of African American and Native American Catholics, the ecclesial picture becomes even clearer. More than half of all U.S. Catholics are not of European ancestry and millions are still struggling with English. There was a time when people in certain parts of the country—the Deep South, the Midwestern Heartland, or perhaps Alaska—could claim exception from the Church's rising diversity. Those days, however, are over as new Catholic communities, especially Hispanics, populate virtually every corner of the nation.

The Church insists on thinking about these matters in terms of the blessings that these changes bring. To serve the coming of God's Kingdom is to engage all cultures in dialogue and proclamation of the Gospel. This engagement is a vast and daunting project with four fundamental dimensions: (1) a personal encounter with Jesus Christ; (2) the transformation of cultures by the power of the Gospel message; (3) the transformation of the social, economic, and political orders along the lines of what Pope Benedict XVI calls "social charity";[49] and (4) ecumenical and inter-religious dialogue leading to the reconciliation of all peoples as desired by Christ.

The Church's evangelizing agenda consequently is demanding and undoubtedly a source of tension, even controversy, because it has countercultural implications. To evangelize is not just about engaging with cultures; it is about transforming them. Ethnocentrism and an exaggerated love of one's nation and culture obscures a truly Catholic identity that effectively gives witness to the faith. Similarly, a perceived need among some seminarians for a high degree of clarity, stability, and certainty may create

---

[49] *See, e.g.,* Pope Benedict XVI, Encyclical Letter *Deus caritas est* (25 Dec. 2005), § 29.

indifference toward or uneasiness with what is different or "other," and thus get in the way of an evangelizer's necessary openness to what is "other" and different. Those who work as *formatores* with today's seminarians (as well as with youth and young adults) report unstable family backgrounds and a lack of basic catechesis. It is sometimes said that these understandably may be a factors in driving young people to a more rigid and fundamentalist way of relating to the faith, one that lacks nuance and fails to deal well with ambiguity. Whatever be the source of this tendency, it must be viewed in relation to the universal mission of all the baptized and especially priests as announced in Acts 1:8 and affirmed in the Second Vatican Council's Decree on Missionary Activity *Ad gentes*. Here priests are encouraged to "be profoundly aware of the fact that their very life is consecrated to the service of missions."[50] In its Decree on the Ministry and Life of Priests *Presbyterorum ordinis*, the Second Vatican Council expands this thought, affirming that the "The spiritual gift which priests receive at their ordination prepared them not for a sort of limited and narrow mission but for the widest possible and universal mission of salvation 'even to the ends of the earth' (Acts 1:8), for every priestly ministry shares in the universality of the mission entrusted by Christ to his apostles."[51]

A healthy concern for orthodoxy or fidelity to authentic

---

[50] Second Vatican Council, Decree On Mission Activity *Ad gentes* (7 Dec. 1965), § 39.

[51] Second Vatican Council, Decree On the Ministry and Life of Priests *Presbyterorum ordinis* (7 Dec. 1965), § 10.

Church teaching ultimately requires a degree of flexibility if indeed the Church is to inculturate the Christian message, that orthodoxy, into each and every culture in accord with the Lord's missionary mandate. That flexibility must entail the ability to prayerfully listen to and enter into dialogue and meaningful relationship with "others"—those who do not profess what Catholics believe as well as Catholics from different cultures. Intercultural competence refers specifically to the knowledge, attitudes, and skills that will prepare priestly ministers to successfully pursue their missionary discipleship of Christ. Among the qualities necessary for a true missionary is an ability to tolerate (not necessarily approve) what is different or outside one's own experience, for the sake of learning about and relating to others. The priest must be able to give to others and to receive from them. As basic ways for approaching its divine mission, the Church proposes dialogue and engagement with cultures and religions other than one's own through contact as well as through study and immersion experiences.

Today in a globalized world Christian mission is not only what the Church does "in mission territories," but also what occurs throughout the developed world where the people of current and former mission territories now find themselves in growing numbers as a result of migration and globalization. In a sense, we no longer "go to the missions"; the missions have come to us! This is the simple fact at parishes, dioceses, schools, and Catholic organizations throughout the U.S. In that sense, the whole country is "mission territory." Are our seminarians and priests prepared for this psychologically, humanly, spiritually, academically, and pastorally?

GUIDELINES FOR INTERCULTURAL COMPETENCE

From 2008 to 2011, the USCCB's Committee on Cultural Diversity in the Church has elaborated guidelines for intercultural competence. This section describes those guidelines and reflects on them.

The first guideline insists on the ability of ministers to frame the question of cultural competence in terms of the Church's mission and its teachings in Sacred Scripture, Tradition, and the Magisterium. Much of the language and rhetoric around intercultural relations in both social and ecclesial circles is understandably derived from non-ecclesial sources. This language owes much to the secular approach of multiculturalism. Business people concerned with attracting new markets for their products and schools and colleges seeking to accommodate diverse student bodies often led the way in shaping the contemporary U.S. approach toward what is called multiculturalism.

While this secular, civic discourse has positive elements, it is simply neither adequate nor appropriate for framing the question of intercultural relations for ministry in the Church. The focus on intercultural competence in the Church flows directly from its mission and identity. Intercultural competence concerns the means to accomplish the Church's purpose. Consequently, today's priests must have an understanding of how the Church's evangelizing mission as mandated in Sacred Scripture, Tradition, and the Magisterium stands on an *ecclesial* as distinct from *secular* understanding of diversity and multiculturalism. It is an urgent need for all ministers to familiarize themselves with the sources of

this multicultural framework, which are outlined in the series of workshops developed by the Committee on Cultural Diversity titled "Building Intercultural Competence for Ministers."[52]

The second guideline concerns how to appropriately communicate in cultures other than one's own. This involves becoming aware of how culture works, identifying cultural differences and styles, and knowing something about the parameters for interacting with cultures. For instance, some cultures are individualist while others are collectivist. This means that successful communication in a collectivist cultural is indirect: the context requires attention to intermediaries like elders or authorities. Individualist cultures, by contrast, tend to communicate rather directly. There are several other parameters like this which establish the framework for successful intercultural exchanges.

The third guideline concerns effective communication with persons of other cultures by familiarizing oneself with specific elements of cultures such as hierarchy, difficult topics that are avoided, and tone and use of language including body language. Effective communication also involves the manner in which decision-making occurs and how conflict is addressed in diverse cultures. This is a basic factor in having successful mechanisms for gaining the real participation of diverse cultural groups in the life and mission of the Church.

---

[52] United States Conference of Catholic Bishops, Intercultural Competencies, http://www.usccb.org/issues-and-action/cultural-diversity/intercultural-competencies/ (last visited 30 Aug. 2015).

The fourth guideline focuses on group interaction among diverse communities and persons and key factors that negatively influence it: prejudice, stereotyping, racism, and ethnocentrism. How are these negative factors identified and understood, and how does one move beyond them?

Intercultural competency for ministry must be rooted in a practical knowledge of how the Church's goal of communion in diversity takes the shape of ecclesial integration rather than assimilation. Intercultural competency requires a strong basis in Sacred Scripture and a Christian spirituality of reconciliation and mission. What models and best practices are available to parishes, dioceses, schools, and Catholic organizations in their pursuit of their mission? Best practices need to be identified, beginning with parishes and moving on to dioceses, schools, and other Catholic institutions. Practical responses to the challenge of intercultural relations, however, must ultimately be grounded in a theology of mission and a spirituality of reconciliation if they are to preserve their Christian inspiration and catholicity rather than merely be expressions of political correctness.

The bishops' guidelines can be integrated thoughtfully into every ministerial formation program. In the case of the PPF, the guidelines can readily be included in a contemporary vision of ordained ministry, which stresses the mission of the priest in the context of a universal and local Church whose evangelizing mission translates into engagement with many cultures. Indeed the focus or target of all the Church's teaching and preaching is understood precisely in terms of culture in the deepest anthropological sense. The guidelines, moreover, naturally fit into the four pillars of priestly formation today: human, spiritual, intellectual, and pastoral. For example, in regard to the human aspect, the PPF describes the priest as "the man of communion…capable of making a gift of himself and of receiving the gift of others,… a man who relates well with others, free of overt prejudices and willing to work with people of diverse cultural backgrounds."[53] In discussing the life of chastity as lived by celibates, the PPF affirms that "chastity cultivates the capacity for authentic self-gift in generative and faithful love. The celibate person renounces the realization of this capacity in marriage but embraces it in a universalizing love extended to all people."[54]

With regard to the spiritual underpinnings of priestly formation, the PPF stresses the Trinitarian source of the priestly vocation and identity from which is derived the priestly mission: priestly spirituality "is a spirituality of communion rooted in the mystery of the Triune God and lived out in practical ways in the mystery of ecclesial communion."[55] The focus is on relationships within the communion of the three divine persons themselves and of them with each and every human person created by God. This Trinitarian unity in difference or diversity is the grounding of the communion, apostolicity, and catholicity which is the Church. All the baptized, especially the presbyters, are called and sent to serve the Kingdom of God, which service consists of a communion with all peoples regardless of culture, race, or social position. By

---

[53] PPF, § 76.

[54] *Id.*, § 78.

[55] *Id.*, § 108.

analogy, one might speak of the relationships among persons in terms of interculturality by which communion in diversity may be realized through proclamation of the word and prayerful listening and dialogue. [56] The eucharistic banquet to which all are invited as highest expression of the relationship of intimacy between God and human beings highlights the priest's unique role in the divine liturgy. This "divine commerce" between God and human beings realized in the Eucharist is a foretaste of the heavenly banquet in which all the nations—that is, cultures, ethnicities, and races—will partake at the end of time. This mystical, Eucharistic, and eschatological spirituality undergirds the bishops' guidelines on intercultural competence, which seek to prepare the whole Church for the heavenly liturgy at the end of time when the Lord will gather people from "every nation, race, tribe and language" (Rv 7:9).

On a more practical note, the PPF's treatment of spirituality highlights the need for priestly ministers to understand and value devotions in their own spiritual life and to "connect with the rich cultural diversity of devotional life in the United States and to appreciate devotional practices of other cultures."[57] Moreover, the PPF points out the apostolic character of priestly spirituality, which shows itself in the way the priest seeks to encounter Christ in other people. The PPF then makes this telling observation: "Especially in a seminary context, seminarians are to learn how prayer is to be lived out in service of others, particularly the poor, the sick,

---

[56] *See id.*

[57] *Id.,* § 110.

sinners, unbelievers, and the stranger..."[58]

In speaking of the purpose of intellectual formation of priests the PPF is very clear: "Intellectual formation has an apostolic and missionary purpose and finality."[59] By "apostolic," the PPF means the commissioning given the apostles by Christ to "go and baptize the nations" (Mt 28:19). Obviously, knowledge about "the nations," that is, cultures, ethnicities, and races other than one's own, is central for carrying out this Great Commission.

CONCLUSION

The priestly vocation, always but especially at this point in history, requires true conversion to the Lord, a choosing to follow Christ. This necessarily demands moving beyond one's comfort zones. Reaching out to others is fundamental, but how is this to happen? New blood and new generations of Catholics, especially immigrants, are bringing life to the Church in the U.S. They provide a strategic focus for the Church's outreach both as potential future priests and religious called to reap more rich harvests of vocations in years to come. While considerable openness has been manifested toward this diversity, seminaries, theological centers, Catholic universities, colleges, and pastoral institutes must continue to unpack the meaning of diversity and the appropriate effective knowledge, attitudes, and skills that will enable ecclesiastical leaders to successfully reach out to others. This

---

[58] *Id.*

[59] *Id.,* 137.

means integrating study, experience, reflection, and prayer regarding cultural diversity into every ministerial formation program. The focus on intercultural competencies profiled in this essay pertains to one of the more necessary means by which the Church will form priests more capable of fulfilling their magnificent calling. Such competencies will enable them to really preach and teach the Gospel of Jesus Christ and form vibrant communities of faith.

Chapter 6

The "Missionary Option": *Evangelii gaudium,* Cultural Competency, and Foreign Priests

Paul D. Turnley

I dream of a "missionary option," that is, a missionary
impulse capable of transforming everything, so that
the Church's customs, ways of doing things, times
and schedules, language and structures can be suitably
channeled for the evangelization of today's world
rather than for her self-preservation.[60]

---

[60] Pope Francis, Apostolic Exhortation On the Proclamation of the Gospel in Today's World *Evangelii gaudium* (24 Nov. 2013), § 27 [hereinafter EG].

The recent influx of foreign priests into the United States has caused a seismic tremor in the Church in North America. Suddenly, the tables are turned and, instead of being a self-sufficient ecclesial enclave spreading the American version of the Good News through our foreign missionaries, in light of the declining number of our native clergy and the rising number of Catholic laity, we have had to import foreign priests not only as temporary replacements but as permanent priests and pastors of our parishes.[61] We sometimes fail to recognize that we have prayed to the "master of the harvest to send out laborers for his harvest" (Mt 9:38), and He has answered our prayers.[62] Are we shocked that the answer is not what we had in mind or, will we, "rejoice always," (1Thes 5:16), for the "Lord has done great things for us" (Ps 126:3)?

I propose that this incursion of foreign priests is a blessing from the Holy Spirit. The Church in the U.S. is in danger of falling "prey to a kind of ecclesial introversion," which can only be avoided, according to Pope John Paul II, by renewal with *mission* as its goal.[63] Foreign priests can help enable the Church in the U.S.

---

[61] Dean R. Hoge & Aniedi P. Okure, "International Priests in America: Two Coming Issues," *New Theology Review* 19, no. 2 (2006), 16.

[62] In the entire first section of EG, the pope highlights God's emphasis on rejoicing in all circumstances, accepting everything in the childlike spirituality of "May it be done to me according to your word" (Lk 1:38) and "not my will but yours be done" (Lk 22:42).

[63] EG, § 27 (quoting John Paul II, Post-Synodal Apostolic Exhortation On Jesus Christ and the Peoples of Oceania *Ecclesia in Oceania* (22 Nov. 2001), § 19).

to accept that "missionary outreach is *paradigmatic for all the Church's activity*"[64] and that the Church, including the Church in the U.S., is "permanently in a state of mission."[65]

By examining the Church in the U.S. under the microscope of *Evangelii gaudium,* we will discover the importance of an objective interpretation of our culture to its renewal. Through understanding the serendipitous cultural competence of the international priest as a facilitator in developing this interpretation, we will be able to actively embrace the "missionary option."

THE NEW EVANGELIZATION

Through the Magisterium, from *Ad gentes*[66] to *Evangelii nuntiandi*[67] to *Redemptoris missio*[68] to *Evangelii gaudium,* the Holy Spirit has progressively brought into focus the call to "missionary evangelization."[69] As set forth by Pope Francis, the "new evangelization … is carried out in three principal settings": (1) "ordinary pastoral ministry"; (2) "the baptized whose lives do not reflect the demands of Baptism"; and (3) "evangelization … to

---

[64] EG, § 15.

[65] EG, § 25.

[66] Second Vatican Council, Decree on the Mission Activity of the Church *Ad gentes* (7 Dec. 1965).

[67] Paul VI, Apostolic Exhortation *Evangelii nuntiandi* (8 Dec. 1975).

[68] John Paul II, On the Permanent Validity of the Church's Missionary Mandate *Redemptoris missio* (7 Dec. 1990).

[69] John Paul II, *Redemptoris missio,* § 2.

those who do not know Jesus Christ or who have always rejected him."[70]

In attempting to identify the place of the Church in the U.S. in this spectrum, we may be tempted to categorize "the traces of God's Spirit in events great and small" according to our own perspective and not God's providence.[71] In the U.S., we may consider the declining number of American diocesan and religious priests, brothers, and sisters between 2005 and 2013 "bad," but it is balanced by the increased number of priestly and permanent diaconate ordinations and graduate-level seminarians as well as the overall Catholic population.[72] Similarly, although the number of parishes has decreased and the number of parishes without a resident pastor has increased, the number of parishes run by someone other than a priest has decreased.[73] These may be signs of a Church regrouping and gathering its strength for a new missionary push.

Many parishes need to look deeper into the reasons for their empty pews and aging populations. Although "nearly one-in-three Americans (31%) were raised in the Catholic faith, today fewer

---

[70] EG, §§ 14–15.

[71] EG, § 288.

[72] Center for Applied Research in the Apostolate [CARA], Frequently Requested Church Statistics

http://cara.georgetown.edu/caraservices/requestedchurchstats.html (last visited 30 Aug. 2015).

[73] *Id.*

than one-in-four (24%) describe themselves as Catholic."[74] Nor can we any "longer depend on rites of passage or pressure from Catholic culture, peers or even family to bring"[75] disenchanted adults or their children back to the Church. Many of these felt their "spiritual needs were not being met" or "found a religion [they] liked more."[76] Of those who do stay, many believe

it's possible to be a "good Catholic" without observing various elements of Church teaching and discipline. Among the 19% of the respondents who considered themselves "committed Catholics," 49% said it wasn't necessary for a good Catholic to attend Sunday Mass every week; 60% said that good Catholics didn't have to follow Church teaching on birth control, 46% the teaching on divorce and remarriage, 31% the teaching on abortion, and 48% the requirement of being married in the

---

[74] Pew Research Center's Forum on Religion and Public Life, "U.S. Religious Landscape Survey: Summary of Key Findings" (2008), http://religions.pewforum.org/reports (last visited 30 Aug. 2015): "these losses would have been even more pronounced were it not for the offsetting impact of immigration"; see also Sherry A, Weddell, Forming Intentional Disciples: The Path to Knowing and Following Jesus (Huntington, Our Sunday Visitor Publishing Division, 2012), 24 ff.

[75] Weddell, Forming Intentional Disciples, 39; see also Francis I, Evangelii gaudium, § 69.

[76] Weddell, Forming Intentional Disciples, 28–29.

Church; and 39% said that good Catholics needn't contribute time or money to help the poor.[77]

According to even our U.S. bishops, our cultural ethic is "a form of moral relativism that is joined, not without inconsistency, to a belief in the absolute rights of individuals."[78]

"Our faith simply becomes a function of the national myth, a function of a certain culture's interpretation of itself and the world."[79] The faith is relegated to "the sphere of the private and personal," and put on a par with all other beliefs.[80] These observations are borne out in the Pew survey: 79% of American Catholics believe many religions can lead to eternal life.[81]

---

[77] Russell Shaw, *American Church: The Remarkable Rise, Meteoric Fall, and Uncertain Future of Catholicism in America* (San Francisco: Ignatius, 2013), Kindle ed., 208–12.

[78] United States Conference of Catholic Bishops, *Ministry to Persons with a Homosexual Inclination: Guidelines for Pastoral Care* (Washington, DC: USCCB, 2006), 14–15; *see also* Allan F. Deck, "Intercultural Competence: The Opportunities and Challenges of the Present Reality," *Seminary Journal* 18, no. 2 (2012), 9; and Francis I, *Evangelii gaudium*, § 61.

[79] Deck, "Intercultural Competence," 9.

[80] EG, § 64.

[81] The Pew Forum on Religion & Public Life, *U.S. Religious Landscape Survey: Religious Beliefs and Practices: Diverse and Politically Relevant* (Washington, DC: Pew Research Center, 2008), 4.

If we refuse to believe that the Church in the U.S. is hemorrhaging, we will "end up in a state of paralysis and acedia."[82] We will experience "the gray pragmatism of the daily life of the Church, in which all appears to proceed normally, while in reality faith is wearing down and degenerating into small-mindedness. A tomb psychology thus develops and slowly transforms Christians into mummies in a museum."[83] Based on these findings within the American Church, we can no longer deny we are at least in setting two of the mission field of the new evangelization—the baptized whose lives do not reflect the demands of Baptism.

A CASE FOR AMERICAN *AD GENTES* STATUS

However, if we examine the Church in the U.S. from the perspective of *Evangelii gaudium,* U.S. Catholicism is definitely in stage three. It is experiencing "exculturation."[84] Christianity, including Catholicism, has ceased "to form part of people's cultural universe."[85] Catholic enclaves are rapidly disappearing; "God has no Grandchildren."[86] Though in theory, 75% of the U.S. population is Christian, "the world we live in is not a friend of the gospel, no

---

[82] EG, § 81.

[83] EG, § 83.

[84] Weddell, *Forming Intentional Disciples,* 15.

[85] Anthony M. Abela, "Catholicism: The End of a 'World'?" *The Sunday Times* (5 Oct. 2003), 56 (reviewing Danièle Harvieu-Léger, *Catholicisme, la fin d'un monde* (Paris: Bayard, 2003)).

[86] Weddell, *Forming Intentional Disciples,* 39; *see also Evangelii gaudium*, Chapter One.

matter how superficially 'religious' American culture may still sometimes seem. It has contempt for Jesus Christ, contempt for the Cross, and contempt for the people who carry their own cross and follow him."[87] We are, in reality, the object of our own mission *ad gentes.*

The world, including the U.S., has lost what Pope Francis aptly labels "the joy of the Gospel."[88]

> The great danger in today's world, pervaded as it is by consumerism, is the desolation and anguish born of a complacent yet covetous heart, the feverish pursuit of frivolous pleasures, and a blunted conscience.... This is a very real danger for believers too. Many fall prey to it, and end up resentful, angry and listless.[89]

As a nation, we fail to see our economy as one "of exclusion and inequality."[90] We refuse to join the pope in saying "no" to the new idolatry of money, "no" to a financial system which rules rather than serves, "no" to inequality which spawns violence.[91] We do not recognize, let alone accept, that "inequality is the root of

---

[87] Shaw, *American Church*, Kindle ed., 48-50.

[88] EG, § 1.

[89] EG, § 2.

[90] EG, § 53.

[91] EG, §§ 53–60.

social ills," that no problems can be resolved without resolving basic economic discrimination.[92]

Our cultural woes are not limited to the idol, mammon. Science is another idol, our animism encouraging us to believe we can find all the answers by examining creation. African and Asian bishops castigate our social communications as lacking "due consideration to [their] priorities and problems ... [and] their cultural make-up," and "threatening traditional values, and in particular the sacredness of marriage and the stability of the family."[93]

The central issue of modern American Catholic life is the temptation to accommodate, to compromise, to get along, and to fit in—and then feel good about it. We accept tepidness in the name of pluralism. We put diversity of belief and behavior above truth. We place the individual above the common good. We elevate "tolerance" above love, justice, and real charity. None of this converts anybody. It does the opposite. It provides people with alibis for indifference and inaction, and it leeches away their faith.[94]

---

[92] EG, § 202.

[93] EG, § 62.

[94] Shaw, *American Church*, Kindle ed., 58–61.

THE NEED FOR CULTURAL AWARENESS

"The simple unambiguous proclamation of what the church teaches is not enough.... The church teaches that the gospel must be translated in a way that it can be received by others. Doctrine becomes life through culture."[95] As Pope Francis points out, "[i]t is imperative to evangelize cultures in order to inculturate the Gospel." In "profoundly secularized countries, it will mean sparking new processes for evangelizing culture, even though these will demand long-term planning."[96]

The Mexican-born Archbishop of Los Angeles, José H. Gomez, observed:

> ... we all need to be better students of American culture, to understand our culture's worldview. We need to understand this culture's values and assumptions. We need to understand the impact this culture is having on our Catholic identity, on our people's faith and their ability to know and believe in Jesus. We need to understand our culture in order to convert it, in order to lead men and women toward the truth.[97]

---

[95] Deck, *Intercultural Competence,* 11–12.

[96] EG, § 69.

[97] Archbishop José H. Gomez, "The Formation of Holy Priests and the New Evangelization," *Seminary Journal* 18, no. 2 (2012), 16.

Cultural awareness is enhanced by the perspective of comparison and contrast with alternate cultures, as anyone who has lived abroad knows. The Holy Spirit has given the Church in the U.S. a great gift—an ability to see our own culture through the eyes of the "hidden" foreign-born 25% of U.S. Catholics, that is, the Hispanic Latinos, Africans, Afro-Caribbeans, Asians, and Pacific Islanders.[98] A recent convert observed: "In my former church it was just us. But in the Catholic Church, you see priests and people from all over the world. The Catholic Church is truly universal."[99]

Even in the melting pot of U.S., we cannot demand that these peoples express "their Christian faith" by imitating "modes of expression which European nations developed at a particular moment of their history, because the faith cannot be constricted to the limits of understanding and expression of any one culture."[100] International priests can help us reevaluate "the naïve insistence of mid-twentieth century giants like John Tracy Ellis and John Courtney Murray that the American way still constituted the best hope for both the Church and all mankind."[101] While the USCCB's

---

[98] *See* Mark Gray, Melissa Cidade, Mary Gautier & Thomas Gaunt, *Cultural Diversity in the Catholic Church in the United States* (Washington, DC: CARA, 2013), 7, 10.

[99] Aniedi Okure, "International Priests in the United States: An Update," *Seminary Journal* 18, no. 1 (2012), 39.

[100] EG, § 118.

[101] Jeff Mirus, "The Rise and Fall of the (American?) Church," CatholicCulture.org (23 May 2013) (reviewing Russell Shaw, *American Church: The Remarkable Rise, Meteoric Fall, and Uncertain Future of Catholicism in America* (San Francisco: Ignatius, 2013)).

inculturation program works to incorporate Catholics from diverse cultures to work and worship together in a mostly Caucasian setting, a simultaneous program should enable these target populations to reexamine, call into question, and offer alternatives and remedies to our present predominantly white, individualistic, consumer-driven, disintegrating American ecclesial culture.

THE PARISH PRIEST: MISSION OR MAINTENANCE

The Church in the U.S., under the leadership of its bishops, "is likewise called to missionary conversion" "To make this missionary impulse ever more focused, generous and fruitful," Pope Francis encourages "each particular Church to undertake a resolute process of discernment, purification and reform."[102]

In light of our cultural turpitude, priests "'cannot passively and calmly wait in [their] church buildings'; [they] need to move 'from a pastoral ministry of mere conservation to a decidedly missionary pastoral ministry.'"[103] The parish priest, foreign or domestic, can no longer afford to focus simply on the administration of the sacraments to the practicing Catholic remnant but must truly extend his pastorate to all within the geographical boundaries of his parish, including the fallen-aways, ecumenical brethren.[104] Because of its great flexibility, Pope Francis exhorts that the parish,

---

[102] EG, § 30.

[103] EG, § 15 (quoting Fifth General Conference of the Latin American and Caribbean Bishops (CELAM), *Aparecida Document* (29 June 2007)).

[104] *Cf. Code of Canon Law*, cc. 518 and 519.

can assume quite different contours depending on the openness and missionary creativity of the pastor and the community.... This presumes that it really is in contact with the homes and the lives of its people, and does not become a useless structure out of touch with people or a self-absorbed cluster made up of a chosen few.[105]

We must admit with the pope, however, "that the call to review and renew our parishes has not yet sufficed to bring them nearer to people, to make them environments of living communion and participation, and to make them completely mission-oriented."[106] Parishes do not conform to his vision of "a Church which is bruised, hurting and dirty because it has been out on the streets, rather than a Church which is unhealthy from being confined and from clinging to its own security."[107]

FOREIGN PRIESTS AS MISSIONARIES

The vast majority of international priests "describe themselves as missionaries coming to help the church in the United States."[108] Having the mindset of a missionary, they are more apt to view their parish as a mission field, unlike their American counterparts and

---

[105] EG, § 28.

[106] EG, § 28.

[107] EG, § 49.

[108] Hoge and Okure, "International Priests: Two Issues," 15.

congregations.[109] "The missionary's enthusiasm in proclaiming Christ comes from the conviction that he is responding to that expectation."[110] International missionary priests share with the American bishops Jesus angst: "I have come to set the earth on fire, and how I wish it were already blazing!" (Lk 12:49).[111] International missionary priests exalt in the portion of God's "spirit poured out on all flesh" (Acts 2:17; Jl 3:2). They experience the depth of the Pope Francis' definition of man: "I am a mission on this earth; that is the reason why I am here in this world."[112] The American Church needs the charisma and the vitality of international priests.

Like "the first missionaries to America," today's international priests must be "serious students of the indigenous cultures they found here."[113] Priests from poverty-stricken Third World Countries are able to consider our "Native American" disposable consumerism with much more detachment and critical judgment than we for whom loaded grocery shelves are taken for granted.[114]

---

[109] "The reason seems to be that Americans see their country as one that sends missionaries, not receives them..." Hoge and Okure, "International Priests in America: Two Coming Issues," § 21.

[110] John Paul II, *Redemptoris missio*, § 292.

[111] *Cf.* particularly the webnars at USCCB, Leadership Institute Programs, Track III, New Evangelization, http://www.usccb.org/beliefs-and-teachings/how-we-teach/catechesis/leadership-institute/programs-track-3.cfm (last visited 30 Aug. 2015).

[112] EG, § 273.

[113] Gomez, "Formation of Holy Priests," 15.

[114] USCCB, Issues and Action, Promise to Protect, Pledge to Heal: International   Priests   2010,   http://www.usccb.org/issues-and-

We should consider them as "precious allies in the commitment"[115] to the universal church and its traditions, for theirs is "an evangelical discernment, the approach of a missionary disciple, 'nourished by the light and strength of the Holy Spirit.'"[116]

THE QUALIFICATIONS OF THE INTERNATIONAL PRIEST

"Moving across cultures is not for the weak or the faint-hearted, and not every foreign-born priest can do it."[117] However, those who can, who have "cultural competence,"[118] may provide invaluable observations and suggestions.

First, by virtue of their being in the U.S., they possess at least a workable knowledge of our culture.[119] Foreign priests, after surviving the initial stages of culture shock, euphoria, and adaptation challenges, can begin to evaluate and integrate the old

---

action/child-and-youth-protection/upload/2010-International-Priests.pdf.

[115] EG, § 257.

[116] EG, § 50.

[117] Hoge & Okure, "International Priests: Two Issues," 20.

[118] Len Sperry, "Becoming Culturally Competent is a Process, Not an Event," *Seminary Journal* 18, no. 2 (2012), 43.

[119] A follow-up survey is needed to ascertain the depth of understanding by most foreign priests about Sperry's "particularly facts about ethnic values, mores, rituals, cuisine, language, social class differences, issues about acculturation, disability, religious beliefs and practices, gender codes, and age and generational differences." Sperry, "Becoming Culturally Competent," 43.

ways and the new, judging the strengths and particularly the weaknesses of each.

Being transplants, international priests in the U.S. possess the "capacity to recognize one's own cultural worldview and biases, as well as the capacity to recognize a cultural problem or issue of another individual or individuals in a particular cultural situation,"[120] as some did when surveyed about their position in America.[121] In addition to their international orientation and training, many religious priests have had international experience in "missionary countries" before beginning ministry in America, a multi-cultural experience which geometrically enhances their perspectives.[122] Hoge and Okure point out international priests "can help us reevaluate parts of American culture—like weak family ties, waste of resources, and so on—by being a mirror for Americans to see ourselves from outsider's eyes."[123]

Being men of God, most international priests at least try to "respond in a respectful, empathic and welcoming manner, as well as recognize the likely impact and consequences of specific attitudes, words and actions on another individual or individuals in a particular cultural situation."[124]

---

[120] *Id.*, 43.

[121] *See* Fernando A. Ortiz & Gerard J. McGlone, "Model for Intercultural Competencies in Formation and Ministry: Awareness, Knowledge, Skills and Sensitivity," *Seminary Journal* 18, no. 2 (2012), 37–38; *see also* Okure, "International Priests: Update," 37.

[122] Hoge & Okure, "International Priests: Two Issues," 19.

[123] *Id.*, 16.

[124] Sperry, "Culturally Competent," 43.

PROBLEMS OF ACCEPTANCE

Sometimes their congregations or diocesan priest colleagues rebuff international priests.[125] As foreign-born priests have reported, "the attitude of American superiority and constant questioning to validate your authenticity makes one doubt the universality of the Catholic faith."[126] "We preach one church, one family, yet the way you are treated tells you that the oneness does not include you."[127] "Our pastoral expertise is needed within the church but we are not invited to hang around."[128]

I suggest we need more than just the pastoral expertise of international priests. We need both their foreign eyes and their missionary perspective to identify and reach the Anglo-Saxon lost sheep of the house of America. If we change our rationale for hiring them from strictly plugging parish holes to true missionary outreach, the fact that they are from a different part of the world would not be considered a drawback but a definite asset.[129]

---

[125] "When you come, it is like they are torn between seeing the necessity of your presence and the needs of the ministry here, and the fact that you are an intruder. They give you the idea that this is just by the-way, and you are not going to be accepted on a permanent basis." Ortiz & McGlone, "Model for Intercultural Competencies," 37–38; *see also* Okure, "International Priests: Update," 37.

[126] Okure, "International Priests: Update," 37.

[127] Ortiz & McGlone, "Model for Intercultural Competencies," 37–38.

[128] *See id.*, 38; *see also* Okure, "International Priests: Update," 37.

[129] "They see the part of the world you come from rather than the fact that you are a priest of the Catholic Church." *Id.*, 37–38.

While foreign priests can be a great help to us, their inculturation into the U.S. is also important. Some come with ecclesiastical misunderstandings that have to do with power and communication. Some must get use to the fact that we do not place priests on pedestals, particularly in light of priest scandals. "Others dislike any lay involvement in parish leadership."[130] An attitude against lay leadership may stem from "laity running parishes [and] international priest ... [being] often seen merely as dispensers of the sacraments."[131] Finally, although they may "voice strict standards on controversial moral issues like cohabitation or homosexuality,"[132] they provide the balance we need to keep our moral pendulum from swinging too far left.

WORKING AT ACCEPTANCE: *TIKKUN OLAM*

We Catholics in the U.S., individual dioceses and parishes, along with international priests, are all "asked to obey his call to go forth from our own comfort zone in order to reach all the 'peripheries' in need of the light of the Gospel."[133] "We are thus 'co-operators with God' (Rom 8:28), joining in the 'repairing of the world,' or *tikkun olam,* as the Jewish people beautifully put it."[134]

---

[130] Hoge & Okure, "International Priests: Two Issues," 17.

[131] Okure, "International Priests: Update," 37.

[132] Hoge & Okure, "International Priests: Two Issues," 17.

[133] EG, § 20.

[134] Richard Rohr, Richard Rohr's Daily Meditation, "First Fruits" (12 Feb. 2014), *available at* http://myemail.constantcontact.com/Richard-

The Church grows not by proselytizing but "by attraction."[135] We are called to share the foreign missionaries' conviction "that, through the working of the Spirit, there already exists in individuals and peoples an expectation, even if an unconscious one, of knowing the truth about God, about man, and about how we are to be set free from sin and death."[136]

We are called to go forth from our sanctums of sacramentality to be the *lumen gentium*. With Pope Francis, we

> do not want a Church concerned with being at the centre which then ends by being caught up in a web of obsessions and procedures.... More than by fear of going astray, my hope is that we will be moved by the fear of remaining shut up within structures which give us a false sense of security, within rules which make us harsh judges, within habits which make us feel safe, while at our door people are starving and Jesus does not tire of saying to us: "Give them something to eat" (Mk 6:37).[137]

Foreign priests with missionary zeal can help the Church in the U.S. go forth to become "a community of missionary disciples who take the first step, who are involved and supportive, who bear fruit

---

Rohr-s-Meditation--First-

Fruits.html?soid=1103098668616&aid=sObdwHDBreU.

[135] EG, § 14.

[136] John Paul II, *Redemptoris missio*, § 292.

[137] EG, § 49.

and rejoice." They can teach us "that the Lord has taken the initiative, he has loved us first (*cf.* 1 Jn 4:19), and therefore we can move forward, boldly take the initiative, go out to others, seek those who have fallen away, stand at the crossroads and welcome the outcast."[138]

Foreign-born priests will help us heed the Pope Francis' call, "let us try a little harder to take the first step and to become involved ... by word and deed in people's daily lives." Let us "take on the 'smell of the sheep' and the sheep will be more willing to hear [our] voice." "Evangelization consists mostly of patience and disregard for constraints of time." International priests can help us find "a way to let the word take flesh in a particular situation and bear fruits of new life, however imperfect or incomplete these may appear."[139]

"SO WHAT ARE WE WAITING FOR?"[140]

"Being a Christian is not the result of an ethical choice or a lofty idea, but the encounter with an event, a person, which gives life a new horizon and a decisive direction."[141] "Every Christian is a missionary to the extent that he or she has encountered the love of God in Christ Jesus: we no longer say that we are 'disciples' and 'missionaries,' but rather that we are always 'missionary

---

[138] EG, § 24.

[139] EG, § 24.

[140] EG, § 120.

[141] EG, § 7.

disciples."[142] "The ultimate aim should be that the Gospel, as preached in categories proper to each culture, will create a new synthesis with that particular culture. This is always a slow process and at we can be overly fearful."[143] We must learn to trust the Spirit's faithfulness, if church renewal and reform, if re-evangelization and the missionary option are ever to succeed. Part of that trust is expanding our vision of the cultural competency international priests bring to their position. "To each individual the manifestation of the Spirit is given for some benefit" (1 Cor: 12:7).

"The Church in the United States faces an absolutely new and absolutely real kind of mission territory every day now, filled with intractable pastoral challenges ... and we need a new Pentecost."[144] International priests are certainly not the whole answer. But they can be part of the solution if we choose to see "the missionary option" as a new paradigm outlined for us by Pope Francis, and we do "not allow ourselves to be robbed of missionary enthusiasm!"[145]

---

[142] EG, § 120.

[143] EG, § 129.

[144] Shaw, *American Church,* Kindle ed., 83–89.

[145] EG, § 80.

Chapter 7

St. Mary's Seminary's Program in Communication Skills Instruction

Elizabeth Carrow Woolfolk, Ph.D.

INTRODUCTION

The need for professional intervention to modify speech articulation for international seminarians in the United States has become apparent in the last few years. The number of prospective priests coming to America from Africa, Vietnam, and Spanish-speaking countries has multiplied. Some of these young men come with little or no knowledge of English. Others, while having an adequate use of English vocabulary and syntax, use the phonemic system of vowels and consonants in their native language as a substitute for the phonemic system of English. Although the speech of the latter group is often adequate for informal communication, it may be a handicap when attempting to address an audience of parishioners. Mispronunciation and misarticulation can interfere with the comprehension of a sermon or homily.

Listeners become frustrated and some even leave a church because of this frustration.

Many seminaries and even some parishes have attempted to address this problem. Although there may be success with one or two individuals, the problem as a whole has not been remediated. Plans are often ineffectual because the seminarians or priests, as the case may be, are not fully convinced of the need for assistance or are too busy to give the attention and time needed to modify their speech. In other instances, the program is too costly, particularly if those for whom it is developed are not interested in investing their energies. The challenge is to formulate a plan that will address both issues.

After outsourcing a speech program to a local university for two years, St. Mary's Seminary in Houston realized that approach was neither financially nor linguistically effective. In the summer of 2011, the administrators at the Seminary decided to develop an in-house model program for improving the pronunciation and articulation of international seminarians. The administrators realized that such a program would require trying different approaches to solving the problem and selecting those procedures that appeared most effective and economical. They also understood that the development of such a program would take two or three years.

PLANNING THE PILOT PROGRAM

Planning a program in July to be implemented in August was not an easy task. The number of seminarians that needed assistance

and the number of instructors needed for assisting them were unknown. The need for instructors had to be met first, so requests for qualified professionals were placed in the neighborhood church bulletins for three or four weeks in July. Surprisingly, there were numerous individuals who wished to volunteer. Among those that wanted to help were four certified speech pathologists and five teachers of English as a second language. In addition, the volunteers included four or five individuals with degrees in related subjects, such as English. In the latter part of July, the seminary administration and staff met with the volunteers to review the program. A coordinator was selected from among the volunteers and the time for meeting with the seminarians was set from 1:00 to 3:00 pm on Friday afternoons, except for those Fridays on which religious events had already been scheduled.

The administrators and coordinator then reviewed general issues and tasks with the volunteers. Points covered included the following.

1. Previous attempts at providing speech assistance to the international students had not proven successful as far as the seminarians themselves were concerned. Many of them would find reasons to miss the classes. One task of the volunteers was to convince the students of their need for help and to make the classes as interesting as possible.

2. Faculty members also needed to be made aware of the importance of good speech intelligibility. For example, a homily is not effective unless it can be understood. An essential ingredient of the program was faculty support,

particularly because changes in speech articulation take time and significant amounts of practice are required before improvement is noticed.

3. Related to point 2, both the administration and faculty needed to respect the time set aside for speech lessons. If the students were not allowed flexibility for attending speech classes or if other jobs were given to them during class time, they would not consider their attendance at class important.

4. Although the volunteers did not receive compensation, they could not treat their responsibility lightly. By being well prepared and punctual, they would communicate to the students that what is being done is important.

5. If there had been time before the session started, the professional coordinators would have provided in-service training for the volunteers. Such training, in addition to demonstrating methodologies in speech intervention, addresses such tasks as keeping attendance records, preparing lesson plans, and documenting progress so that a substitute can know exactly what has been done and what needs to be done. In the demonstration program, these tasks were covered during the semester instead of at its start.

The most important of the instructors' tasks was that of administering the speech modification program itself. We had a number of components of the speech program; some we changed and others we dropped as we proceeded.

SPEECH PROGRAM COMPONENTS

This section briefly considers various components of the speech program, including: assessment; a mini-course in American phonetics; methodology in speech modification; expansion of speech knowledge to other experiences; grouping the students for instruction; audio-visual support; and the volunteers themselves.

Although we had little time to do a complete assessment the summer before we started the program, we plan to include it in the program at the beginning of each subsequent semester. Such assessment consists of measuring the student's articulation of American English phonemes and American grammatical morphemes. A rating scale highlights evaluation of word and phrase stress in sentences, appropriate intonation patterns, and general intelligibility. The results of the testing provide the guidelines for instruction and obviate the necessity to start all the students at the same level of training. Students want to begin at the point where they belong. We found that nineteen young men satisfied the requirements for eligibility in the program—that is, the speech they used contained sufficient phoneme errors to reduce intelligibility for listeners.

Topics included in the mini-course in American phonetics were: (1) structure and function of the speech mechanism; (2) description of and distinction between consonant and vowel sounds; (3) production of American English consonants according to place of articulation, manner of articulation, and voicing, and their comparison to consonants of other languages; (4) place of modification of the oral cavity for the production of vowels; (5)

rules of stress of substantive words in sentences as well as the lack of stress of grammatical morphemes; and (6) use of the International Phonetic Alphabet.

During the first semester of the school year, forty-five minutes of a two-hour period were set aside for the mini-phonetics course. However, because of the students' other seminary obligations, only about six classes took place. Because the program during the previous year had not been successful, the coordinator believed (and still believes) that some indicator of accountability needed to be a part of the course, such as university credit, a certificate for passing, or a final exam—anything that would encourage the students to master the content.

The class was meant to provide the students with a theoretical basis for understanding speech production, to assist them in analyzing and correcting their own errors, and to help them hear and understand production differences among the phonemes of their own language and between their native language and American English. Unfortunately, because of limited time, the phonetics class was dropped from the program for the year immediately following the pilot program and the emphasis shifted to phoneme production techniques.

What methodology in speech modification did the pilot program employ? The procedures used for speech intervention were standard ones used for error modification, including: (1) ear training—teaching the students to hear error sounds when they occur in isolation, in words, and in sentences; (2) discrimination—having the students compare the error sound with the target correct sound and indicate if the sounds differ; (3) production—

having the students produce the target sound either by imitation or by teaching the placement of the articulators, first using the sound in isolation, next in words, and lastly in sentences.

One of the most difficult steps in changing speech pattern is incorporating new patterns into daily life experiences. Most international students have a number of incorrectly articulated sounds. Some of their target sounds are not actually 'wrong,' but even a slight deviation in one sound can make a word appear to be a different although similar word. Changing one sound and carrying it over to conversational speech or to sermons and homilies takes an almost infinite number of repetitions. If it is hard to change even one sound, again, consider how difficult it must be to change a number of sounds in all the words in which such sounds appear and to do so when trying to use speech as a medium of communication. Consider having to make these changes when your central focus is study and spiritual development. It's not an easy task!

One activity that appeared to successfully motivate the students to practice was a presentation of readings from the Bible by those seminarians who would not be at the seminary the following year. This presentation took place at the final meeting in May, and among the invitees were the former archbishop of the Diocese of Galveston-Houston, the rector and vice-rector of the seminary, family members, and friends. Each seminarian practiced his excerpt, focusing on the sounds that were troublesome to him. The seminarians made the effort to articulate slowly, stress appropriate words to elicit meaning, and use good intonation. Many believed that this event was successful in accomplishing its purpose.

Because we had not had the opportunity to evaluate the speech and language of the seminarians completely when we started the program in August, we had little criteria for putting them into instructional groups. Grouping the students for instruction was necessary because there were nineteen seminarians who needed help and thirteen volunteers, only seven of whom had any previous experience with helping adults change speech patterns. The groups were not constant because some of the seminarians or some of the volunteers would be absent from time to time. Furthermore, the error sounds differed for the individuals within the groups, and the differences made individualizing instruction difficult.

We changed the grouping the students for the second semester. The seminarians were divided into three teams of approximately the same size and having more or less the same error patterns: African, Vietnamese, and Spanish-speaking (Mexican and Columbian). Assigned to each team were four or five volunteers—two professionals plus two or three aides. Each team was further divided into pairs having the same sound errors that needed remediation. This general approach was more effective, particularly for students who were able to get individualized instruction.

The group format also made it possible to work on other communication features important to speech intelligibility: syllable accent in words, word stress in sentences, intonation, rate and volume—the suprasegmentals of speech. Sessions for rating the above aspects of speech provided feedback to the students from individuals not directly involved in the instructional program.

We were fortunate to have available the latest audio-visual

equipment to display charts and graphs in teaching the phonetic course. Computers allowed the students to listen to special language discs and imitate sounds, words and sentences. Additionally, each student had his own digital recorder for practice outside of class.

The volunteers created charts and tables for the course in phonetics, word lists for practice with selected sounds, and forms to plan lessons, chart progress, and rank performance. The words that occur in the priest's spoken portion of the Mass were classified according to initial, medial, and final sound to allow the seminarians to concentrate on specific error sounds.

The response to our request for volunteers was extraordinary. The volunteers represented churches from all over the city, some quite a distance from the seminary. At least four of them had fulltime positions; these received permission to leave work and make up time later during their free time. One was a Vietnamese physician who left his office to donate his efforts to help his countrymen. The volunteers were conscientious about attending, thereby signaling to the student the importance of the task of modifying his speech. A few even attended seminary services where one of the international students was reading an epistle or preaching. Most of the volunteers stated a desire to return the following year.

LESSONS FOR MOVING FORWARD

All in all, we believe we had a successful year. The seminarians were more enthusiastic about the program in May than they had been in August. One of the deacons, who helped in a local parish, reported that parishioners who did not know he was in the program told him how much he had improved during the three months he was there. The speech instructors recognized significant improvement in many cases. The improvement was gradual and therefore not necessarily noticeable to those who came into contact with the students on a daily basis.

An evaluation of the 2011–2012 program in "American Phonetics" (formerly called "accent modification" or "accent reduction") helped us arrive at some changes that may make the program more effective in the future:

1. Because Friday afternoon is at the end of the week of graduate theology classes and other obligations, the day for speech class and instruction should be changed.
2. Even within a specific language group, each student has unique misarticulations, making it necessary to work with each on an individual basis. We have tried to provide such individual work.
3. Because there is no other day when all the students are available at the same time, we decided that each student should receive two lessons during their free periods during the week.
4. The most effective instructors were the speech pathologists and those with a background of teaching English as a second language. The seminary administrators were willing to hire three part-time professionals to work with the international students during the day. Their salaries

together amounted to about the salary of one full-time professional.

5. The seminary will also provide speech classes to international priests already working in parishes.

6. Having volunteers for the program created goodwill and infused energy into the program, so we would like them to continue in some capacity.

7. Long-term planning envisions having a laboratory for speech and language so that the seminarians can have a place to practice "out loud." One student told us that he practiced in the shower even though others thought he was "crazy."

In thinking back on the American Phonetics program initiated in 2011–2012 at St. Mary's Seminary in Houston, Texas, we believe that, for a beginning program, it was a success. Most, if not all, of the seminarians were more intelligible after taking the program. The choice of the program's name—American Phonetics—was fortuitous, acknowledging, as it does, a broad scope of speech-related issues—cultural, psychological, emotional, and linguistic. Attention to the multitude of factors having a role in change helped convince the seminarians that we were all together in our attempts to create for them a new way of communicating without having to give up the old. We were no longer just 'modifying their accents.' Many features of the program were experimental: the volunteers, the course in phonetics, the group work with suprasegmental phonemes, the feedback from outside listeners. Seminary administrators could evaluate the relative value of each component and determine which to change and which to continue, taking into account the factors of purpose, time, money, and availability. They viewed the program as one in the process of development, able to bring back at a later time the pieces that were omitted and to restructure the parts in a new way. The administrators will continue to act with knowledge that the effectiveness of priests from countries outside of the U.S. depends, to a large extent, upon their ability to communicate with clarity in English.

Chapter 8

Holy Apostles College and Seminary's English as a Second Language Program: Preparing International Students for Success

Caitlin Seadale Celella

Holy Apostles College and Seminary, located in the middle of Connecticut, is a unique place where priests, deacons, seminarians, brothers, sisters, and lay students study side by side. With bachelor and master degrees offered in both philosophy and theology, students are attracted to Holy Apostles from many different states and countries. Of the 160 students who take classes on campus, over 40% are receiving services from the English as a Second Language (ESL) Department.

The ESL department has the goal of preparing students to succeed in rigorous English-based courses. Comprised of two professors—one full-time and one part-time—the department offers five core courses with teaching practices based on research concerning second language acquisition. The ESL department offers to each student individual tutoring with native English-speaking volunteers and access to a small ESL library, as well as workshops on pronunciation, avoiding plagiarism, and properly citing sources. Jim Cummins' seminal research on English language acquisition found that grade-level students require a period of five to seven years, on average, to approach norms in utilizing academic English.[146] Even with such a small department, most of the students at Holy Apostles need only two to three years in ESL courses before they are prepared to enroll in non-ESL, credit-bearing courses. This success, achieved within such a small timeframe, is due to two things: a research-based curriculum and a teaching methodology that serve to provide maximum practice time in a classroom environment that lowers students' affective filter, and a comprehensive writing program that prepares students for the rigors of academic writing in English.

The five core ESL courses, which range from beginner to advanced levels, focus on practice, accuracy, and confidence. Practice is needed to acquire the new language, accuracy to master the language and succeed in English-based courses, and confidence to ask questions and utilize the language in the presence of native speakers. Most importantly, practice results in moving language from students' short-term memory to long-term memory. Practice takes a great amount of time. Therefore, students who enter Holy

---

[146] Jim Cummins, "Age on Arrival and Immigrant Second Language Learning in Canada: A Reassessment," *Applied Linguistics* 2 (1981), 132–49.

Apostles' ESL program as beginners or intermediate English speakers are enrolled in three ESL courses. This provides the majority of students in the ESL program with 4.5 hours of English practice, four days a week.

SECOND LANGUAGE ACQUISITION

To outline how one learns a second language, Barry McLaughlin writes: "second language learning is viewed as the acquisition of a complex cognitive skill. To learn a second language is to learn a *skill,* because various aspects of the task must be practised and integrated into fluent performance."[147] Taking three ESL courses per day assists students with acquiring English, a new skill. When beginning to learn a second language, students are engaged in controlled processing, which "involves the temporary activation of a selection of information nodes in the memory, in a new configuration ... [it] requires a lot of focused attentional control on the part of the subject, and is constrained by the limitations of the short-term memory."[148] Through much practice, "sequences first produced by controlled processing become automatic. Automatized sequences are stored as units in the long-term memory, which means they can be made available very rapidly whenever the situation requires it, with minimal attentional

---

[147] Barry McLaughlin, *Theories of Second Language Learning* (London: Arnold, 1987), 133–34.

[148] Rosamond Mitchell & Florence Myles, *Second Language Learning Theories,* 2nd ed. (London: Arnold, 2004), 100.

control on the part of the subject."[149] Students spend a great amount of time in classes, which provides the time necessary to move language sequences from short-term memory to long-term memory. Having moved their English language skills to their long-term memory, ESL students are able to access the sequences quickly and with less attention.

CLASSROOM ENVIRONMENT

Providing students with time to practice their English skills is just as important as providing them with the classroom environment to support language learning. To achieve this aim, Holy Apostles' ESL program strives to provide a classroom environment that lowers students' affective filter. The affective filter, introduced by Krashen in 1985, is defined as "a mental block that prevents acquirers from fully utilizing the comprehensible input they receive for language acquisition."[150] "Anxiety, lack of confidence, and lack of motivation" are the factors associated with this mental block, and the presence of these factors in the classroom has been shown to lead to slower or less thorough language learning.[151] Though Holy Apostles' ESL students are in general extremely motivated, their ESL classroom environment has

---

[149] *Id.*, 101.

[150] Stephen D. Krashen, *The Input Hypothesis: Issues and Implications* (London: Longman, 1985), 3.

[151] Marysia Johnson, *A Philosophy of Second Language Acquisition* (New Haven, CT: Yale University Press, 2004), 48.

been designed to ease anxiety and induce confidence by creating an encouraging and supportive learning community that is driven by a stable pattern of classroom language and activities, sheltered instruction practices, and formative assessment.

One complete series of books, Cambridge University Press' *Interchange* Passages, provide the template for a stable pattern of classroom language and activities in Holy Apostles' ESL program. Course levels I, II, and III are entirely based on the first three levels of *Interchange* books; while course levels IV and V use *Passages 1* and *Passages 2*, respectively. Each course focuses on English practice according to the lessons and activities provided in this series of books. This is a successful model because the books integrate new grammar and vocabulary with practice in the four language domains: listening, speaking, reading, and writing. Therefore, skill practice is integrated. For instance, a speaking activity with a partner necessitates both speaking to a partner and listening to a partner. A writing activity may feature speaking to a partner about their topic as well as writing. Such activities reinforce all four language domains and lead to extended practice time during every class. Basing every class session on the book is valuable because students know exactly what to prepare for the next class, can follow along in class easily, and know what to expect in terms of classroom activities.

The ESL classroom environment at Holy Apostles has been structured so that the target language is the only element that changes from day to day. This lowers students' affective filter, as their anxiety is reduced when they know what activities and teacher speech to expect in class. For example, every class session has the same structure: attendance, prayer, and then work in the student book or workbook. The language for each activity is the same in every course. The request for a prayer is always "Would someone please start us with a prayer?" When there is a picture accompanying an activity in the book, the professor's always asks, "What do you see in the picture?" Students know that when they see a picture in the book, the professor is going to ask that exact question. Also, every unit ends with a short article for reading practice. The procedure for the reading activity is exactly the same in each ESL course. The professor says: "Look at the title and picture. What do you think this article is about?" After receiving spoken answers from students, the professor always gives the same instruction: "Read the article and underline words you don't know." Students find comfort in knowing the order of activities and the professor's language: the stability frees them to focus on the target language being practiced in class and reduces their affective filter.

Grammar structures are taught in the same way in all ESL courses at Holy Apostles. The professor introduces the structure and writes simple sample sentences on the board, and students work to formulate the grammar rule according to what they see in the sentences. Students tend to remember the rules more frequently when they have deduced the rules themselves. The professor then writes one sentence frame, or beginning to a sentence, on the board and requests that students complete the sentence. Speaking practice continues until every student has offered at least one sentence aloud. Then students begin the task of speaking with a partner before they write sentences including the grammar point. As speaking is a productive skill almost always mastered before writing, allowing students the time and space to create and speak their sentences is a valuable mode of practice before moving to writing.

Unlike many other classes, Holy Apostles' ESL classes allow students the time and environment to complete the sentence frame with spoken answers at their own rate and without raising their hands. In this way, oral practice—which always precedes written practice because of the difficulty of writing—becomes a forum for students to practice speaking sentences with the new grammar with teacher support, gentle teacher correction, and repetition by the students. Although students will sometimes accidentally offer their sentences aloud simultaneously, the two students quickly decide which one should speak first. This forum model also allows for immediate feedback from the professor, including correction of students' language as well as praise and positive reinforcement.

For an example of this forum model, when learning about modal verbs, the following sentence frame may be written on the board: "In the winter, I must ____." Students take time to silently formulate their answer and then chime in when no other student is speaking. This practice serves to lower students' affective filter in that it gives students the time they need to formulate the entire sentence. While some students need only ten seconds to answer, other students may require a minute or more before they feel comfortable enough to offer their sentence. Students also receive the error correction and large amount of speaking practice they need before moving on to write their sentences or produce less structured sentences with partners.

SHELTERED INSTRUCTION STRATEGIES

The ESL department utilizes many research-based teaching strategies from a model called "Sheltered Instruction." The Sheltered Instruction "approach was first introduced in the early 1980s by Stephen Krashen as a way to use second-language acquisition strategies while teaching content-area instruction."[152] The approach "teaches academic subject matter and its associated vocabulary, concepts, and skills by using language and context to make the information comprehensible."[153] Though initially formed and recommended for grade school classes, Sheltered Instruction teaching strategies are effective in any classroom, as they strive to make classroom content accessible to learners. Holy Apostles' ESL program employs many of these recommended strategies and activities, such as practicing with and emphasizing key vocabulary. Before the start of each unit, students are given a list of the new vocabulary that will be used in that unit. Students are responsible for defining the words on their own, and pronunciation practice occurs during class before the unit begins. Each word is written phonetically on the whiteboard and students repeat the words after the teacher with a focus on copying the professor's sounds and syllable stress. The vocabulary lists are utilized during various classroom activities that rely heavily on many of the new words.

---

[152] Jana J. Echavarria & Anne Graves, *Sheltered Content Instruction: Teaching English Language Learners with Diverse Abilities* (Boston: Pearson, 2007), 56.

[153] *Id.*

Students can also recognize the words in spoken language, pronounce them, and add them to their productive vocabulary.

Other Sheltered Instruction teaching strategies employed by Holy Apostles' ESL professors are: using comprehensible speech; allowing sufficient wait time for students' responses; checking students' understanding; and modeling. Using comprehensible speech is vital, as students need to hear English spoken slowly in order to be able to understand classroom speech. The professors emphasize that "[s]peech should be at a natural but slower rate than normal, and enunciation should be clear."[154] In addition, instructions are given at least three times and are delivered in the exact same language each time. For instance, when instructing students to open their student books, the direction is always as follows: "I'm in the student book, page ten." [three second pause] "I'm in the student book, page ten." [three second pause] "I'm in the student book, page ten." The repetition allows students to hear the same language many times and understand the given direction. When instructors provide different language each time, students often are still trying to understand the first sentence when they are presented with the different language of the second sentence.

Affording students sufficient wait time is also important. Students need at least fifteen seconds to formulate their answer to a question and prepare the English they will use to answer the question. Because Holy Apostles' ESL program uses the forum model for answering questions, students are given minutes to formulate their answers and present them aloud. Checking

---

[154] *Id.*, 151.

students' understanding, another Sheltered Instruction strategy, occurs regularly in the forum model. For example, just before each of the books' activities ends, the professor asks, "Do you have any questions?" This is a good time for the professor to gauge student learning or to locate possible gaps in students' knowledge or skills through the students' questions. After a listening exercise, ESL students at Holy Apostles will often ask, "What was that word you said at the end?" or "What does this word mean?" These questions provide insight into what students heard or did not hear during that activity.

Finally, modeling is an integral part of how people learn a skill. From the day we were born, we have been watching those around us as they model skills; we later emulate them as we strive to gain those skills. Modeling language is vital for this same reason. Holy Apostles' ESL professors often model accurate pronunciation and syllable stress of new words as well as entire sentences and grammar structures. For instance, after each student has finished reading a unit's article, the professor will say, "Let's read this together." The professor then reads the first paragraph of the article with the students repeating each sentence chorally. Then each student reads a sentence aloud in turn, with the professor correcting the student's accuracy in pronunciation and syllable stress.

FORMATIVE ASSESSMENT

Along with employing Sheltered Instruction strategies, Holy Apostles' ESL program utilizes formative assessment daily, with little emphasis on summative assessment. This works to create an effective learning environment by lowering students' affective filter. The program focuses on students' practice, accuracy, and confidence in gaining English skills and knowledge, instead of on grades and studying for a test. Formative assessments includes "formal and informal processes teachers and students use to gather evidence for the purpose of improving learning," while summative assessments "provide evidence of student achievement for the purpose of making a judgment about student competence or program effectiveness."[155] Formative assessment is used in the ESL program daily; professors use students' classroom speech and writing to gauge where students have gained knowledge and skills and as well as where students have gaps in their knowledge or skills. This assessment then informs the professors' teaching; should students remain unable to master a grammar structure after one class period, the professor continues practicing that same grammar structure during the next class. In this way, students are constantly monitored and assessed informally, and the information received from students' output informs the teaching and pacing of the courses. Students feel challenged to learn but not rushed or pressured. This is the preferred form of assessment in the ESL department, with summative assessment only occurring every two or three weeks in the form of a short quiz after completing two units in the book. The focus on formative assessment lends itself to lowering students' affective filter, as students and professors alike

---

[155] Jan Chappuis, *Seven Strategies of Assessment for Learning* (Boston: Pearson, 2014), 5.

are interested in students' practice, accuracy, and confidence, rather than their formal test scores. This places less pressure on students and causes less stress than a classroom that is driven by how well students do on formal tests.

WRITING PROGRAM

The ESL program features a comprehensive writing program that prepares students for the rigors of academic writing in English. A report on the key findings from the National Literacy Panel on Language Minority Children and Youth recommends: "given that English language-learners have more difficulty acquiring text-level skills, efforts to build their comprehension and writing should be targeted intensively throughout the years of schooling."[156] Precisely because learning to write in one's second language is far more difficult than learning to speak, read, or listen to one's second language, the ESL program features a comprehensive program that prepares students for English academic writing. The writing program has four components: weekly writing assignments, one-on-one meetings with professors, controlled composition exercises, and free writing.

---

[156] Diane August, "The Development of Literacy in Second-Language Learners: Key Findings from the National Literacy Panel on Language Minority Children and Youth and Instructional Implications," *STARlight: Research and Resources for English Learner Achievement* 5 (Dec. 2007), 3.

Upon entering the Holy Apostles' ESL program, each student receives a composition book with a short checklist inside the front cover. This book and checklist serve as the basis for the writing program. The one or two writing questions assigned weekly provide students with the opportunity to practice vocabulary and grammar lessons from that week. For instance, a unit on prepositions of time may lead to a writing question asking students to describe their daily schedule. They have the chance to apply their knowledge of prepositions of time in that assignment. Weekly questions are given on Wednesdays, students write and self-edit their work over the weekends, and then the books are collected on Mondays. Students are given the freedom to write as little or as much as they wish every week. They are aware that writing is the best form of practice and that they choose how much they want to practice and improve. The checklist in each composition book starts with the same two questions for everyone, with professors and students adding to their personal checklists over time. The checklist first asks two questions. Do my subjects and verbs agree? Did I use the correct verb tense? These two questions cover the majority of mistakes made by ESL students and provide helpful guidelines for students reviewing their work before it is collected.

Once students have completed their weekly writing, their composition books are collected and each student in beginner and intermediate courses meets with a professor one-on-one. There is a set weekly schedule so that all students know when they will meet with the professor to edit their work. Meetings are held in the professor's office and focus on the students' writing. Professor and student read the student's work aloud together in order to hear possible mistakes or awkward phrasing. When a mistake arises, the student is asked to find the mistake. If needed, the professor helps the student locate the mistake and then asks how to fix it. For instance, the professor may point to a phrase and say, "Many book. What does this noun need? Is it plural or singular?" In this way, the professor models the thought process for students so they can emulate the process later. Students also take responsibility for finding and fixing their mistakes, as they are preparing to edit their own work when they move into non-ESL courses. When the professor and student team finish reading and editing the student's written work, they review the mistakes and look for patterns. These mistake patterns are added to the students' checklist for the following week of writing. Some students look at their mistakes and realize they often forgot articles, while advanced students often omit or choose erroneous prepositions. In this way, students are able to identify their writing issues and keep an ongoing list of what they need to improve in the future. The meetings also provide the time and space for students to talk with professors about any issues they are having in class or in the dorm. Rapport, trust, and confidence are built quickly with one-on-one weekly meetings, as are individualized writing checklists and editing skills.

The third component of the writing program is free writing. Each Thursday, students write for the first ten minutes of each class period. The prompt is a thought-provoking question or a photograph and the directions are simple: write as much as you can for ten minutes and do not worry about accurate grammar. One of the students' favorite prompts was to describe a day in the life of rosary beads. In addition, professors never look at students' free writing or correct it. Because writing is the language domain that is generally the most difficult to learn, many students feel anxious or nervous as they sit down to write. Ann Raimes (1983) recommends free writing to increase fluency and decrease negative feelings about writing: "As they do this kind of writing more and more often ... some find that they write more fluently and that putting words down on paper is not so frightening at all."[157] Holy Apostles' ESL students begin with only a few sentences when they first begin free writing. After a couple weeks, they write much more and appear less anxious when faced with a blank sheet of paper. Many students are able to easily track their free writing improvement, since they have written more and more each week. This improvement builds confidence. This activity concludes with an invitation to share their writing with a partner or with the whole class. Sharing stories, ideas, and experiences from their free writing contributes to a tight-knit classroom of students.

The final facet of the writing program is controlled composition, which occurs during the first part of each class session on Wednesdays. In contrast to free writing, controlled composition allows students to concentrate "on one or two problems at a time; they are thus spared from tackling the full range of complexity that free writing entails."[158] Similar to the ESL class sessions, the stability of controlled composition exercises allows students to focus on one or two points of language without

---

[157] Ann Raimes, *Techniques in Teaching Writing* (New York, NY: Oxford University Press, 1983), 7.

[158] *Id.*, 95–6.

worrying about the entire scope of writing. Raimes described the exercises as follows: students "are given a passage to work with; they do not, therefore, have to concern themselves with content, organization, finding ideas, and forming sentences ... [they make] a few specified changes, usually of a grammatical or structural nature."[159] Holy Apostles' ESL professors utilize simple paragraphs from a large store of easy and intermediate ESL online reading exercises. Students in each class period receive copies of one paragraph with one instruction—to change something in the text. For instance, one instruction may be to change the subject "men" to "a man." This necessitates changing the subjects as well as the verbs. Students may be asked to add articles or to change all of the verbs to the present continuous tense or to the simple past tense. Classes of more advanced ESL students are often asked to change sentences from active to passive voice or to add prepositions where necessary. This is a helpful exercise, as students are able to focus on one point of grammar. Professors also use this exercise to reinforce or review grammar lessons.

CONCLUSION

In conclusion, the ESL program at Holy Apostles College and Seminary is successful in preparing students for rigorous seminary study in English. This is accomplished over two to three years of intensive study with a research-based curriculum and teaching methodology. The classroom environment and professors'

---

[159] *Id.*, 97.

teaching strategies and activities—featuring Sheltered Instruction strategies and formative assessment—lower students' affective filters. This enables students to gain a large amount of knowledge and to hone their skills in an encouraging and supportive environment. The ESL department's comprehensive writing program, which every student begins upon entering ESL courses, provides students with the practice, accuracy, and confidence they need to write effectively in academic courses in English. Holy Apostles is truly a blessed place with motivated and hardworking students; everyone learns and supports each other in their journey to learn English, achieve in higher education, and serve the Church.

SEGMENT 2

One Missionary Priest's Experience

Life and Lessons of a Priest from a Warzone: A Memoir

Rev. Robert Obol

The Life and Lessons from a Warzone is a memoir that discusses the events that occurred almost on a daily basis during the time of unrest in Pajule and northern Uganda in general. Fr. Obol reflects on the role of faith, providence, community, and reconciliation in a warzone. He shares the enduring lessons that he has learned about life and himself from working in such an environment. It is his hope that sharing these experiences will educate those who have not had the experience of war about what life is like in a warzone.

It was a crisp October night in 1985 when a group of unknown gunmen attacked Buda – the town in eastern Uganda where my father worked and lived with his family. When the gunshots started at two in the morning, my father immediately got up from bed, dressed hurriedly, and ran from his room to the other end of the house where my cousin Jildo and I were sleeping.

In the culture of the Acoli people, it is generally believed that when a person is asleep he is not to be awakened in the middle of a gunfight. There is a cultural assumption that it may be one's luck that a person sleeps through an exchange of gunfire. There is also the fear that awakening a person in the middle of one's sleep may make him disoriented, and if he were to fall into any danger or harm after being roused, the party who woke him up would be blamed for the injury or death. Because of this, most people do not wake up someone who is asleep because they would not like to live with the guilt of being responsible for any harm that was caused. Further, it is culturally presumed that an attacker in his right conscience will show decency and respect for a sleeping person, since he is harmless. So, my father and Jildo let me sleep.

My father asked Jildo to remain in the house and take care of me. He was afraid that if the attackers were to overrun the town, which was defended and protected by less than twelve policemen, he would be their primary target since he was the manager of the only bank in town. It was always presumed that the bank manager had the key for the repository where the money was kept. If the attackers were to overrun the police guard post, they would have come to seize him so he could take them to the money.

So, my father escaped out of the house through the back since the front entrance faced the direction of the town, where most of the gunfire was concentrated. The house had a four-meter wall around it. To get out of the house, he carefully opened the wooden door, trying not to agitate a rusty bolt that often made a lot of noise, and once he had made his silent exit, Jildo locked the door behind him.

At around five a.m., the guns fell silent. The few policemen had stood their ground and pushed back the attackers. To be certain all was safe, my father returned to the house at six a.m. He was shivering and exhausted and had not slept the entire night. My cousin also was unharmed; he had diligently kept watch at my bedside all night. On my part, I had slept throughout the night. It was only at breakfast that they told me how intense and frightful the night had been for them.

Such incidents were the norm in 1985. As a young boy at the time, I recall that in the news coverage there was much chaos and violence in the country throughout the year. In the southwestern parts of the country, the rebel army known as the National Resistance Army (NRA) was fighting the government of the Uganda People's Congress (UPC), led by President Milton Obote. It was common to hear news of attacks and ambushes in that part of the country and even of land mines being used to blow up civilian passenger vehicles.

PREPARATION FOR THE PRIESTHOOD

My family passed the Christmas holidays of 1985 in Madi Opei, When January 1986 arrived, we departed Madi Opei and returned to Buda in the Eastern part of the country where my father worked. We got to Kitgum town in a military lorry, since this was the only means of transport available. There we climbed aboard a military truck that was traveling from Kitgum to Mbale. The truck belonged to a high-ranking military officer in the army and since the driver had armed escorts, we felt that we would be safe. On reaching

Buda, a man called Naki, who worked with my father at the local bank, informed me that I would begin my seminary training in a week's time. I had passed the seminary entrance exam, which tested skills in English language, math, science and social studies.

My journey to the priesthood had begun with a few words to my father: "Daddy, I want to join the seminary." He had replied, "If that is what you feel, we shall discuss it with your mother in the evening." On that very evening, after some discussion, both parents gave me their blessing to join the seminary.

On January 18, 1986, I started my final year of grade school/primary seven at St James Preparatory Seminary in Achilet, Tororo. I traveled with my father, and eventually we arrived in Tororo City, where the seminary was located about four miles away from the city center. When I met the rector, Father Wet, he congratulated me on working so hard to qualify for seminary studies. I was excited to be admitted. When I saw some seminarians with whom I was already acquainted, I ran to them, and the first thing I asked them to do was take me to my place in the dormitory. The excitement made me forget my father, and in fact he returned home without us saying farewell to one another.

As I started my preparatory seminary training, the war between the government of Tito Okello and the NRA rebels was still raging. The rebels were getting closer and closer to Kampala, the capital city of Uganda. Even during our first week in the seminary, we were aware that the war was intensifying, but we had ceased following it keenly since none of us had a radio and we were young, being between the ages of twelve and fifteen years. So we relied on what we were told by the seminary authorities.

In the course of our first week of classes, we kept hearing rumors that Kampala had fallen into the hands of the rebels. On Friday it became apparent to us that something significant had happened in the country because in the middle of the night we heard a lot of gunshots from the direction of Tororo, in particular near the military barracks of Rubongi that was along the road to our preparatory seminary at Achilet.

The following morning, our first Saturday in the seminary, we woke up to chaos. From the compound of the seminary, we could see government soldiers fleeing with their families in trucks filled with looted property and household items, while others searched for any vehicle that they could forcefully take from its owners.

On seeing the chaos, it became apparent to us that the NRA had overthrown the government of Tito Okello Lutwa. That day marked the beginning of the lack of peace for northern Uganda. Most of the soldiers of the deposed military regime fled northwards across the border of Uganda to camp in South Sudan. On August 25, 1986, after these former government soldiers were attacked in their Sudanese camps, most of them fled back to Uganda and started to fight, against the new government.

The year 1986 brought great change to the country. For most of the years since Uganda had gained independence in 1962, the country had been ruled by Northerners, and for the first time real political and military power had passed into the hands of Southerners. This change also gave an opportunity to the rest of the country to express their true feelings about Northerners, who are for the most part of Luo or Sudanic origins.

Achilet Preparatory Seminary was in the eastern part of Uganda, an area culturally dominated by the Jophadola, who are also of Luo ancestry. So the Jophadola naturally made up a large part of the student body. The majority of the students, however, were composed Bantu: Bagishu, Samia, Bagwere, Baganda, etc. The other ethnic groups were the Iteso, who were a sizable number, and the Sabiny, who were very few. The Iteso and Sabiny were neither Luo nor Bantu.

I was one of only two Northerner seminarians in the seminary. Although we were only in our early teens, the two of us experienced a shocking level of hostility and prejudice. Much resentment was expressed toward me because I was a Northerner and a person of Luo origin – and consequently I was labeled as one of the "killers." In the course of any argument or a discussion with a fellow seminarian, that seminarian would remind me I was a Northerner. Other students would mock me by mimicking a government soldier of the former regime breaking into a house speaking Swahili (the official language of the army) with a northern accent. This was often done to make me feel bad or to silence my point of view. For the first time I realized the very deep divisions in my country that I could not ignore.

I admired the comportment of most of our teachers, both priests and laymen. Whatever their own biases, they never directed any hostility to me. In fact, I felt safe and protected by them. Normally no students tried to either justify or publicly propagate their racial and political prejudices, although they often came to the fore in the midst of outbursts and heated arguments. More often they demonstrated such prejudices subtly.

At the end of 1986, I completed my preparatory seminary schooling at Achilet. In March of the following year, I joined the high school at St Pius X Seminary in Nagongera, which was about twelve miles away from Tororo. My education at the seminary high school would normally have taken six years, but I was to study at the school for only four years, until the age of eighteen.

At that point I decided to study in a school that was not a Catholic seminary. I was even willing to go to a public high school. I had four reasons for doing this.

First, I considered studying in a non-seminary environment to be an essential part of my process of discernment. I had joined the seminary when I was thirteen years old, and I felt that I should make comparisons and contrasts between life inside and outside the seminary before making a final commitment.

Second, I wanted to confirm my vocation. I had always felt that God wanted me to be a priest. Although I knew that leaving the seminary would expose my vocation to many risks, I was convinced that my burning desire for the priesthood would weather any storms that would come my way.

Third, I believed that two years out of the seminary would give me the opportunity to return to my diocese. I had joined the seminary in Tororo because my father was a civil servant. But I had hoped that if I were to pursue the priesthood I would be able to join my home diocese of Gulu.

Fourth, as a seminarian, I was required to belong to a parish. Because my parents no longer lived in Tororo, however, it had become almost impossible to be part of a parish there.

In May 1991, I joined entered the Catholic high school of St Charles Lwanga Kasasa in Masaka, which was run by the Brothers of Christian Instruction. This was not a seminary, but the school rules were strictly enforced. Its dominant ethnic group was a Bantu tribe called the Baganda. Here I had to work hard to fit in and be like the rest of the students. I believe that at the end of two years I was like them in everything. But at the end of those two years, the fact that God was calling me to be a priest became clear. My love and desire for the priesthood had increased. When I thought about being a priest, I experienced inner peace; the thought of any other path left me restless and inwardly turbulent.

After completing high school at St Charles Lwanga Kasasa, I returned to my home diocese and joined the college seminary of Alokolum in Gulu. Alokolum was in the Northern part of Uganda, and thee I studied philosophy for three years. Following that, I interned for one year at Lacor Seminary High School, Gulu, before continuing my studies at Ggaba Seminary in Kampala. For four years I studied theology in Ggaba, and some completed my preparation for ordination as a Catholic priest. The seminaries for both philosophy and theology were national seminaries comprised of a multiplicity of tribes. Issues of ethnicity and regionalism would arise, but were not hostile. My seminary training gave me the opportunity to learn the ideas of students from different parts of the country, and to see things through their eyes.

At a cultural level, this deepened my self-awareness, especially with regard to how people looked at my tribe and region. It was a moment for me to reflect on my own cultural and tribal attitudes toward them as well. I discovered that when it comes to the crime of tribal bias and prejudice, no one has clean hands. We Northerners have our own biases and prejudices toward the Bantu tribes; for the most part we see them as cowards, liars, and thieves, who cannot be trusted. Above all, I believe that this awareness of my own cultural assumptions and prejudices toward others and my own awareness of their tribal and cultural prejudices toward me made me at ease in dealing with them, because I always believed that beyond the prejudices they were real people with good hearts and intentions.

The high dropout rate from the seminary of Gulu throughout the 1990's weighed on me heavily. Most of the seminarians abandoned their training for the Catholic priesthood at different stages of their formation for one reason or another. At the end of August 1994, the beginning of the academic year 1994–1995, I participated in the annual general meeting with sixteen other college seminarians. Only two of us eventually became priests. Priestly ordinations were rare in the diocese. Watching my contemporaries leave the seminary was depressing, but their departure strengthened my resolve to persevere. I was convinced that even if I had many choices about what to do with my life, God still needed young men like me who were open to giving up other opportunities in life to serve Him; and I believed that I could do it.

The vocation crisis in the Diocese of Gulu at the time worried everyone. In August of 1997, when I reported to Ggaba Seminary, I was the only student from my diocese; yet the neighboring diocese of Arua that was carved out of the diocese of Gulu had forty seminarians. The faithful of Gulu wondered whether they would have priests to serve them in the near future, while the priests worried about the continuity of their ministry and wondered why young men were not drawn to their vocation. For the seminarians in the diocesan seminary high school it was equally devastating, because whenever a college seminarian left his training, they lost a role model or someone to whom they looked up. So I was firmly convinced that my choice to be a priest would contribute toward restoring faith, hope, and stability in a Church that was experiencing a crisis of self-confidence and self-doubt.

ORDINATION TO THE PRIESTHOOD

In June 1999, when two years remained before my ordination, I had a memorable encounter with one of my clansmen. We had gone to Madi Opei, my father's birthplace, to visit the gravesite of his elder brother, who had passed away two months before. By this time my home parish had not had a priest assigned to it for three years. Throughout the many years that I had been a seminarian, I'd had plenty of support from my family and my adopted parish of Christ the King, but almost no open encouragement from any members of my father's clan.

Many of the paternal relatives kept asking me questions like "Robert, what are you still doing in the seminary?" "Why are you, a young, intelligent and handsome man, wasting yourself in that place?" "Can't you find something better to do with yourself?" "Why do you intend to kill the clan and tribe?" I avoided as much as possible entering into arguments, since I knew that I would not be able to convince them. I personally understood their ambivalence, indifference, and at times, their hostility to me becoming a priest, since they placed married life above everything else. Because I was the firstborn in my family, they expected me to get married and raise children to keep the family line alive – and at a certain point be a leader of the clan. If I became a priest, it appeared that I would abandon all these sacred cultural responsibilities and obligations.

So in the evening, as we were getting ready to leave for Kitgum, Onesimo, a crippled gentleman supporting himself with a walking stick, came to me. He told me that he had something important to discuss. I had not seen or met him before. I think he was in his early forties, but he looked much older. In our short dialogue, I could tell that he was not a regular churchgoer but he intensely loved the parish church of Madi Opei and the priesthood. He told me that he had a request to make of me, and I promised him that I would do what I could for him. He said:

> Robert, do us the honor of becoming a priest. See what is happening in our parish? We have not had a priest assigned here for almost four years; whenever we ask for one to be appointed here, we are always told that there are very few priests in the diocese. If you become a priest, it will be hard for them to always tell us that there is no priest to be assigned to our parish since we shall ask them to assign you to work here as our son. You never know; you might become our voice as well.

These words moved me deeply because they expressed the sentiment of a community that was experiencing a void. It needed a spiritual father and leader. At the same time, this request gave me some satisfaction because I could see how much progress the community had made in its values. In the past all that they had cared about was that one married.

When I was young, I was attracted to the life of the priest as one who gives personal attention to any person who comes to him, even one whom he does not know. As I matured, I became more attracted to the priesthood because of the humanity and self-offering of Jesus Christ. Onesimo's thoughts and concerns served as an inspiration to me. He reinforced my conviction that if I were to become a priest, it would be for the service of others, and not for any personal benefit.

The following year, on July 15, 2000, I was ordained a deacon in Gulu cathedral. One year later, on August 18, 2001, I was ordained a Catholic priest at Christ the King Parish in Kitgum. One day before my priestly ordination, I met my bishop; and in our discussion, he expressed his intention to appoint me to Pajule parish, which had been run by the Comboni missionaries for the last forty years. He informed me that the missionaries were soon leaving care of this parish to the diocesan clergy. There was talk in the course of the preparations for my ordination that I might be assigned to teach in the diocesan seminary high school; but the bishop thought that I needed a more holistic experience, and so directed me to start my priestly work in a parish setting.

My priestly ordination was an occasion of great joy for the people. Since the elevation of Gulu diocese to the status of an archdiocese in 1999 and the arrival of a new bishop, no one from the diocese had been ordained a priest. The last ordination under the former bishop had taken place almost four years ago. Moreover, the venue for my ordination was Christ the King, my adopted parish. In Uganda, we identify the parish where a seminarian's parents, or at least his father, were born as that seminarian's parish; most of the time, it is located among his clan members. Neither of my parents were born at Christ the King, although I had lived and grown up there. The members of the parish had supported me at each and every stage of my seminary training. Many of them saw their own dreams and prayers fulfilled in my becoming a priest.

It was close to eleven years since a priestly ordination had taken place in Kitgum vicariate, in which my ordination took place. Because of the insecurity, most ordinations were done in Gulu vicariate at the cathedral itself. Among the thousands who came to my priestly ordination, some were witnessing a priestly ordination for the first time in their lives, and this day would mean much to them. It was a remarkable moment in the lives of the children and youth as well.

When the ordination Mass was about to begin, my sister Palma sat next to me with the rest of my family, relatives, and clan members. They were all waiting for the moment when my parents would present me to the bishop for ordination. I remarked to her: "Palma, in all my life, I have not seen you so colorfully and elegantly dressed as you are today." Her answer was most surprising: "Robert, a few minutes from now, I am going to be substantially changed forever; I will no longer be called Palma only but the sister of a priest." Her response reflected the pride and joy that everyone had in my becoming a priest.

There was also much elation in the Madi Opei parish because I was going to be the first priest from the parish or the clan. The last person who had gone so far in his training was my father, who had left the seminary in 1970. Some of them told me this: "Father Robert, from now onward when the priests of the diocese are assembled for a liturgical celebration marching in procession, we shall be proud to point out that you are one of our very own."

My mother later told me of her unique experience at my ordination. When the prayer of consecration came to an end and it was announced that I was now a priest, she felt like a heavy weight was taken off her shoulders and she breathed a huge sigh of relief. She then realized how stressed she had been all the years I was studying to be a priest because I could have dropped out or been dismissed at any time.

A PARISH PRIEST IN PAJULE

On October 4, 2001, I reported to Pajule Parish to begin an eventful period of my life and work. As I took up my duties, the security town's security deteriorated as large groups of rebels belonging to the Lord's Resistance Army or LRA crossed the borders of South Sudan into Uganda.

As a newly ordained priest in Pajule, I faced the challenge of loneliness. The missionary order that had run the parish for nearly forty years typically assigned two or three priests there together, since their constitution required priests to live in community. This is not the case with the diocesan priests. My pastor Fr Peter Olum and I were charged with the pastoral care of two different parishes, Pajule and Puranga. This meant that often we would be alone for weeks.

After the first three days in Pajule parish with my pastor, Fr Peter left for a full week to attend to the affairs of Puranga parish. I could not believe the solitude and the loneliness that his absence brought in the evenings. During the day, the parish was very busy, since close to a thousand people were participating in different activities within the parish, the elementary school, the nursery school, and the tailoring school. At the end of the day, however, total silence fell over the parish grounds. In short, in the evenings, the place was like a ghost town. I really wondered within myself if this was the priestly life for which I had prepared and longed. While studying at seminary, I had become accustomed to living with many people. Life as a priest at Pajule was vastly different. The parish was on a vast piece of land that was close to forty acres, with the rectory at its center. I felt like my only neighbors were the many buildings around the rectory. With the exception of the convent, the nearest homes were those at the edges of the parish.

Loneliness, however, was only one of the challenges I faced as a parish priest at Pajule. Since the beginning of the war in 1986, the missionary priests who had previously staffed Pajule parish had served as visible signs of solidarity, hope, and perseverance to the community of Pajule and the neighboring parishes that had been deserted. Unlike many parishes in the archdiocese that were closed for long periods because of the deteriorating security situation,

Pajule was closed for three months only when the lives of the priests were in actual danger.

Finding myself constantly in situations in which I had to act fast and be a part of decisions that could save lives or put my life and that of others in danger sometimes made me ask myself if the many years of training to be a priest had prepared me for it. I had always thought of my work as doing parish administration, dispensing the sacraments, planning the schedule for parish activities, celebrating the Mass, delivering homilies, and explaining church teachings. Although I was well aware that, as a priest of the Archdiocese of Gulu archdiocese, I would have to deal with the insecurity of the LRA war in one way or another, it never dawned on me that I would be at the epicenter of the conflict. I found myself holding not only pastoral meetings but also security meetings.

Another challenge for me was accepting the decisions made by my pastor. As the pastor, Fr Peter had the final say on most facets of parish life. When his decisions were about priestly ministry and parish administration, it was easy for me to go along with him. But when it involved the safety of the community and of us, I personally needed to be convinced that he was doing the right thing and his judgment was correct. Many times, I asked myself: "What would I do if I were certain that his action or inaction would put his own life, mine, and those of the community in danger?" Because of this, when it came to security issues, the decisions that we made were arrived at through consensus. We needed to be in agreement, since both of us were placing our very lives on the line.

After we both agreed that we needed a military detachment set up in the parish, my pastor went to consult other community leaders before we formally requested the army to be deployed in the parish. All the community leaders supported the idea, and I then went on his behalf to meet the military commander in the barracks. But I was told that he was away. I doubted this, since the soldiers at the entrance to the barracks had informed me that he was in. When there is plenty of insecurity, commanders are reluctant to make commitments or provide security guarantees to anyone for fear that if something goes wrong, they will be held accountable. I believe that the commander had instructed those at the lower ranks to tell me that he was not around. So I met the army intelligence officer instead.

He assured me that every evening about 150 soldiers would be deployed around the parish and its surrounding area. I was skeptical of this assurance, although I did not express my skepticism to the officer, since I knew that the total number of the soldiers in the town was less than three hundred. If they were to place such a large number to cover the parish area alone, it would not be possible for them to protect the entire town.

When I look back, it was as if a divine voice were speaking to the military through us two priests. Pajule was attacked on a massive scale by the LRA three weeks later. If they had responded to our request to place a detachment at the parish, the military would have been able to fight the LRA on two fronts. Since they did not respond to our request, the military was forced to fight from the barracks only.

When the rebels began firing in town, most people fled on foot in the direction of the parish, but they turned before they reached their destination since it was equally unsafe. Some of the people who had attempted to take refuge at the parish said that they found it "hotter" or more dangerous than the town because the parish had its own assigned group of rebels in addition to others who were firing heavy support weapons at the military barracks near it. The rebels shot indiscriminately at the people running into the parish compound. Fortunately, no one was killed or injured by the bullets since there were so many buildings to hide behind.

Furthermore, the many buildings in the parish echoed the gunshots and shells that were being fired and produced frightening noises and harsh dissonant sounds. Many people who could not reach the parish took refuge in the parish cemetery. Most of them literally spent the night among the dead with the gravestones as their camouflage. This showed the extent of their desperation. Many people in Pajule, like the rest of Acoliland, believe that the cemetery contains the spirits of the dead and some of them are evil ones that cause harm to human beings. Under normal circumstances most people would never consider taking refuge in a cemetery.

After lying on the floor for only a few minutes, I heard a loud bang on the back door leading to the dining room of the rectory. Most of the doors and windows were made out of steel because of the violence, but if the rebels could not break through them, they would break through the actual walls of the house. The walls were weak, having been erected before there were concerns about war and insecurity. Then, I heard a deep voice, cruel and fierce, like that of a wild animal: "Father, Father, Father, open the door. If you do not open the door, we shall kill you this evening." This was said about five times. As they were ordering me to open the door for them, they were also jumping and kicking on it very harshly. At this moment, the visiting priest and the young boy who were lying on the hard cement floor hid under my bed.

I knew at once that it was useless to hope that the rebels would not get in, since they had taken control of the place. I was afraid that they could begin to fire into the house. The longer I hesitated the more infuriated they would become and the more likely they were to commit havoc in the parish. It was time to act.

I called to the visiting priest, who had been a priest for sixteen years and had personally met the rebels on many occasions. In fact, his primary reason for coming to Pajule parish was to re-establish contact with them. When I bent down under the bed, however, he appeared cold and pale. He was in a terrible state of shock. On several past occasions he had been betrayed by the military authorities who allowed him to meet with the LRA and then sent soldiers to attack the rendezvous site. This attack apparently triggered memories of those past occasions.

I got up and shouted loudly from the hallway, "Do not knock down the door; I am coming to open it." In fact, many who were hiding in the parish compound heard my shouting within the house. This moment changed my role in the parish;

from then on, I made many more decisions. I needed to warn the rebels in advance that I was coming to open the door because I was afraid that they would fire through the door and kill me instantly. When they heard my voice, which was indeed very deep and authoritative, they all stopped stomping on the metallic door. I opened it and came face to face with armed LRA rebels fresh from the bushes.

Seeing LRA rebels standing at the door of the dining room, all of them bare-chested with guns and fixed bayonets, I felt that I had come face to face with death and human cruelty in its worst form. Since it was getting dark, I could not distinguish their faces clearly, but I could see that they had very dark, shiny skin, as if they had smeared a lot of oil on themselves. All of them appeared to be very young men in their early teens, and only one of them was near my height and most likely was about eighteen years old. The whole place smelled of smoke and gunpowder.

The rebels looked surprised to see me. They were so fearsome, and yet, I looked cool, composed, and calm. At this moment I think I made a big mistake because I kept quiet and retreated to my Catholic priest persona, allowing them to take control of the situation. Because the rebels understood the language of authority and are used to commands, I should have been more assertive and asked them questions like "What do you want? What can I do for you? Who is your commander?" This would have been risky, but it might have succeeded.

Since I stood silently before them, one of them shouted a question at me: "Who are you?" This question triggered many ideas in my mind, and I had to process very quickly the implications of any answer that I might give. In Pajule parish I was called by several titles. Many called me "Pare Matidi," which in the local language meant the young priest since I was newly ordained; I appeared very small in their eyes and I was the associate pastor as well. A few in the parish called me by my first name, Father Robert, and while at school I was called by my middle name, Nyeko. But I decided to tell them my last name, which hardly anyone used. So I told them that I was Father Obol. I could see that they looked surprised; it was a name that they could not connect to any that they had heard before. I was afraid that the priests in the parish might have been accused of being critical of them in our homilies and that when they came into contact with any of us, they would cause us bodily harm.

Then the tallest among them ordered me, "Sit down." I sat on the floor without any argument or resistance. They were afraid to have me stand because I was larger and appeared stronger than most of them. They might have also been concerned that I would knock one of them down, fight, or even grab a gun. I sat on the floor at the entrance of the door to the dining room, and within a second I was surrounded by eight rebels. They all had guns with knives fixed at the top, pointing at my head, holding the triggers like they were about to fire. Suddenly I could not believe the position I was in. The sight was like a crown of bayonets, and making the situation worse was that two days ago, I had gotten a haircut and shaved my head completely bald.

One of the rebels asked me in a very cruel and rude voice if we had a radio-call. I admitted that we did have one since I did not want to risk my life for a piece of property. Another one shouted at me, "Get up and take us to the radio-call." While trembling, I got up to lead them to our rectory sitting room. The radio-call was the only means of contact between our headquarters and other parishes of the archdiocese of Gulu. The rebels always targeted the radio-call, since they could alter the frequencies to their own in order to communicate with other rebel units, and in particular with their bases in South Sudan.

Indeed, I was lucky that the radio-call was in the parish at the time. If it had been broken and I had taken it in for repair, they would not have believed me and would have tortured me to produce it. As I led the rebels to the sitting room, I could not believe how the environment in the parish had changed. There were gunshots being fired everywhere. Even though I grew up in an environment with such insecurity, I had never before intentionally got up to walk in the midst of so much gunfire. I was shaking so much that I could not walk straight. I knocked myself against the dining table and later again against another chair, and in the process one of rebels tried to kick me down but missed my legs.

When we reached the room where the radio-call was located, the rebels immediately ordered me to sit down again. They were very afraid that I could fight back, and so they did not want to take any chances. It was a real fear on the part of the rebels, since many people in northern Uganda have had the chance to work in the armed forces and have had military training.

In the sitting room, the rebels asked me for the location of the radio-call. I showed them where it was, and they immediately grabbed it and started disconnecting it from its antenna. As I sat down on the floor, I watched how my things and those of the parish were being looted; but above all, I marveled at the speed with which the house was being emptied of any property. There were rebels instructing some of the women prisoners what they were and were not to loot. Others were commanding those in the lower ranks to make sure that they had checked under each and every bed and made sure there was no one hiding underneath. This was something revealing for me because it showed to me that the LRA understood the psychology of most of the people in the society. From this moment I promised myself that I would never go under the bed whatever the circumstance. While I could not see any of their faces in the darkness, I heard their stern orders and warnings. The rebels could see much better in the room, since they were the ones with torches.

Although they were in control, I could feel that they were under much pressure and wanted to conclude their mission as soon as possible. They were taking anything they could find so long as it was portable, including things that I believed they did not need, like my motorcycle headgear. I knew quite well that they did not have motorcycles or ride them in the jungles. All the tablecloths and curtains in the house were being pulled down, torn to pieces, and converted into bags. In fact, the rebels in the house looked more like very experienced thieves than people who had differences with the government of Uganda. Within five minutes the sitting room was empty.

In the parish, we had a large and heavy video screen that we often lent to the reception center for recreational activities. I saw one of the rebels try to pick up the screen from the house, but it was too heavy for him. He succeeded only with the help of another rebel.

Then the rebel soldiers remaining with me in the sitting room ordered me to take them to the location of the parish food store. At the time we had very little in our own store. But CARITAS had plenty of food supplies at the reception center. I did not intend to lead the rebels to them. Once again they instructed me to get up and lead them to the rectory food store, and I agreed since I knew that they would not find much there.

But as I got up, I heard a huge blast in front of the church. One of the rebels had fired a portable mortar from the direction of Pajule parish at the military barracks. The sound alone was nerve-racking, and the vibrations made everything shake. I physically trembled in the midst of the rebels and almost fell down. One of rebels, seeing me quivering, shouted at me, "Father, we do not tolerate cowards; we kill them." I kept quiet.

During the time I was with the rebels, they appeared not to be bothered by the sounds of gunfire and huge blasts. In fact, it seemed like a normal working day for them. Their only interest was in knowing the direction from which the bullets were coming. They seemed to be able to distinguish between the sounds of the gunshots being fired by them and by the government soldiers.

Then, another rebel came into the room and was assigned to make sure that I did not escape. He was about sixteen years old. I introduced myself to him and tried to make him a friend. I have always had the belief that I make a natural connection much more easily with men, however cruel they may be, than with women, so I was willing to take a chance here. In the brief talk we had, I discovered that, unlike the rest of the rebels, he seemed kind and respectful. Seeing how tense and frightened I was, this rebel soldier assured me that they would not harm me. But he wanted me to be taken to meet their commander, Charles Tabuley. The idea of going to meet the LRA commander really frightened me. Later, he asked me to lead him to the priests' food store, which I did. There was not much in the room to take. There were things like beans, engine oil, and one crate of beer. He had an interest only in the engine oil, since the rebels needed it for oiling their guns.

Next we went outside the house to the back of the rectory. By this time the gunshots had ceased and the grounds had calmed. I had calmed down as well. The rebels were now fully in control of the parish, camp, and town, and they had surrounded the government troops in Pajule military barracks. I could not believe I was among them while they were looting and running all over. I thought, "so this is what the rebels look like." They spoke the local language very fluently, if not even better than us.

Parked next to the kitchen was the car of the visiting priest, a Suzuki Samurai. The rebels begin to vandalize it; one of them broke the front windshield with the butt of his gun. Another rebel brought dry grass. Some of them began opening the fuel tank that was very tightly sealed, and others rushed to provide a box of matches to set it ablaze. When I saw this, even though I was their prisoner, something happened to me that I believe was a divine voice. I shouted at them with force and authority in my voice like I was back in control of the place. The sudden courage that I had was surprising.

"Do not burn my vehicle; you know that I am the priest here. My duty is to help people; how will I help people if I do not have a car?" To my surprise, one of the rebels told the rest to leave the vehicle alone. I wanted to take advantage of this, so I asked who their leader was, but none of them was willing to reply or talk to me. I could sense that there were several groups in the parish, each with a specific task to perform. I had hoped that by negotiating with their leader I could minimize the damage they were doing to the place.

As I stood at the veranda of the rectory, which was two steps high off the ground, a rebel soldier who was about the age of eleven flashed his torch onto my face. The time was now about six forty-five p.m. He had a stick in his hand and raised his gun and pointed it at my chest. Suddenly, I could not believe what I was seeing; it was like a scene from a movie. He had his finger on the trigger and was ready to fire at any second. He challenged me to say anything provocative to him, and then he would shoot. My reaction at seeing this was disbelief, like it was a scene from a hunting exercise, except that this time I was the target. I also felt pity for this young boy; he was a victim of his circumstance. If he had not been abducted by the rebels, he would not be threatening to kill me. In the eyes of the young boy, I could see so much hate, rage, and contempt for me; and yet I could not tell its source. Since I knew the psychology of the child-soldiers, I remained silent and did not attempt to talk to him. I did not want to give him any excuse for shooting me. When he saw me quiet, he lowered his gun and told me that I had survived. He went into the house and looted some bars of soap from my bedroom. When he returned he said, "You are lucky; I wanted to make you lie down on the ground to cane you, but I am pleased that I got some good things from your room."

If I had not been silent, he would have killed me just to make a name for himself and help build a notorious reputation as the one who had killed the Catholic priest. This was one of the reasons why some children who were forcefully abducted stayed and voluntarily became rebel soldiers themselves. They felt that being in the rebel army gave to them privileges and power over adults, whom they could humiliate, torture, and kill. They would not have such power and control if they lived in society like the rest of us. However horrible their actions were, it made these young rebel soldiers feel powerful.

I also noticed that this young boy hated my physical appearance. He castigated me for being physically big. The rebels had always associated being overweight with a level of comfort in life. I believe this is an important distinction that has to be made. In western society, being overweight is seen as a disease since it is an indication of poor self-care and there are many diseases connected to obesity. In many sections of African society, on the other hand, being overweight is a measure of comfort. In fact, people who have put on weight often times are envied. Since the conditions of living were very hard for most of the rebels in the jungles, many of them hoped that when they were in control of Uganda, they would also put on some weight. Further, the rebels looked at someone who is fat as a government agent or a person benefiting from the status quo. This was a source of resentment to them since they believed that they were suffering in the bushes. I noticed that continuing to stand in their midst drew a negative reaction from them, since they took it to be a hostile posture, and I sat down like a real prisoner.

I could also see how childlike and childish they were in their behaviors. Some would come out of the house with a lot of excitement about things they had plundered whose name or use was unknown to them. They would tell their colleagues that they had gotten something very precious, and when they could not identify it, they would run to me to assist them. It was like thieves asking the owner of the property to identify their loot and its value before they went away with it.

Then a rebel soldier brought some luggage from the house and placed it at my feet. He intended for me to carry it when we began to leave for the jungle as abductees. But I declined to move my hands to pick it up. If they were to abduct me, I wanted them to take me like one of their officers – that is, I would not carry any of the loot. This step made me know that the rebels intended to take me along with them to the jungles.

As I sat down surrounded, the rebels received the good news that plenty of food had been found on one end of the building.

In fact, there were close to two hundred bags of corn that had been supplied by the organization of the World Food Program to feed the returnees in the parish. They all ran to that side of the building, and for the moment, they left me alone.

I immediately began to think of what to do. I did not want to be abducted and go with them into the jungles. The LRA walked on foot with their captives for hundreds of miles in a single day, and I knew that I would be unable to do so. I was also barefooted, since I had left my room abruptly without having had any time to put on my shoes. And even if I had, my regular shoes were not appropriate for walking in the bush; they would have caused terrible blisters on my feet. In the month of January, as was the case in Pajule and Acoliland as a whole, people set all the dry grass on fire to clear the fields for the coming planting season. Sharp shoots were left that could pierce bare feet. Such injuries were very common on the feet of the returnees at the reception center.

Because of this, I took the risk to go back inside the house. The rebels were still looting the rectory while flashing their torches. I passed near some of them, since it was now totally dark. They could not recognize that I was not one of them, and in fact some of them mistook me to be among them. While in the rectory, I immediately made up my mind to enter the pastor's office. This was the one room that the rebels had not broken into since it had a strong door. I took its key, which hung above the door. This key was an interesting one. It was half its normal size, for it had broken several years back, but it still worked and so there was no need to have it replaced. But opening this door was a problem. Because it was dark and I was panicking, I failed to place the key in its hole to open the door. What I did then was place the key in my pocket and return outside. I believe that this failure was in God's plan for me.

I could see that the rebels were very absorbed in looting the place and did not care about their surroundings at all. Surprisingly, some idea came to my mind that I had to leave. Otherwise, I would be abducted. The fate of some of our seminarians who were home for the holidays and had been abducted a couple of months ago at a place called Adilang came to mind very vividly. This made me act.

If I were to escape, there was only one direction that I could take – sideways from their midst, eastwards to the main gate of the rectory, while leaning against the wall. When I reached the gate, it was unlocked since the rebels had broken it open. I could not go through it, however, since beyond the gate the security lights of the parish elementary school illuminated its surroundings. The time was about 7:30 p.m. The parish church, which was in the same direction as the elementary school, appeared to be the only place that the rebels were plundering, but I could not enter it since its security lights also were on. Even if I had taken a chance, I did not have its key with me at the time, so it would have been impossible for me to get inside.

Since I could not pass through the gate, I made up my mind to go north. I ran from one building to another for a distance of about five meters and hid behind the wall of the CARITAS store, listening to see if anyone was trailing me. As I stopped, I heard one of the rebels shout, "If you run, I will shoot you." I immediately held my breath. I had to take this threat seriously. If an LRA prisoner of war tried to run away and was caught, he or she was to be executed on the spot. I was not certain if the LRA rebel soldier was warning someone else or me. After about five minutes, I realized that the threat addressed to me.

During this time I again paused to consider what to do. I made up my mind to escape from the parish. I needed to go through the pigsty and then climb over the rectory wall. My instincts told me that no LRA soldiers were present, so I ran for about fifteen meters. I was lucky that my instincts were correct. If I had made a miscalculation and there were a single armed LRA rebel lying on the grass, he could have shot me. I jumped into the pigsty. The pigs ran around making a lot of noise and squealing loudly. I wished this evening they could have observed some silence. I stopped and was quiet for a moment, listening. When the rebels heard the pigs run and squeal, I heard one of them say, "It is the stupid animals making noise; there is no trouble." Throughout this conflict, the animals that the LRA rebels resented and despised most were the pigs, although the origins of their negative image of pigs was difficult to explain.

When I realized that there was no one following me, I quietly crept through the pigsty to climb the wall. But the pigsty had a four-meter-high wall around it with barbed wire on top. There were also broken bottles cemented on top of the wall to prevent anyone from trying to climb over the fence. The height of the wall was slightly above my shoulder. I supported myself by holding onto the roof of the reception center, which was the building attached to the pigsty, and lifted my body up. As I held onto the roof of the reception center, I got another surprise. I received an electric shock that made me jump down and almost fall. I had touched an iron sheet that had contact with a live electric wire. This made me abandon the idea of supporting myself against the rooftop.

At this particular moment, I felt like a moving body without a spirit inside me. I felt like my soul had left me and I had been shaken to the core of my being. My breathing had changed; the sound was like someone else and not me. It was loud, warm, and stale. I felt as if a red-hot flame burned in my chest. I felt like I never had before; I smelled death in the air. I was convinced that I was in the early stages of death, and I thought that many people who died in the war passed through this same phase. I held on to the barbed wire and the tiny pillars on top of the wall with my bare hands. I lifted myself up with them and gently placed my bare feet on the broken bottles and jumped over the wall of the pigsty and the parish. My height was a great asset to me since I am six-foot-three. The surface of the ground on which I had set foot was hard and rough, and since it was now dark, I could not tell what I might have stepped on. I immediately touched my feet to see if I was bleeding; fortunately, I was not. I did not even have a scratch on my hands or my feet from the barbed wires, sharp edges of the broken bottles, or the rough surface.

When I was on the ground, the next problem that I had was where to go. I was out of the parish walls, but with nowhere safe to go. The rebels were almost everywhere. The place that came immediately to my mind was my garden of sweet potatoes to the north. There, I hoped that I could hide under the leaves. However, from that same direction I could hear the voices of many rebels shouting and calling out to the catechists and their families to open the doors for them and let them in. East was the direction of the camp for the internally displaced persons. The activity at the camp was more frightening than the activity anywhere else; it was like hell had broken loose. I heard gunshots and gunfire in the camp and endless screams and pleas from the camp dwellers for their lives to be spared. I heard the rebels trying to break open doors and using axes to smash some down. The nuns' residence was located on the southern side of the rectory. Fortunately, all the nuns were away for vacation, but some people regularly spent their nights at the convent. The residences of the other catechists were situated on the western side of the rectory. I heard rebels forcing the catechists' doors open as well. There was no safe place for me to take refuge, and yet I had to move. If the rebels were to find me, they probably would not leave me alive.

I ran for about fifty meters toward the camp, hoping that I could lie down and hide behind the wall of the nursery school, for it had some grass around it. As I was running, I was breathing very abnormally, and I felt like my lungs were bursting. A long time had passed since I had done any serious physical exercise. Suddenly I heard the steady voices of several men instructing me not to run, so I stopped. These were not rebels, but four men of the parish. They immediately recognized me and instructed me to lie down. They were afraid that if I continued to run, I might be killed in a crossfire between the rebels and government soldiers. So I lay down next to them, and for the moment these men forgot about themselves and came closer to comfort and support me. I was breathing very heavily, and I believe that any passerby could have heard me from a distance. Looking at them, I recognized two of the four men. I had hired them to build and renovate part of the wall around the pigsty that had fallen down several years ago. These men were builders in Pajule who would go to the area bars in the evenings and take some local brew. They were not regular churchgoers. They came to church only if a relative or someone important in the area died.

One of these men taught me some things about faith that I will never forget. First, that the Christian faith is a communal experience. That is, in a faith community, we feed and survive on the faith of one another. There are moments when the community relies on the priest to strengthen its faith, and there are also times when the priest needs the witness of faith in the community to keep his own faith alive. Second, a priest will never be able to tell the impact of his work upon the people that he serves. This is what he whispered in my ears, words that I will continue to remember as long as I live: "Please, Father, be calm and do not be afraid, God will take care of us tonight; we have not committed any crime. And if anything bad is to happen tonight to any of us, it means that God has allowed it to happen." I could not believe what I heard. His words were filled with so much faith, and yet I did not want to entertain the idea that something might go wrong this evening. For over one year I had been preaching to the community to have faith and trust in

God's protection, and today was my turn to get the same message through him.

Within a few minutes, we started to see the rebels lead captives from the camp in a single straight line. Most of them were men and young boys who were carrying their loot, and some captives that were walking too slowly were being beaten. There were a lot of screams and cries in the air. They came close to where we were but passed us by. This was a difficult moment for me. I knew most of the people being abducted and tortured. I felt so much pain for them, but at the same time, there were too many conflicting and confusing feelings inside me: sympathy, fear, horror, terror, pity, concern. It felt like I had lost any sense of balance and the primary instinct directing me was now my personal survival.

As I lay there, I asked myself disturbing questions. Why do I have to go through such a terrible experience? I was also very frustrated with God and I asked Him, why do you make us very helpless and place us at the mercy of such violence and evil? The armed rebels who were now in control of the place could kill any of us if they wished. At the same time one of the messages I had preached months ago on the Feast of the Baptism of Our Lord came to mind. The readings reflected on the reason Christ desired to be baptized: to share with humanity the joys and the pains of life. Within myself, I began to think that maybe this was also a moment for me to share in Christ's pain and that of my parish community.

Within a few minutes, we saw four men. They were bare-chested coming toward us with their shirts wrapped around their waists. They were searching the grass with their torches; they almost passed us by, but they suddenly stumbled upon us. When they saw us, they asked us a question that was very sarcastic: "What do you think that you are doing? Do you think that you are hiding?" In fact, their question was appropriate. We were, in fact, behaving like ostriches. When an ostrich is in danger after running for its life for quite a long time and cannot proceed anymore, it hides its head in the sand and presumes that it is safe and the problem is gone. This was a similar situation to us; apart from burying our faces in the ground, we had very little grass that was covering us. We did not know how to respond to this question, afraid that any clumsy answer could be used as a pretext to harm us. One of us was really smart and creative. He dodged the question and said: "When things started, we were caught up here."

The rebels started to interrogate us and demand personal items. Personally, I had nothing since I had run out of the rectory abruptly. They asked for garden boots to protect their feet from thorns, but none of us had any. Then, they asked for watches; again none of us had one. Of the five of us, the other four were simple villagers who did not put on watches; they often told the time by looking at the sun. I started to get worried because I thought that they would harm us in frustration, since they had failed to get anything of value out of us. Fortunately, one of us had his transistor radio with him. At the time of the attack, he was at the market and had bought a saucepan and had placed the saucepan on top of the radio. It was common practice among men in Pajule to walk around in the evenings with their radios in their hands listening to the local news programs. So after a short search, the rebels got the radio, and it satisfied them to have gotten something out of us.

All along we were lying facedown as the rebels asked us questions, but now they wanted to identify each one of us. They began to flash their torches into our faces. I had not said a word since they found us. One of us twisted and turned on the ground, since he was lying on the grass uncomfortably, and a rebel soldier took this as an excuse to cut his back with a sharp object shaped like an axe. The object was small in size and had a very sharp blade, and this gentleman started to bleed. I could tell from the faces of the rebels that they did not recognize any of the four men, nor did they have any particular interest in them apart from getting what they could from them.

Then, it came my turn; I kept on looking down till they insisted that I look at them. The rebels were not willing to leave without identifying me. One of them flashed his torch into my eyes and asked me a question that almost made me have a heart attack. "Are you the priest? Are you the priest? Are you the priest?" He asked almost seven times. I knew that my moment of death had arrived.

I believe that it was easy for the rebels to sense that I was different. As a priest, I live in a society that is very poor, but my lifestyle is that of a person who is middle class. Even if I am not paid a salary for what I do, I have more opportunities and a better support system than most people. Because of this, my physical appearance, body, complexion, dress, and feet looked different from the other men. In short, my external features made me a person of interest.

I was very frightened and did not know what to say. I paused, stammered, murmured. The answer I gave held the key to my life or death. I was not certain whether these four rebels had been assigned to look for me since I had escaped the rectory. If so, my chances of surviving were less than two percent.

I therefore refused to disclose my identity or confirm that I was a priest. The furthest I could go was to tell them that I worked in the parish. As one of the rebels was getting very insistent on knowing my identity, another intervened by asking a question. I believe in my heart that this rebel soldier wanted to help me out and cool down the tempers of the others. This rebel changed the subject from my identity by asking if they had taken the radio-call. I confirmed to him that the radio-call was the very first thing they took when they entered the rectory. So it was somewhere with one of them. Then this rebel soldier told the others to leave with him. This was a great surprise, because even if they did not do additional harm to any of us, they could still have forced us to go along with them to carry their loot. I attribute this to divine protection.

As they left, I wondered what would have happened if any of us had tried to run away in the heat and panic of the moment. I was certain that the person would have been stabbed or shot dead. When the rebels had gone, I calmed again. It was around 9:00 p.m. I climbed inside the wall of the nursery school, which was the next building. The four men instinctively followed. Fortunately the man who had been cut was not bleeding profusely; by placing his hand against the spot he was able to stop most of the bleeding.

One of the men was sickly and began to cough very loudly when what we needed was dead silence. Because he was coughing so hard, his colleagues ran away from him, and yet he did not want to be left alone and ran after them. At this moment, we whispered to each other that we all needed to go our separate ways rather than be killed together. I ran outside the wall of the nursery school and squatted under a mango tree at the edge of the soccer field of the elementary school. From there, though it was dark, I could see the cemetery, the teachers' quarters, and the camp, since all were located across the soccer field.

I was now a distance of about four hundred meters away from the rectory. While under the mango tree, I began to see the rebels flash their torches nearby, and this almost scared me to death. I was taken up by fear and panic. Fortunately, at this time, there were no gunshots being fired. So, I climbed the mango tree and hide between the trunks. Thee I kept wishing and praying that no rebel soldier would come under the tree and flash his torch upward. Within a short while, I found that the trunks of the mango tree were not comfortable and it was getting cold. Later, I realized the great danger to which I had exposed myself: if there had been a resumption of gunfire, I could have been hit by a bullet. This was one of the stupidest decisions that I made throughout the war. One of the lessons that I learned was that in situations of intense and extreme danger, one should rely on one's intellect all the time rather than emotion. A single misstep may determine whether one stays alive or gets killed.

The top of the mango tree was also a bad place for me because from it I could hear almost everything that was happening nearby. Whenever I heard something fall or break in the rectory, I could feel a sharp and pricking pain in my heart. I heard the rebels break open the door to my pastor's office; this made me almost fall off the tree. I was becoming hysterical because I had wanted to hide in the room's ceiling. It felt like they had gotten me once again. Immediately, I knew that I had to climb down from the tree and go somewhere else. I guessed that the time it was nearly midnight. The moon was so bright; the only place with some vegetation was the garden below the soccer field, but there was no cover to get there.

Nonetheless, I took the risk to run from one end of the soccer field to the other in the moonlight. I was lucky that I did not meet any rebels and that none of them saw me before I entered the garden, which had been harvested a few months back. It was almost half the size of the soccer field and it was large enough to hold hundreds of people. My biggest concern was scorpions, since they liked such places. It would not be fatal, but the pain would last for at least twelve hours. I was also afraid that there could be snakes in the garden, but I was also certain that snakes rarely attacked unprovoked, and if I did not step on one, I would be fine. I enter the garden without any incident but immediately discovered that it was very smelly and uncomfortable because most of the people used it as a latrine. I had to negotiate my way to find a spot that was dry. Even though it was dark, I found a very small space, but I had to lie completely still or end up soiled.

This was the beginning of one of the longest nights of my life. Even at eight hundred meters away from the rectory, I was not yet certain if I had survived death. I could still hear the rebels shouting and ordering the people in the camp to open the doors of their houses or be killed, and there was sporadic shooting along with the cries of mothers and children pleading for their lives. About fifty meters from me, there was a gunman who fired bullets continually into the air as the rebels attacked the camp. It was difficult to tell his identity, but I could only guess that he was a rebel soldier who watched the perimeters as the rest of the rebels looted the camp. I felt powerless, wondering at the number of people I would find injured or killed the following morning if I survived this horrible night

I had heard many people tell of times when they were forced to flee their house and spend the night in the bush, but this was the first time I had done it. It made me appreciate my bed. After thirty minutes of lying on the bare, hard ground, I felt restless and exhausted, and I just wanted to get up and sit. But I could not since there were still bullets flying all around. I had basically two options: to lie on my back or to lie on my stomach. But within a very short time I became restless in either position. Lying on my stomach was very uncomfortable and irritating; it felt like I was constantly being pricked by a needle on account of the rough ground, the dry grass and roots, and the remnants of the stalks of the cereal crop planted in the garden. A better position for me was on my back, but this placed my ears close to the ground and heightened my sensitivity to my surroundings; I felt that I could hear what was occurring as far away as five miles, and this was nothing but violence.

Furthermore, the moonlight made my situation more precarious. It was so bright that the garden became very illuminated. The stalks of millet stood about five feet tall, but most of them had been trampled when the people ran through, and some had been eaten up by termites, so very few were left standing to provide any meaningful camouflage.

Intermittently, as the gunshots and explosions subsided in the night, I kept on asking myself a number of questions: God, why are you doing this to me? Why do I have to go through such a terrible experience? Why do I have to be killed after working only for one year and a few months as a priest? As I continued to reflect on the above questions, I heard a baby who might have been about five months old cough and begin to cry, and I realized that the mother was lying on the ground about ten feet away from me. The baby was coughing and crying because it was getting too cold, and yet, there was hardly anything that the mother could do to keep it warm. In fact, this woman had run from her house in the camp with only her baby and dear life. If the situation were a little bit better, I could have shown her some sympathy or said something to encourage her, but I did not want to frighten her or draw the attention of the gunman firing close by. I dared not speak to her.

As I continued to think about my agony, I tried to make some sense of it, since it seemed that it would be impossible for me to continue to live my life without being resentful and bitter toward the rebels and the parish for having exposed me to so much danger. Searching within myself for a spiritual message out of this ordeal, I came to the conclusion that God had allowed me to spend the night in this garden with a purpose, however horrible the experience may have been. He wanted me to share in the suffering and pain of my people so as to be able to empathize with them. From now on, when others told me their stories of being attacked or abducted or spending the night in the bush, I would fully understand end empathize.

At around two a.m., as the rebels started to withdraw, they began to set the houses ablaze. The skies were filled with tongues of fire, and the people who were still in the camp appeared to be inside a big bowl of fire. At that very moment, I saw hundreds of children between the ages ten to fifteen run to the garden where I was and lie down. What surprised me most was that I began hearing the rebels sing the songs that we normally heard on the FM radio stations. This was an indication that they listened to and monitored whatever took place in society through the radios they stole.

As the rebels retreated, the government soldiers who had been surrounded in the barracks engaged them in a gunfight. I could hear each side hurling abuse and curses at the other. The government soldiers were shouting at the rebels and calling them thieves while the rebels were responding and calling them cowards, as if the two sides had so much hate for one another that gunshots were not enough to do the job unless they were accompanied by words of contempt.

At approximately 6:00 a.m., I made the sign of the cross and thanked the Lord for keeping me and everyone else who had survived safe through the night. I asked God to give me the strength and courage to face the challenges that I would now find. As I got up to go to the parish, there was a little sunlight. A small girl of about eight years old who had been lying down close by got up to follow me. When I saw her, I asked her to remain where she was until we were certain there were no more gunshots. I was confident that she was safe where she was and could return home to the camp or come to the parish later, but my concern now was for her safety.

The aftermath of this attack was terrible. Four people had been killed: two in the parish and two in the town itself. On the parish grounds, a truck was set ablaze and burnt to ashes, and the rectory was partially destroyed by fire. The church itself survived. Since the beginning of the war, the parish compound was the only place where most people felt safe. Whenever they were feeling unsafe, they took sanctuary at the parish. The parish's value as a symbol of security and protection had been taken away from them a single evening.

A few people who had nowhere to go, mostly mothers with very young children, spent their nights at the convent. Before bedtime, I would recite the rosary with them. After prayer, I would wish them a good night and reassure them that they were safe. This was the most unusual experience that I have ever had. As I bid the people assembled a good night, they looked at my eyes very intently. It seemed I appeared to them like a superhuman. They would cling to each and every word of reassurance from me. Even if I was the man of God in their midst, deep down inside I was as worried and scared as all of them.

During this time, we experienced concern and displays of solidarity from the authorities of the Archdiocese of Gulu. They were concerned about my own security and my mental state. But since the rebels had taken the radio-call, our one reliable means of communication with those outside Pajule, I had to go to a place called Oguta to speak with them. It was the only place nearby that had some limited cell phone network coverage, which was indicated by a single bar on the cell phone. Oguta was on the road to Kitgum, about five miles away from the parish, and was a dangerous spot since LRA rebels passed through it on a regular basis.

To some in the archdiocesan administration, the experience I had gone through was too much for someone who had been a priest for just one year and a few months. This came out clearly in my discussions with the Vicar General of the archdiocese, Msgr. Matthew Odong, who wanted me to leave the parish immediately and go to Gulu. I was opposed to the idea. The Vicar General reminded me politely: "Father, it is a matter of obedience for you to heed this directive to come to Gulu; it would be good for you to get out of the place to recover from what you have gone through." On my part, I told him: "I appreciate your prayers and concern for me, but as a matter of conscience; I cannot leave or abandon the parish since I believe that it would be the wrong thing for me to do."

The stand that I took to defy the directive of the Vicar General was unusual, but I felt that I had good reasons for it since I was the only one who knew the actual situation on the ground and the needs of the people. The diocesan authorities were focused on me as an individual, and not on the people who looked to me as their shepherd. I was convinced that if I had left the place at this particular moment, the morale of the people would have totally collapsed. They had already lost their symbol of security, the parish. It would be too much for them to learn that the priest, now their only hope, had also abandoned them.

I firmly believed that I could still continue to be their voice and would have the capacity to use my influence and status to talk to nongovernmental organizations that needed a credible contact on the ground in order to channel aid to the people. Further, the church was the only visible and viable structure on the ground. Scarcely any functioning institutions remained. There were no journalists or local reporters who could inform the rest of the country or the world about what was happening. As a religious leader, I believed I could use my influence to speak about the plight of the people to the political and military authorities in the district, and if I left, the people would lose this important voice. Furthermore, I believed that my presence would check military abuses on the population, though they were rare at the time. My presence would mean that any abuses that took place would become known outside Pajule, since I could report this to the ecclesiastical hierarchy for steps to be taken. In short, I was concerned lest the only center of authority in the community that was independent from the military be silenced.

Since I would not leave the parish, the diocesan authorities had to make some accommodations for me. The Vicar General and Fr

Peter planned to go to Lira, an hour's drive from Gulu, and find a driver who would take the risk to come to Pajule to bring me funds and clothing. I badly needed money. The rebels had left the house and my food store empty. My only remaining articles of clothing were a pair of trousers and a shirt I put on at the time of the attack. As the Vicar General and my pastor left Gulu for Lira, they reflected on the attack my subsequent refusal to leave the parish, and they pondered: "If a young man who has been a priest for one and half years is taking the risk to be there with the people because of his faith in Christ and his desire to serve Him, what about us, who were both ordained priests almost sixteen years ago? How can we not take the same risk and go to Pajule?" So they resolved to make the dangerous journey to Pajule – a journey dependent upon faith for both of them. Only one driver was willing to risk the road called Hajji, and he would charge four to five times the normal rate of transport on the one-hour trip from Lira to Pajule. He never stopped anywhere along the road, even if he met rebel soldiers along the road or an ambush on the way, he drove through.

When Fr Peter and Fr Matthew reached Pajule on Saturday at around four p.m. We were surprised and happy to receive them since we were not expecting them. They were astonished to find us calmly preparing for Sunday Mass, in the midst of our ruined town and parish.

The following day hundreds of people attended Mass. Most of the town and camp dwellers came, irrespective of their faith traditions, to listen to the message of the Vicar General. In the middle of the celebration, the director of CARITAS also arrived. The community of Pajule as a whole appreciated the solidarity of the leadership of the Catholic Church, and the risk that these two officials took to come meant a lot to us. I heard positive comments from inactive churchgoers: "You see the Catholic Church; when they are faced with a problem they support one another."

Before the end of the Mass, the Vicar General blessed every space in the parish with holy water: our living rooms, the rectory, the convent, and the reception center where the two killings had taken place. After Mass, the community breathed a sigh of relief. It felt like God was once again in charge. Later that same day, they all returned to the headquarters of the Diocese in Gulu. Father Peter could not stay: his journey to Pajule with Fr Matthew was unplanned, he needed to pick up his personal belongings in Gulu, and he had to report the urgent needs of the parish to the bishop.

THE PRIEST AND THE REBELS

My first meeting with the LRA rebels in April of 2003 was not something that I had wished for or planned. I was in Gulu on parish business and needed to return to Pajule. The only available transportation entailed traveling with representatives of the Acholi Religious Leaders Peace Initiative. Acholi was an umbrella organization that brought together a group of cultural and religious leaders seeking peace in northern Uganda. The delegation was headed for Koyo Lalogi, where it would meet with the LRA, and the driver of the vehicle was the brother of one of the rebel commanders. We left Gulu via Lira, driving toward Pajule. I was to be droped me off in Pajule parish before the delegation went on to meet the rebels. By this time, in order to promote dialogue with the rebels, the government of Uganda had designated the whole of Lapul sub-county, in which Koyo Lalogi was located, a ceasefire zone.

As we were approaching Pajule, the delegation members began to panic, breathe loudly, and shift nervously. They pleaded with me to accompany them to meet the LRA rebels. I was very hesitant. My personal rule when traveling at the time was that once I had decided on a plan, I would not change it; I believed my first choice was the safer one, arrived at with divine guidance. Moreover, the LRA was often suspicious and hostile to visitors they did not expect or invite. As the delegation insisted, however, I resolved to accompany them. As the only Catholic priest in the group, I suddenly took on a new role representing the Catholic Church.

The junction to Koyo Lalogi was about one mile from the main center of Pajule. I was greatly surprised when we encountered two rebel soldiers very near to the main road, less than five hundred meters from the junction. This came as a great shock to me because this spot was very near to town. It indicated that the rebels constantly observed who was going in and out of the town, and if they had any ill intentions they could easily carry them out. These two rebel soldiers had advance information that a delegation from Gulu was coming to their base. They stopped us, assuring us that it was safe to proceed and that we would meet more rebel groups ahead.

After driving for fifteen minutes into the bush, we met a large group of rebels who were excited to see us. Their attitude was festive, as if we were coming to a picnic. There was a lot of youthful excitement and happiness among them. Most of them were in their early teens. Several boasted of having their own personal guns, and others bragged about their large numbers in the place, and that even if the government soldiers were to try to attack them they would never be dislodged. Some of them came and introduced themselves to us, but they all had fictitious names like the crocodile, cow, goat, rabbit, or guinea fowl.

As we traveled deep into the jungle, we could hardly see what was ahead of us since the grass covered all the roads into Koyo Lalogi. The little we could see were marks of destruction: burned buildings, crumbling walls, and abandoned houses. The primary signs that people had once lived there were the orange and mango trees that were in the compounds. At this time of the year in early April 2003, the trees were full of ripening mangoes and oranges, but there were no people to pick and eat them.

The elementary school of Koyo Lalogi was the only permanent building left standing. Its renovation had not been completed before the place became insecure. When it was raining heavily, the LRA rebels used it for shelter, or for cover when there were any suspicious planes flying overhead. This trip was remarkable for me, since Koyo Lalogi had a large role in our fears since the resumption of conflict in 2002. From Koyo Lalogi, the rebel commanders regularly would send out units around Pader District to attack passenger vehicles and steal food and supplies.

As the time came for us to leave, we boarded our truck to depart. The speed with which we left was striking. Before a journey we normally would say a prayer through the intercession of St Christopher, the patron saint and protector of travelers, but this time we forgot. Yet there was plenty of need for us to pray, since we were about drive through rebel-infested jungles. As the car was leaving the place of the meeting, Nyeko Tolbert Yardin, the rebel commander, came forward and stopped the driver and asked us to get down. "Father," he said, "as a man of God, you have not blessed us; bless us before you leave." As I got out of the vehicle, I wondered why prayer was important to this LRA officer and, above all, what would I pray? Did it make sense to pray that God bless the rebels, despite their murdering and plundering? What if they were not happy with my prayer and felt that I had judged or criticized them? I asked God to provide me with the words to say, and I believe that He did. The prayer went something like this:

Lord God, as your minister, you know that we all love this land. I would like to thank you for the beauty of Acoliland and its people, children, soil, skies, and rivers. You have blessed this land with every good gift.

Unfortunately, we cannot enjoy your many gifts in this land. Because of this war, we are refugees in our own land. I pray that you bless every sincere effort by the government of Uganda, the LRA rebels, the people of Uganda, and the religious and cultural leaders toward peace in Acoliland.

We concluded by reciting the Our Father and the Hail Mary.

The rebel commander seemed moved and pleased with my prayer, and asked that on a future visit I bring them rosaries. I responded that I could not make any promises since we did not have rosaries in the parish and we rarely traveled because of the security situation. During the attack on the parish, the rebels stole all the rosaries in the house. Some of them, which I had bought in Rome when I went for the beatification of two of our catechists in October 2002, were engraved with John Paul II's picture.

As we boarded our vehicle and left the rebel base, I pondered many theological questions on prayer. Why did these rebels value prayer? Did they pray to the same God that we all do? What did prayers mean to them? What did reciting the rosary mean to them if in the evening they lined up along the roads to shoot and kill innocent people?[160]

One evening in the middle of June 2003, after our night prayers and supper, we two priests in Pajule went to bed. Before falling asleep, Fr Peter customarily listened to some world news on the radio at a very low volume. That evening, the BBC reported that the Ugandan Army had intercepted a communication from the LRA high command in the South Sudan instructing LRA fighters in Uganda to kill any Catholic

---

[160] The beliefs of the LRA are obscure; most of us did not know or understand them. For example, they purported to believe that Uganda as a state ought to be ruled and guided by the Ten Commandments. This was puzzling to most Ugandans, since the LRA frequently murdered innocent people, despite the fifth commandment, "Thou shall not kill."

priest that they found in Gulu. We were sixty-one priests being targeted. Since my ordination almost two years earlier, no other priest had been ordained in the archdiocese.

When Fr Peter heard this grim news, he immediately brought me to listen as well. What we heard made both of us very nervous. We wished one another a safe night and promised that we would discuss the news report in the morning. We were always aware that we served in a very risky place, but this rebel threat put the spotlight on us. We could not take it lightly because our parish was at the epicenter of the conflict; most of the other Catholic parishes in Pader District had closed. The two priests who previously had worked in the parish were ambushed and murdered while traveling; their deaths also weighed heavily on our minds.

The following day we considered our options. We had basically two choices. The first was to pack up and leave. The second was to continue working while making new security arrangements.

As we agonized on our next steps, my pastor was firmly of the idea that we should move out of the parish as soon as possible. He was of the view that we could return once in a while and conduct Masses and administer sacraments when we considered it safe. At the parish we had two vehicles in running condition that we could use to flee to Kampala or to Gulu. Kampala was almost three hundred miles away from the conflict area and would give us a moment to rest from all the violence. This option was not practical, however, since it would require money to live there. The headquarters of the archdiocese was located in Gulu, where we could stay in one of the parishes or institutions. Gulu, however, was not safe earlier. The LRA rebels had recently abducted close to forty-one seminarians in Gulu. Moreover, I feared that in Gulu we would seem like shepherds who had abandoned their flock.

One factor that complicated our deliberations was the community of religious sisters. Four sisters lived at the parish and ran the schools. If we, the two priests, were to flee from Pajule, we could not leave them behind. Yet these sisters were central to the community. Running one of the two remaining elementary schools still operating in town, they served nearly 1,500 children. If they were to move out, there was a real possibility that everything would come to a halt. We made sure that the head of the sisters participated in our deliberations.

We considered the devastating impact on the community of the departure of its priests and sisters. For almost eighteen months, the strength of the community had been built on the Church and the continuous presence of at least one priest. I knew that God alone protected us from the dangers of working in Pajule, since the army had failed several times. Since the attack of January 23, 2003, however, they had also learned their lessons and become more vigilant, deploying around Pajule on a twenty-four-hour basis. I believed we were safe within the town. Personally, I also felt spiritually and theologically challenged by the situation we were in, and I continued to ask myself, if I ran away from the parish, how could I ever ask my congregation to have faith and trust in God for their security? What kind of credibility would I ever have as a shepherd among them?

This was something that created some friction between us, the two priests. We could not agree on what to do to take care of the people and our own lives. My pastor was firmly for the idea of periodically returning to the parish, while I was convinced that we should stay in the parish, but with more soldiers assigned specifically to protect the place. The head of the sisters supported my position. Because we could not arrive at an agreement, we consulted the diocesan authorities.

When we called the Vicar General, however, he told us they did not have any directives for individual parishes. He merely told us that priests and their communities must take necessary precautions. So we resolved to write a letter to the military authorities in Pader District headquarters, requesting them to beef up security around the parish. We stated clearly that without a guarantee from them to provide us with additional protection, it would be foolish for us to continue working in Pajule.

After writing our letter, we traveled to Pader District headquarters to hand-deliver it. The journey was very stressful because the road had been cut off for several weeks, since the rebels had been abducting travelers. It was a wet and rainy season, and tall grass had grown on both sides of the road, such that in many places we could hardly see more than fifteen meters ahead. We traveled separately, Fr Peter in his truck and me on my motorcycle, because we did not want both of us to be blown up or killed in the same vehicle.

On reaching Pader town, we met the political and military leaders, who were very understanding. The civil and political leaders in Pader did not want Pajule parish to be closed, since they knew how important our presence was to the whole community. They immediately held a security meeting and resolved to assign soldiers to protect the rectory and parish premises, in addition to the protection that the parish had as part of the town as a whole. That very evening we saw several soldiers stationed specifically to protect the parish. This was a great relief.

In view of the death threat looming over the Catholic priests of Gulu, we reduced our travels outside Pajule to the minimum. Within Pajule, which had a radius of three miles, we were safe. But occasionally we had to visit the chapels outside Pajule. The majority of the chapels had been closed, and most of the people assembled in the chapes at Pader and Acolibur. These places had close to thirty thousand people each, and once in a while we had to take the risk to go to minister to them. Whenever we traveled to these chapels we put on our clerical shirts or cassocks, thinking that the rebels might hesitate to attack us if they clearly see we are doing God's work. When we had not visited a chapel for a number of weeks or months, someone would come to us on foot or bicycle and relate that the Christian community would like to receive the sacraments. The people usually wished to receive the sacraments of baptism, penance, and the Eucharist. If we took two to three months between visits to a chapel, we would baptize from seventy to one hundred babies in single Mass.

Around the time that the military boosted security on the parish grounds, I received a memorable letter from my sister

Silvia, the sixth born of the nine children in my family. Silvia wanted to update me about what she was doing in Kitgum, as she was looking forward to starting college that coming fall semester. She also wanted to learn how I was taking the threat of the LRA to kill the Catholic priests. She wrote: "Father Robert, we heard the news that the LRA rebels have ordered the killing of priests; hearing this made me deeply troubled and worried about you. I want to know what you have made of this news. Remember, Father, I will always be praying for your safety and that of the other priests of the Archdiocese." The concern and love expressed in this letter moved me very profoundly. I wrote back thanking her for her letter and her prayers. I also informed her that we were fully aware of the threats against our own lives as priests, but that God had been protecting us in our work. I promised her that I would avoid taking any unnecessary risks.

Working as a priest in a dangerous area put much pressure on my family. Whenever they heard of an ambush along the roads, an attack on a parish, or a raid on Pajule, they thought of my safety. The best intercessor for me to God was my mother; she daily would say a rosary for my safety. Although Kitgum, where my parents lived, was just forty-five minutes away from Pajule, because of the insecurity I could visit them only once every six to nine months.

FROM PAJULE TO THE UNITED STATES

The news that I would leave Pajule for the United States of America was most shocking to me. In late June 2004, as I was returning from vacation in the Archdiocese of Tororo, the Vicar General called to inform me that the bishop had something important to discuss with me. So I postponed my return to Pajule in order to meet with the bishop in Gulu, not knowing what to expect.

I reached Gulu I found that the bishop had left the day before. In the evening after dinner the Vicar General invited me to his living room and presented to me the prospectus of a university. He broke the news that the bishop had gotten a scholarship and wanted me to study at Walsh University in Canton, Ohio. When I heard this, I was shocked; I did not have any plans to for further studies at the moment. The Vicar General went on to say that the bishop was well aware that Pajule parish was celebrating her Jubilee Year, but he had made up his mind that I go to graduate school in the United States within two months. When he had presented me with the documents and the communications, I thanked him and told him that I needed to pray about it.

My selection by the bishop to take this scholarship troubled me in several ways. However insecure and risky life was in Pajule parish, I found my work fulfilling since it gave meaning to my vocation as a priest. Because of this I considered working in it as the most important thing in my life at the time, and I was willing to forego other opportunities. I was also concerned about the damage that would be caused to the morale of my parishioners by my abrupt departure. I had built a strong relationship with the community, and I could not imagine how to tell my parishioners that I was suddenly leaving in the midst of the parish Jubilee Year. This strong bond and vibrant spiritual life in the parish made it possible for us to add two additional Sunday Masses to the Mass schedule.

Upon returning to Pajule I was confused and drained. I felt lost. The parish community sensed something was going on inside me. I head them ask one another questions such as, "Our priest these days looks very low spirited and depressed; what is happening to him?" I reassured them that I was fine. Pajule was a hard place, but I knew how to live and survive in it. It was a big parish with about sixty thousand people. To be entrusted with such a significant responsibility after being a priest for only three years was a big achievement. If I were to go to school, I had to give it up.

One question that continually returned to my mind was, "What is the United States of America like?" I had seen movies made in Hollywood and some of them were about life in the USA, but I was certain that most of them were fictional. I also wondered what theological discipline I would study. I always believed that academic studies in the United States were more secular and liberal. Other times, I wondered what student life would be like again: staying awake for long hours in the night to complete assignments, a tiny space to live in, and sitting in class for many hours listening to professors.

Despite these misgivings about the timing of a trip, I had always admired certain things about the United States of America as a country. Its political system periodically allows citizens to choose new leaders freely and fairly, and those who hold political office most of the time reflect the popular will. The institutions of the USA serve the interests of citizens other than those who are in power. Real political power is in the hands of the people and not the military. The citizens are free to speak on all subjects, including security and threats to their country.

After two weeks in Pajule, I returned to Gulu to meet the bishop. I still had mixed feelings about leaving Pajule to go to school in the United States of America. But I was now leaning toward accepting the offer and beginning to think more and more that it was what God wanted me to do. I also felt that it would be beneficial to my future ministry as a priest, even if it did mark the end of my ministry in Pajule. I asked the bishop to allow me report to school in January of 2005 instead of August 2004, so I could serve in the parish untill the end of the year and celebrate the Parish Jubilee day on December 8, 2004. The bishop listened attentively, but reaffirmed his earlier decision. He informed me that the university was expecting me at the end of August 2004. I was left with less than two months before I reported. Despite my misgivings and disappointment, I chose to obey the bishop and to trust his judgment.

Back in Pajule, I set up structures for the Jubilee Year celebration in the parish, ensuring that it could function without me or my successor. We also established committees for publicity and fundraising. Yet I could not communicate to the parishioners that I was leaving the place; I feared that revealing that news would give rise to many questions for which I had no answers. In fact, I had no information to give to my parishioners about who would succeed me in the parish aside from some rumors.

Before going for my visa appointment at the embassy, I had in my possession a number of documents from several sources including letters from my bishop, the schools that I had attended, and the secretary general of the Uganda Episcopal Conference. With these documents, including the university admission to the United States, I felt confident that I would easily be granted the visa.

At the American embassy in Kampala, the practice at the time was first come, first serve. This meant that I had to arrive very early in the morning in order to secure a visa appointment. For every visa appointment at the embassy, whether it was successful or unsuccessful, one had to pay one hundred dollars. The first time that I went for an appointment, there were close to four hundred people waiting at the gates. Since I arrived early and had all my documents in order I was allowed in for a face-to-face interview. When my turn came, a lady sitting behind tinted windows asked for my documents, which I showed her. She glanced at them and told me that they were not granting me the visa because my documents did not specify that I had room and board. I left the embassy very disappointed because I had put so much work and time into preparing for the appointment. Nonetheless, I was confident that if I got assurances and clarification from the university, things would be fine. So I immediately sent them an e-mail asking them to send me a fax confirming that my scholarship covered room and board that I could take to the embassy. Then, as the weekend was drawing near, I left for Pajule.

I returned to Kampala on Tuesday, since the university faxed their confirmation letter over the weekend. The following morning I went to the American embassy, and this time I was certain that I would be granted the visa. Because it was a second and separate visit, I presented one hundred dollars once again for the visa interview. When my turn came, I presented the documents that I had and the fax message from the university indicating that I had room and board. This was a different lady from the first visit, and she cursorily looked at my documents and the fax message and then asked for my grade-school certificate, which in Uganda is the primary leaving exam certificate. This request was strange because rarely do we present a grade-school certificate for anything unless it is the only certificate that a person has, and I was going to graduate school. The visa application process appeared to be a game of cat and mouse, since with each and every visit the rules changed. It seemed focused on finding a reason to deny granting a visa.

Before returning to Pajule, a friend advised me to call the public relations officer at the American embassy and register my complaint, which I did. I passed the cell phone number to my bishop, who called him after two days and discussed my plight with him. The second visit to the embassy had left me stressed, drained, demoralized, and devastated. The emotional pains that I was going through at the embassy were self-inflicted; if I decided against pursuing education in the United States, I would be spared these troubles. As I was returning to Pajule, I made up my mind that if my bishop had not talked to the people at the embassy and received assurances that I could get a visa, I would not return to the embassy, and I would forget the idea of going to school altogether.

A week later, the public relations officer at the American embassy called me and told me that the status of my application had been reviewed and my chances were good. I needed to bring all my supportive documents, and they were not going to charge me any new visa fees for this appointment. I left what I was doing in Pajule and hurried to Kampala, since my third appointment at the embassy was scheduled for the next day at 12:30 p.m. I reached Kampala at midnight the night before.

As I entered the US embassy from the side gate, I found everyone nice and friendly to me this time. This time I met a much older man, who looked at my documents and cross-examined me. He asked where I came from and what I did and why I was choosing to go to school in United States. He asked me more details about the school, its ownership, and scholarship policy. I could answer some of the questions but not all, since I did not know how the university system operated in the United States. Still, he appeared satisfied with my answers and told me to return to pick up my visa the following day at 3:00 p.m. I was excited and relieved. I felt like running out of the embassy and calling friends to tell them that I had been granted the visa. The following day I picked up my visa – one of the nine people in total whose application had been approved out of hundreds.

The morning I was to leave the parish, I offered Mass in the parish church and said farewell. Close to one hundred people attended, which is a large crowd for a weekday. I told the congregation that even if I was going to a distant land as a student, they would always be in my thoughts and prayers. I promised them that I was going to approach my education with the same commitment and determination I had when things were difficult among them. After the Mass, when we were outside the church, I had the chance to say good-bye to each one of them individually. This morning was the last occasion on which I experienced their affection and warmth. About fifteen couples came to meet me in my office and shared things that I had not expected. They talked about how my three years working among them had touched and transformed them as individuals and as couples. Others described the positive changes my leadership had brought into the lives of their children.

When it was almost time to leave, at midday, the altar boys and liturgical dancers that had celebrated Mass with me for the last three years came running to see me off on their class break. This was one of the hardest moments for me. Leaving Pajule was not an idea anymore; it was a reality now. I found this time to be very painful and felt a profound sense of separation, since I was not sure if I would ever return. I loosely quoted Ecclesiastes 3:1–8, saying that three years ago was the time for me to come to work in Pajule as a newly ordained priest, and it was now time for me to leave. I went on to say to those assembled that I was thankful for my time among them. As I finished my farewell speech, I saw my altar boys, liturgical dancers, and parish staff struggle to hold back tears, which made me emotional too. As I drove through town, many stood by the roadside to say good-bye. Once again I saw a lot of sadness in their faces, and some stopped the vehicle for a final hug. One woman, who had a son called Tony and was always referred to as "the mother of Tony," stopped me and said: "Father, it is a sad day that you are leaving, but we put everything in God's hands."

I spent about three days in Kitgum saying farewell to my family and close friends before journeying to Kampala for my flight. Both of my parents were excited about my going to school in the United States, but for different reasons. My father saw it as an opportunity to get more knowledge and broaden my perspective on life, but my mother was happy because I was getting escaping the dangers of Pajule.

On September 29, 2004, I flew to the United States. School had begun six weeks earlier; the process of procuring a visa delayed my arrival. This was my first truly long-distance trip alone. I fell asleep only to wake up at Brussels. At the beginning of the flight the waitress wanted me to eat since we were starting a long flight, but I declined since I was too tired. As the plane traveled further away from the continent of Africa, I felt the physical separation from my own people, and the immersion into a foreign land. The further I traveled, the more composition of the passengers changed: most of those who boarded the plane in Entebbe were black; as we approached the United States, most of the passengers were white.

The trip from Europe to the United States extremely long, and the different entertainments on the plane did little to take away the sense of boredom as we flew over the ocean. At times it felt like an endless trip, which once again gave me a moment of introspection. I began to ask myself: "Why do I have to travel such a long distance away from home?" Once in a while I would remind myself that I must be going for some really serious business in the United States. While I was lost in thought, I heard the air hostess announce that we were flying over the state of Maine, and that in less than an hour we would land in Newark. This was a great relief for me, but I still had to take a connecting flight from Newark to John Hopkins International Airport in Cleveland, Ohio.

When we landed and I got out of the plane, my level of anxiety rose. First, the size of Newark was intimidating. Second, I had to change flights and make sure that my luggage was placed on the next flight. I was worried that I would not be able to identify my luggage and transfer it to the next flight. Fortunately, I was able to check my baggage on the flight to Cleveland. Third, having coming from a country that is almost 99.9 percent black, I was thrown into a sea of white people; I seemed to be the only black person among them. All the men and women looked alike in my eyes. They were polite, but they spoke too fast. I was fortunate that I came from an English-speaking country and was able to communicate, even though I could see those around me strain their ears to understand me.

I rushed to the gate to board the flight for Cleveland, with the help of some people who gave me directions. As soon as I entered the plane, its door was closed; I was the last person to board it before it took off. When I reached Cleveland, I expected to take a taxi to Walsh University, but Fr Jino Mwaka, a student priest from my diocese was waiting for me. It was exciting to meet him, as we had not seen each other for almost two years. He had come to the United States at the height of the insecurity in Pajule. We had been contemporaries in the seminary, but he was four years ahead of me. As soon as we picked up my luggage, we headed to the airport parking lot, which was another big surprise for me. It was the first time I had seen such a large parking lot with several levels, and I had never seen so many cars. In Uganda, most cars park on the side of the street.

When we began to drive out of the airport, another surprise for me was the amount of space and the sizes of things. The road signs appeared really big to me, and the highways were also extremely wide. The many roads leading to different destinations were striking, too. This was the first time I had seen two or three lanes of cars moving in the same direction and two or three more going in the opposite direction. The number of cars and above all the high speed at which they traveled amazed me. I kept wondering how each car could keep within its lane, and most of the time I was afraid that the car behind us would smash into our car since they all drove very fast. The roads in Pajule were dirt, narrow, and single lane. When two vehicles came from different directions, one vehicle, usually the smaller one, had to go to the side of the road and wait for the bigger one to pass.

Father Jino was filled with happiness to see me. He had just bought a car and he was learning his way around. In the excitement, he gave me his road map and asked me to read it and guide him as we drove to Canton, Ohio. Can you imagine a person from Pajule who has spent less than two hours in the United States being asked to guide a driver to an unknown destination? I looked at the map for a few minutes, and could not interpret it. It made me feel more tired and exhausted. In the years to come, I often joked with Fr Jino about how he had traumatized me by asking me to read the map.

Before going to Walsh University, he drove me to the Catholic parish of Our Lady of Perpetual Help in Aurora, Ohio, where he lived as a priest in residence at the time. We entered the church and thanked God for my safe trip to the United States. I loved the church, which was not the traditional rectangular church but round, brightly lit, and with plenty of space. The cleanliness was remarkable, and I wondered how it was kept so clean. I could not see dust on anything. The grass on the compound was cut and level. Being September, the skies were clear and bright, and the air was cool.

Father Jino later took me to Walsh University in Canton, Ohio, where I was welcomed by the Brothers of Christian Instruction, with whom I would reside. My arrival in the United States marked not only the end of my ministry in Pajule but also the conclusion of a significant phase of my life. At the same time it marked the beginning of a new ministry as a priest and a student in the United States.

I presently am working in the midst of a five-year contract serving as a hospital chaplain in Kansas City, Kansas. After that, I will return to Uganda. The contrast between living and working in Pajule and the United States is remarkable. In Pajule, my very life seemed to hinge on divine providence, since mortal danger lurked everywhere and at all times. In the United States, I experience certainty, peace, and order in my day to day activities

To have had the training as a chaplain and to have the opportunity to work in a hospital in the United States is a great blessing. Pastoral ministry to the sick has been a personal passion since my seminary days. In Pajule parish I attended many sick people who had been displaced and were living in the camps. For a long time, I desired to get some professional training and experience in the area, which thankfully I am now receiving. Uganda, unlike the United States, lacks a developed pastoral care system and structures to care for the sick, such as hospitals with chaplains. I hope to use my knowledge and experience to make a contribution toward developing such structures and programs for pastoral care of the sick back in my own country.

CONCLUSION

Further, it is a fact that the many years that have passed have created some distance between me and the raw feelings and trauma caused by the war. And yet I know that the impact of the war will live with me for the rest of my life, and there will even be times when I find it difficult to articulate it. I remember in my first days as a student at Walsh University in 2004, a fire truck drove onto the university in the middle of the night and honked its horns very loudly. When I heard the loud sounds in the middle of my sleep, I was gripped with fear and wanted to run out of my bedroom, thinking that the LRA were breaking into the place. Minutes later I realized that I was now in the United States – the bedroom where I lay was smaller, cramped, and brightly lit compared to my previous one in Pajule, which was more spacious and darker, since power outages were common. In fact, it took me almost two years to be healed from the fright of any loud sounds and bangs. Even after spending almost eight years in the United States, the blasts and the sounds of fireworks for Independence Day celebrations on July 4 every year bring back the memories and tensions of a rebel attack. Whenever Independence Day is approaching, I always worry about how I will pass the day.

While most of my time in the United States has been spent going to school, I have had the unique opportunity to meet many people and learn from them about their culture. I am today much more attentive to cultural similarities and differences. At the same time, this has made me more appreciative of the uniquely distinct values of my own Acoli culture. For example, I have come to the realization that while all people may desire justice, we achieve the same goal differently.

Although I was exposed to many life-threatening situations as a young man and priest, I now look at my service in Pajule as a great privilege from God. In limited ways, I had the opportunity to alleviate the sufferings of my people. Moreover, my ministry in Pajule increased my faith. I am more than ever convinced that God has a purpose for me. It is this same God who led me from Pajule to the United States and has sustained me throughout my graduate studies and ministry in this country. During my ministry in Pajule, I often ate, drank, and chatted with a person who was killed the next day. The question I always asked myself was this: "Why do some of the members of my community get killed, and though I have taken the same risks as they did, I keep on surviving?" This made me come to the conclusion that if I am still alive today, God must have a purpose and a mission for me to accomplish.

Studying in the United States gave allowed me to step out of the center of violence. I have had the time to reflect and write down my recollections. Through my graduate studies, I have acquired knowledge that I believe has made me more insightful, self-confident, and a better writer. It is my hope that my education and priestly ministry in the United States will enrich my service in Uganda and in the Archdiocese of Gulu, when the time comes for me to return home and again work among my people.

In the hands of my parents in 1972. The little child who would one day be a priest.

At the Alokolum seminary chapel, I am seated third from the right. We are singing our hearts out because from an early age we were taught that one who sings prays twice.

Before the end of my ordination Mass, my bishop asked me to bless him. I had
received new powers as a priest through him and he wanted to be among the
very first to experience their spiritual benefits.

After I had been ordained a priest before the final blessing, my bishop with great excitement told the congregation that he had a brand new priest that he wanted to introduce to them. For the first time he referred to me as "Reverend Father." He told them that I would be the 61st priest serving in his diocese and he was giving me a personal name, "Rubanga Mar," meaning "God is Love."

Soon after my ordination to the priesthood with my bishop, parents and the clergy who participated in the Mass.

Here I am standing next to the vehicle of a local businessman that the L.R.A. set ablaze at the parish. I was convinced that one day I would tell the story no matter how long it would take.

Within minutes after I returned from my first night ever in the bush in January 2003. Most of the people assembled at the parish were in a state of shock and wondering what might have happened to me.

As the chaplain of Pajule Reception Center I attend to one of the former child soldiers. However difficult their ordeal, it did not prevent most from making a successful transition to a new life.

The inside view of Pajule parish church and the congregation. In the warzone, the only place where most people heard a refreshing idea and felt some peace and joy was at the celebration of the Mass.

SEGMENT 3

Country Reports

Colombia

The geography of Colombia is diverse, spanning tropical seas, ocean waters, rugged mountain ranges, and rainforests. With the Caribbean Sea in the north, the Pacific Ocean in the west and borders with Panama, Venezuela, Brazil, Peru, and Ecuador, Colombia is also famous to tourists for its twin chains of the northern Andes Mountains and lowland Amazon basin.[1] Geographically, Colombia is rich in natural resources. Spiritually, this land has also prospered from several centuries' worth of Catholic heritage and tradition, beginning in the 16th century when explorers from Spain brought with them Catholic missionaries. In the subsequent centuries, the Colombian Catholic Church has grown and thrived, producing a unique and diverse combination of Spanish, indigenous Indian, and African cultures that is beautifully expressed in Church liturgies and customs.

In its 600 years of existence in Colombia, Catholicism has crossed many ethnic boundaries and become deeply embedded within Colombian culture and society. While the Colombian population has mixed ethnic origins, a dominant majority of its people are members

---

[1] David Knowlton, "Colombia," *Worldmark Encyclopedia of Religious Practices*, vol. 2, *Countries: A-L*, ed. Thomas Riggs (Detroit: Gale, 2006), 236–41, here 236.

of the Catholic Church. Of its approximate population of 41 million, up to 94% are Christians, and 81% of these, Roman Catholic.[2] At least formally, nearly all Colombians are some type of Christian. The minority that are not Catholic belong to other religious groups in Colombia including various Protestant churches, Seventh-day Adventists, Mormons, and Jehovah's Witnesses, and there are also small communities of Jews, Muslims, and practitioners of indigenous and African-influenced religions.[3]

EARLY CHURCH HISTORY

At the time that the explorers first came to Colombia, this land was the seat of important Indian chiefdoms. These tribes were central players in the region at that time, and even today continue to play a vital role. Many Colombians can trace some roots back to these indigenous groups. As a result of centuries of ethnic mixing, today almost 60 percent of the country's population is considered *mestizo*, or of mixed Indian descent.[4] Yet the path to this point involved many layers and hundreds of years of struggle and partnerships in the aftermath of the Spanish settlement there.

Along with the first explorers and opportunists, Spanish missionaries in Colombia also set out to bring the Gospel message to new lands. Beginning with the Franciscans in 1508, missionaries

---

[2] *Id.*

[3] *Id.*

[4] *Id.,* 241.

carried the faith even to the most remote parts of Colombia.[5] Their work did not only cover religious education, but as with many other foreign missions, the Church sought to improve basic social services as well.

> The missionaries erected the church in which the converted congregated, built hospitals and ran schools in which were taught reading, writing, arithmetic, chant and above all Christian doctrine. Along with these efforts, the missionaries became the defenders of the Chibcha people, who were otherwise mistreated and exploited without mercy by *encomenderos* seeking slave labor for their plantations.[6]

From early times, there seems to have been a special partnership between at least some indigenous tribes, like the *Chibca*, who found support from Church leadership. Another group at was the large number of African slaves that were brought to Colombia to work the mines and plantations.[7] They too had to be taken into consideration by the Catholic Mission. It is estimated that more than a fifth—and perhaps as much as a third—of its population is of African origin.[8] The number of Colombians today who are of African descent really

---

[5] "Colombia, The Catholic Church in," in *New Catholic Encyclopedia*, 2nd ed., vol. 3 (Detroit: Gale, 2003), here 851.

[6] *Id.*, 851

[7] "Colombia," in *Junior Worldmark Encyclopedia of World Holidays*, vol. 2, ed. Robert H. Griffin & Ann H. Shurgin (Detroit: UXL, 2000), 154–54.

[8] Knowlton, 241.

shows how large this original African contingent was.

With the convergence of these three cultures, the Spanish (Western) with the indigenous Indian and African, it is therefore not surprising that there were differences in language, traditions, and beyond. At the forefront, there were disputes with respect to doctrine and the customs. For example, some customs conflicted with native customs, such as polygamy and idolatry.[9] Yet, the struggles were not only with communicating Catholic norms to the local tribes and African slaves. The preaching of the gospel among native tribes sparked serious resistance on the part of witch doctors on the one hand and hypocritical Spanish slave owners on the other.[10] In different ways, each of these groups benefitted from the missionaries.

Language, clearly, posed another central challenge. It was not so much the acquisition of a foreign language that was so bad, as it was the ability to learn *multiple* languages. With backgrounds as diverse as these groups, just as missionaries succeeded in mastering the language of one community, the language of the next would again confound their efforts to communicate the word of God.[11] To bypass these linguistic hurdles, these communities relied more upon action than spoken or written word to learn the ways of the Church. In this way, native Indians and Africans were able to see the new religion in practice.[12] The action of evangelization through church ritual was an important teaching of this time, but it also laid the groundwork for many of the Catholic Colombian traditions of today.

---

[9] *Junior Worldmark*, 153–61.

[10] *Id.*

[11] *Id.*

[12] *Id.*, 153–54.

POLITICAL IMPACT

In the early days of colonial government, relations with the Catholic Church were naturally favorable. When the governmental structure changed after national independence from Spain, so too did the status quo for Colombian Catholics. After their 1824 independence, the country was embroiled in a long series of often violent struggles around the church's place in society and its relationship to the state.[13] These struggles have primarily concerned land ownership and the seizure of private property, clergy appointments, and other matters of economic welfare. On these matters, Church leaders attempted frequent mediation between rebel and government officials as a way to end the bloodshed.[14] Conflict was not only concerning the Church, but involved the larger society as a whole, and are mostly related to corruption in the government, which leads many groups to take up arms, defending their own interests.

At times there have been resolutions to suspend violence and work on a resolution. Though there are some movements that have seen success, the violence continues. In some years it has even amplified. After years of increasing violent crime, such as kidnappings, murders, 1999 saw a new trend by guerilla groups that left hundreds dead by the year's end.[15] Through today there have been several rounds of peace talks that have mostly been unfruitful and leave many disappointed. For example, one of the proposed

---

[13] Knowlton, 236–41.

[14] "Colombia, The Catholic Church in," 852.

[15] *Id.*

solutions was disarmament, providing incentives to turn in weapons. But like other resolutions, this one has fallen short. Disarmament processes have allowed many combatants to reintegrate into society, yet a significant sector has rearmed.[16] The people of Colombia continue to be threatened by these militias and the constant threat of another breakout. In response, the Church, portions of the government and non-governmental organizations tirelessly continue to advocate for those who are victimized by violence and other injustice.

CULTURE AND SPIRITUALITY

The practice of the faith in Colombia, as in most other places, varies from place to place or according to one's economic class. Tendencies in religious observance in Colombia are similar to other Western nations, where the upper class or intellectual elite by large do not faithfully observe their professed faith if they have one at all. According to one study, "upper-class

> Colombians, with few exceptions, expect to be married in and buried from a Roman Catholic church have their children baptized, and treat first communion as an important rite of passage. However, in between these family landmarks and the principal festive occasions of the church calendar, they are not always faithful in their religious practice. The intellectual elite, as in so much of the Western world, is largely agnostic, although its members may still observe some of the formal

---

[16] *Id.*

ceremonies out of a respect for cultural tradition, to satisfy more devout family members, or simply for the festive value of the events. The upper-middle class tends to be more observant, and the same can be said of the peasant populations in Antioquia, the eastern highlands, and certain other regions."[17]

The degree of involvement is subject to many different factors beyond these terms, but generally speaking, these are considered normative.

Since culture and society is a mixture of Spanish, Indian, and African cultures, the expression of Christianity bears resemblance to these groups. One encyclopedia describes the influence of

Indian and African culture as particularly evident in the popular Catholicism of Colombia. Indigenous and African religious practices continue within this common, often extra-official, form of Catholicism. For instance, many Colombians of African heritage who are officially Catholic also maintain links to the broader culture of the African diaspora through forms of music and dance and through a sense of religiosity related to spirits and spirit possession.[18]

One's location in Colombia has made an impact on how assimilated the community is. Some parts of Colombian society have

---

[17] Rex A. Hudson (ed.), *Colombia: A Country Study*, 5th ed. (Washington, DC: Library of Congress, Federal Research Division, 2010).

[18] Knowlton, 240.

evolved their own expression of Catholicism, a development that has been a cause for difficulty through the years. In Colombia's highlands most indigenous peoples were assimilated into Catholicism; yet, it took longer for lowland peoples to be brought into the mainstream Colombian culture, and as a result they have maintained many more of their religious traditions, including classic Amazonian shamanism.[19]

What results is a combination that is sometimes acceptable and sometimes not in these situations. According to one source, "Since the late twentieth century indigenous religious practices have become increasingly popular among urban middle- and upper-middle-class Colombians. Such people have been particularly interested in employing the various forms of shamanism and traditional healing."[20] Another cultural expression found in indigenous and African practices have combined saints and amulets and are deemed to have the power to bring about transformations in a person's life.[21] In both of these examples, of traditional healing and sacred objects, there is a potential for deviation from what's acceptable and this challenge is one that Church leaders continue to face. Many traditional cultural customs have been completely outlawed as well, such as polygamy.

As complicated as the inculturation of Catholicism might be in tribal communities in Colombia over the centuries of Christianity's history in the country, it is undeniable that the faith has taken root in a majority of the population. The Catholic Church plays a major role

---

[19] *Id.*

[20] *Id.*, 240–41.

[21] *Id.*, 238.

in Colombia, which has been called one of the most Catholic countries in the Western Hemisphere.[22] Despite the challenges inherent in the layers of ethnic groups in Colombia, there are solid devotions that have become cherished traditions, many of which share similarities with Catholics in other countries.

Religion is a significant part of Colombian life, privately and publicly. Colombia follows the traditions of international Catholicism with a hierarchy of sanctuaries and pilgrimage sites based on miraculous images of saints, the Virgin Mary, and Jesus Christ and public spaces, both national and local, are marked by the presence of holy images, such as crucifixes or images of saints, the Virgin, or Christ.[23] These visible demonstrations show on a national level how significant the role of religious observance has been for the people of Colombia. Colombia as a whole celebrates the following religious events as official holidays: the Feast of the Epiphany, Saint Joseph's Day, Holy Thursday, Good Friday, the Feast of the Ascension, the Feast of Corpus Christi, Saints Peter and Paul, the Feast of the Assumption, All Saints' Day, the Feast of the Immaculate Conception, and Christmas.[24] In addition, as a result of colonial practices, each town and social organization in Colombia has a patron saint, and his or her feast day is a major social and religious event.[25] Catholic customs in Colombia seem to vary widely in some ways, such as in the devotion of particular saints or in particular

---

[22] *Junior Worldmark*, 156.

[23] Knowlton, 238.

[24] *Id.*

[25] *Id.*

liturgical expression, but the core doctrine and central Catholic feasts and traditions are shared by all.

One of the predominant cultural demonstrations of the Colombian faithful surrounds the liturgies of Holy Week (*Semana Santa*), considered Colombia's most important holiday. These holy days are observed following strict rituals, many dating to the 1500s and 1600s, where people attend long church services and participate in numerous parades or processions commemorating the Passion, the Crucifixion, and the Resurrection of Jesus Christ.[26] Families commemorate this time by working together to spruce up homes, churches, and churchyards, attending daily Mass, processions and more. Certain towns are known for their Holy Week services, such as Zipaquirá and its underground services or Popayán for its Palm Sunday celebration that draws crowds that some say are compared to those of Seville, Spain. [27] These popular celebrations draw visitors from all parts of Colombia and beyond and are just some examples of major traditions that are upheld annually.

POPULAR FIGURES

Popular figures in early Colombian history were missionaries who initially helped bring the faith to Colombia. Among these were: St. Louis Bertrand and St. Peter Claver, the apostle of the Africans; the Augustinian, Francisco Romero, author of *Llanto Sagrado* (1693); and the Jesuits Alonso de Sandoval (1576–1652), José Gumilla

---

[26] *Junior Worldmark, 156.*

[27] *Id.*

(1686–1750) and Juan Ribero (1681–1736).[28] In more recent times, a couple Catholic leaders that have received popular national attention are *Archbishop Isaias Duarte Cancino* and *Mother Laura Montoya.* Isaias Duarte Cancino (1939–2002), archbishop of Cali, was known for his bold criticisms of guerillas and narcotics traffickers, despite the fact that the Church has generally attempted to avoid involvement in such affairs.[29] His bravery ended up leading to his murder by an anonymous gunman, but he is celebrated for his heroism and commitment to peace. Mother Laura is another notable Colombian popular religious figure, particularly most recently, with her May 2013 canonization.[30] She is now recognized as the first Colombian canonized saint, a fact that many Colombians are happily celebrating through television specials and Mother Laura merchandise. She is loved by many for her work with the indigenous, the marginalized and the poor.[31]

HIERARCHY AND SEMINARIANS

The Catholic Church in Colombia has grown from a single Mission in 1550[32] to a hierarchy of 77 dioceses, including 13

---

[28] "Colombia, The Catholic Church in," 851.

[29] Knowlton, 238.

[30] Jim Wyss, "Madre Laura Named Colombia's First Saint," *Miami Herald* (12 May 2013), *available at*

http://www.miamiherald.com/2013/05/12/3394175/madre-laura-named-colombias-first.html.

[31] *Id.*

[32] "Colombia, The Catholic Church in," 848.

archdioceses.[33] The archbishop of Bogota is just one of three Colombians who, by appointment of the pope, belong to the College of Cardinals and the Colombian Episcopal Conference (CEC) represents the hierarchy as a whole.[34] The Colombian Catholic Church was well organized from its introduction into society in the 16th century, and soon after its arrival was found to be growing rapidly. By the middle of the 17th century Colombia had an exuberant religious life that included a metropolitan see with three suffragan dioceses, numerous parishes and doctrines, appropriate canonical legislation emanating from synods and provincial councils, and clergy in convents and seminaries. [35] From that point forward, the Church has continued to flourish, with increasing influence. Today there are many sources for intellection formation in seminaries or Catholic universities.

Colombia today is seeing a large number of seminarians, even with the growth of Protestant Christianities in the overall South American region. According to recent statistics, the Roman Catholic priesthood numbers, in total, about 8,000, including roughly 5,700 parish priests and 2,300 who belong to religious orders; there are also slightly more than 1,000 unordained brothers in religious orders and more than 17,000 Roman Catholic sisters.[36] Despite seemingly high numbers, the number of priests available for ministry does not keep up with demands. The ratio of Roman Catholic priests to total

---

[33] Hudson, 120.

[34] *Id.*

[35] "Colombia, The Catholic Church in," 850.

[36] Hudson, 120.

population, at one in 5,575, is not really adequate to meet the needs of the church but is among the highest in Latin America.[37]

Even still, many Colombian seminarians and priests choose to answer the call to serve in lands away from home. Colombia consistently ranks at the top in U.S. statistics as the country of origin for foreign priests and seminarians. In 2011–2012, there were 118 seminarians from Colombia, the second highest of all 81 countries that sent seminarians.[38] Some of these are studying in the United States but will return to their home countries, yet a majority of them are going to be ordained for a diocese in the United States. Even with the challenges of serving parishioners who are "different" than they are, these priests have enriched the communities where they live with their experiences and outlook. The benefit of this exchange is often two-way.

As grateful as U.S. dioceses and parishioners are to receive Colombian priests, there is no question that Colombia has dire needs of its own that require the service of many faithful and dedicated priests. The Colombian Catholic Church is active in public ministries and is often in the national spot light. To this end it has organized ministries at the archdiocesan and diocesan levels to perform outreach, as well as a chain of universities and schools to train people in Catholic doctrine and to influence secular learning.[39] By utilizing

---

[37] Id.

[38] Mary L. Gautier, Catholic Ministry Formation Enrollment: Statistical Overview for 2011–2012 (Washington, DC: Center for Applied Research in the Apostolate, 2012), *available at* http://cara.georgetown.edu/Publications/Overview2011-12-FINAL.pdf.

[39] Knowlton, 240.

resources like the internet and news media, the Church is able to promote important values. Strategies such as these have proven as effective tools in the effort to build peace in this war torn nation.

CHALLENGES

Concerning Family Life

Colombia faces some of the same challenges that other secular countries face, particularly with respect to philosophies on social issues that are in contradiction with Church values. In its views on marriage and the family the Colombian Catholic Church follows the direction of the Vatican.[40] Lifestyles that are contradictory to these views are at times common, however, such as in the areas of divorce, cohabitation, euthanasia, and contraceptives, and gay-rights. Legally a couple may already obtain a divorce, use contraceptives, and opt for euthanasia, and politically, there are always efforts to legalize abortion and homosexual unions.[41] The Colombian bishops have come out in opposition of these matters and continue to publicly advocate in favor of traditional Church teachings.

Some of these challenges concerning family life are exacerbated by poor economic status. Many poor couples in Colombia, both urban and rural, live together as common-law partners because they cannot afford a Catholic (nor a civil) wedding celebration.[42] Church

---

[40] Id.

[41] Id.

[42] Id.

leaders are using all means possible in order to urge the faithful to be true to Church teaching, despite societal trends and pressures.

Concerning Violent Conflict

Violence has been one of the major problems in Colombia in its contemporary history. It is not only a problem to Colombia, but it is one of the chief challenges to the international community, particularly in South America as it faces a high influx of Colombian refugees. According to the US Conference of Catholic Bishops,

> Colombia has been torn apart by conflict for over 40 years. The war that has raged between the Colombian government, guerilla groups such as the FARC and ELN, paramilitaries, and narco-traffickers has cost the lives of an estimated 50,000 – 200,000 people and has displaced millions of others. According to the United Nations High Commissioner for Refugees (UNHCR), there are currently 3.5 million internally displaced persons inside Colombia, while another 500,000 – 750,000 are seeking refuge in neighboring countries. It is the largest displacement crisis in the Western Hemisphere, and constitutes the seventh largest refugee population in the world."[43]

---

[43] United States Conference of Catholic Bishops, Colombian Refugees: No Solution in Sight, *available at* http://www.usccb.org/issues-and-action/human-life-and-dignity/migrants-refugees-and-travelers/columbianrefugees.cfm (last visited 7 Sept. 2015).

Humanitarian agencies, like Catholic Relief Services, have been operating in Colombia in hopes to alleviate some of these struggles. Catholic Relief Services is working to deliver humanitarian aid to Colombians and their host communities; meet needs for food and non-food assistance; provide psychological, social and legal assistance; and build the capacity of local governments to enable displaced Colombians, and the communities receiving them, to exercise their rights.[44] They are not alone in these efforts, with many other organizations, governmental and non-governmental, that also work to this end.

Governmental agencies as well as local Colombian Church initiatives have also aimed to reduce and ultimately eliminate conflict. Many initiatives and programs enable the Church to defend and promote human rights within Colombian society, especially of the most poor and excluded, who are often the most affected. The Church has made a commitment to contribute to a peaceful solution to the conflict by constantly denouncing violations of human rights—whatever their source.[45] These projects include: the Bishop's Peace Committee, National Conciliation Commission, Week for Peace (*Semana por la paz*), the Jesuit-sponsored Program for Peace, among others.[46]

---

[44]   Catholic   Relief   Services,   Colombia,   *available*   at http://www.catholicrelief.org/countries/colombia (last visited 7 Sept. 2015).

[45]   Catholic   Peacebuilding   Initiatives   in   Colombia,   Catholic Peacebuilding Network, *available at* http://cpn.nd.edu/conflicts-and-the-role-of-the-church/colombia/the-churchs-role-in-peacebuilding-in-colombia/some-peace-initiatives-in-colombia-/ (last visited 7 Sept. 2015).

[46] Id.

The violence has tragically affected almost all parts of society, including Church leaders who continue to be targeted in attacks. According to data from the Colombian bishops, more than 80 priests have been killed in the last three decades, along with five religious sisters, three religious brothers, three seminarians, one bishop and one archbishop.[47] To respond to the call to be a priest or religious can be a daunting discernment, but even more particularly under the threat of violence, yet many Colombians bravely step forward every year to serve.

FUTURE OUTLOOK

If there is one point of consensus in a country marred by division, it is that no one wants war and violence. Peace is an aspiration on the hearts of all Colombians. Everyone wants a home that is safe for their parents, children, and grand children. Despite continued setbacks, the Colombian Catholic Church continues to promote the qualities of peace by directing the focus on what, and specifically who, fuel the conflict. No group can force a ceasefire on another. It has to be brought about together if it will have any lasting effect.

True and lasting peace will have to address the struggles of all, including those who perpetuate the violence. The Bishops Conference of Colombia affirms, "A just peace must address the

---

[47] Catholic News Agency, "Colombian Priest Killed in Continuing Trent of Violence" (5 Feb. 2013), *available at* http://www.catholicnewsagency.com/news/colombian-priest-killed-in-continuing-trend-of-violence/.

underlying social and economic inequities fueling the conflict. Poor and marginalized groups such as Afro-Colombians, the indigenous people, women and youth must gain full participation in Colombian society... Agreements achieved should have broad input, and their compliance ought to be subject to the vigilance of all." [48] True peace to the armed conflict must honor memory and truth, justice and reparation, and must be reached through a process that respects life and the dignity of each person.[49] For peace to work, the hearts of those who use violence as a means of problem-solving must change to reflect a respect for the dignity of all, even those that are perceived as enemies. The Catholic Church in Colombia has provided the framework to build relationships that have been broken and with its considerable impact through media, the internet, and the pulpit, many are able to take to heart this message of peace and goodwill.

Over the years, while it is true that lasting peace has been elusive, it is not because there have not been enough proposals. The passion and commitment that many have shown is a strong testament to the will of the people of Colombia. The bishops described it well in the following statement:

In government circles, in community proposals and in policies developed over the last few years, we find a hidden treasure of proposals and experiences around peace. In the geography of peace, there are peaks of community experiences in which many counties are centers of initiatives that spring from the creativity within the people. It is certain

---

[48] Catholic Peacebuilding Initiatives.

[49] Id.

that this is a creative dynamic born of an active desire, not just a concept or some distant idea about human harmony.[50]

These are the peacemakers who despite continued disappointment and hopelessness still promote the cause of peace. The lesson imparted by all these processes is that the country needs to recognize the richness of these proposals, overcome the erratic and scattered policies found on many levels and convert these proposals into real roads to peace.[51] There are real, tangible solutions on the table. The challenge for the road ahead is both in implementing new positive approaches, while separating from what is flawed and damaging in present crisis management strategies.

If there is any value to be found in the civil war in Colombia, it is in the people who have fought for peace. Many have sacrificed and continue to sacrifice along this path, from the worker who ignore the risks and travels miles by foot to work to make a living for his family, to the to the priest who simply offers the Mass, many innocent and good willed Colombians are showing resiliency and bravery in these everyday tasks. There is a goodness in the selfless service and in sacrifice of these individuals. The Bishops eloquently stated: "There is a long list of community leaders, pastoral workers, human rights defenders, and men and women who have given their lives as they traveled together this path to peace. They have inspired, on all levels, positions taken by the Episcopate, pastoral plans, actions and commitments of the Church and have served as a rich source of

---

[50] Id.

[51] Id.

inspiration.[52] This richness inspired by these community leaders is a reminder that Colombia is not simply defined by its civil conflict. The examples of these individuals is a glimpse into its nation's history that reflects the journeys of a diverse group of people, with backgrounds that could not have been any more different, coming together as one.

---

[52] Hector Fabio Henao Gaviria, Lessons Learned in Peacebuilding in Colombia, Catholic Peacebuilding Network (June 2007), *available at* http://cpn.nd.edu/conflicts-and-the-role-of-the-church/colombia/the-churchs-role-in-peacebuilding-in-colombia/lessons-learned-in-peacebuilding-in-colombia/.

India

Catholics in India make up a statistically small number, only 1.6% of the entire population, and Christians overall at around 2.3%[1]. Given the size of the population, however, India has more Catholics than one might think. At approximately 17 million, the total number of Catholics is comparable to twice the population of New York City. Among other Christian communities, the Catholic representation is the highest in the country, with the larger concentrations in the southern and eastern parts of the state. The rest of the country is predominantly Hindu (80.5%), Muslim (13.4%), Sikh (1.9%) or Buddhist (0.8%).[2]

India continues to experience steady, consistent growth, some of the most impressive in Christianity anywhere in the world. For example, in the Diocese of Asansol, on the eastern side of the Indian subcontinent, the number of Catholics there has almost doubled since the diocese was founded in 1997, while the number of priests has tripled.[3] The spread of Christianity in India varies from region to region, with some areas seeing a much more rapid pace than others, but overall, the rate of growth is quite healthy.

Spread across a geographically immense space, among diverse communities, the face of Catholicism in India is by no means uniform. A Mass in Kerala, India will most likely bear traces of the Syriac language, reminiscent of the ties of early Christians to this community. Another

---

[1] http://news.bbc.co.uk/2/hi/4243727.stm

[2] http://censusindia.gov.in/Census_Data_2001/India_at_glance/religion.aspx

[3] http://catholiclane.com/good-and-bad-news-from-catholics-in-india/

Catholic Mass in Goa, India, would be more recognizable to the Latin Catholic since this community has strong ties with Roman tradition as a result of a centuries' long relationship with Portuguese missionaries beginning in the 15th century.[4]

Given the historical diversity of the Catholics in India, it is not easy to make generalized statements about the practices and traditions of the average Indian Catholic. The Indian Bishops reiterate the beauty of their nation's diversity in saying, "Our country has been noted for its deep spirituality, its saints and sages, its rich diversity of cultures and religions." [5] When a country's inhabitants speak more than a thousand different languages and dialects, something like a quarter of the total number of spoken tongues that exist in the world,[6] one may imagine there is not a single liturgy that all Indian Catholics share in common. In fact, there are dozens of distinct cultures that all represent a wide range of historical traditions.

To put it into perspective for a Westerner, the difference between the culture of a tribal community in the north-east of India and a community in the south of India is greater perhaps than the difference of culture between a Swede and an Italian in Europe. [7] To the outsider, India may not seem diverse with respect to religion either. It may even be conventional in some places to stereotype Indians as most likely Hindu, or perhaps even Muslim or Sikh, but how many Westerners immediately bring to mind Christianity when considering ancient Indian religious practices? Many

---

[4] http://www.pbs.org/wnet/religionandethics/episodes/april-24-2009/ancient-christians-in-india/2754/

[5] Final Statement of the 30th CBCI General Body Meeting The Church's Role for a Better India: http://cbci.in/statements.aspx .

[6] Sahi, Jyoti, "Believing without Belonging? Some Reflections, International Review of Mission 92 no 365 Ap 2003, p 227-230.

[7] Id.

Westerners would suspect that Christianity is a foreign import solely due to the work of European missionaries, but this is not so. Others even claim that Christianity may have a presence in India, but it is an inauthentic one that they may allege was imposed or coerced upon the native Indian population. These claims are also unsubstantiated, however.[8] The Church in India has been influenced by missionaries, but Christianity thrived there well before this time.

The Catholic Church in India bears the tradition of three distinct sources of Christianity at different times. The Church reflects a communion that is comprised of three groups: the Latin rite, the Syro-Malabar rite, and the Syro-Malankara rite. Each of these groups has its own unique history and separate ecclesial structures and liturgies, yet they share a common unity, with Pope Benedict XVI as the head of the overall Indian Church. The local Episcopal bodies manage the Church on the national level and these include:

1.   Conference of the Catholic Bishops of India (CCBI) - Latin Church
2.   Syro-Malabar Bishops' Synod (SMBS) - Syro-Malabar Church
3.   Holy Episcopal Synod - Syro-Malankara Church.[9]

The first on this list is the Latin rite, to which Westerners of the Roman rite would be most closely linked. The other two, the Syro-Malabar and Syro-Malankara, have roots in the first centuries after Jesus Christ. From very early times, there existed on the Malabarand Coromandel Coast a considerable community of native Christians claiming to have received

---

[8] Hull, Ernest. "India." The Catholic Encyclopedia. Vol. 7. New York: Robert Appleton Company, 1910. 12 Sept. 2012<http://www.newadvent.org/cathen/07722a.htm

[9] http://cbci.in/Church-in-India.aspx

the Faith from the Apostle St. Thomas. [10] Since there are no known artifacts and other evidence from this time, this is a point that can not be confirmed, but the community maintains this as a truth and their Syriac liturgy is linguistically very close to the Aramaic of the time of Christ. Over time, this community is believed to have been led by bishops who were of the Nestorian persuasion, common to the Middle East of this period. Syro-Malankara and Syro-Malabar Christians have maintained a continual presence in southern India.

When the Portuguese missionaries came to India by the 15th century, they encountered these early Christians who had been practicing the faith for over a millennium and they considered their views to be tainted from Nestorian influence. They believed, therefore, that it was their moral obligation to purge all documents that contained heresy. The Synod of Diamper of 1599 made official these efforts to bring the community into communion with the Catholic Church. [11]

Of the Catholic Christian communities of India, it is the Syro-Malankara and Syro-Malabar churches that have seen the most growth. Unlike their counterparts in "the Middle East," "Ethiopia/Eritrea," and "formerly communist Europe" excluding the Greek Rite Church in Ukraine, "the Indian Eastern Catholic Churches centered on the state of Kerala" are described as "'lively' and 'growing'." [12] Characterized as "islands of growth," the Syro-Malabar and Syro-Malankara Eastern Rite Churches were described by Archbishop Veglio as "vigorous and growing, despite hindrances." [13]

---

[10] New advent

[11] New advent (Ernest Hull, see previous)

[12] http://www.thehindu.com/news/the-india-cables/article1715617.ece

[13] Id.

Indian Spirituality

Indian Catholics, while they are in some ways different than American Catholics, are similar in other ways, as in their affinity to the Blessed Virgin Mary. "Our Lady of Vailankanni," the Shrine of Our Lady of Good Health, has become a major Indian holy site, and has grown so popular that some now even call it the "Lourdes of the East."[14] A popular practice for Indian Catholics from the Mangalore region on the west coast of India is a festival that celebrates the Nativity of the Blessed Mother. This feast is popularly known as "Monti Fest" and is preceded by special prayers and traditional hymns. The children also make floral offerings to the statue of the Infant Mary.[15] This particular tradition is not only celebrated in India, but has been transported all over the world where Indian Catholics from Mangalore have settled. The September 8th feast is a very special time for this community and when it is celebrated abroad it is considered a glimpse of the culture back at home.[16]

Indian Catholics also share in common with Catholics of the West their devotion to the saints. Although there are comparatively fewer saints from India than other countries, the spirituality of Indian saints is quite rich. It is from the southern part of India where the first female Indian saint, Sister Alphonsa, only recently canonized in 2008, lived.[17] Previously, the only Indian to have been made a Roman Catholic saint was Gonsalo Garcia, who was canonized in 1862.[18] The canonization of Sister Alphonsa is considered

---

[14] Catholic Focus Youtube video. http://www.youtube.com/watch?v=C6SlR98ZZBo

[15] Magalore.com

[16] Catholic Focus Youtube video.

[17] Catholic Focus Youtube video.

[18] http://www.usatoday.com/news/religion/2008-10-10-india-saint_N.htm

to have come at a time when violence against Christians in India was at a high point; many continue to seek the saint's intercession for solace and peace in this time of persecution.

Challenges

As a minority religious community in a divided society, Catholics bear the brunt of much suffering in various forms. Indian Catholics and Christians overall are discriminated against by laws that prohibit conversion to Christianity, violating their freedom of conscience. They also suffer violence and vandalism, and they experience a lack of resources and discrimination in the caste system. Although the caste system is Hindu in origin, it has become part of Indian social life and is also followed by many Christians and others, especially in rural areas. Under the system, society is divided into Brahmins (priestly class), Kshatriyas (warrior class), Vaishyas (trading class) and Sudras (serving class) in descending order of superiority and social status. Dalits are duty bound under the caste system to carry out menial, often degrading jobs for the upper castes while, in many areas, living in segregation from them.[19]

The Indian Bishops, speaking out on the injustices of the system, said: "Recognizing that untouchability and caste discrimination are contrary to the Gospel of Jesus, we will root out this evil, wherever it exists, from within the Church and make concerted efforts to empower dalits. We commit ourselves to join hands with our dalit brothers and sisters in their fight for equal rights and the Constitutional benefits which are denied to them on the basis of religion."[20]

---

[19] "Churches back Buddhist conversions of Dalits," Christian Century 118 no 33 D 5 2001, p 13-14.

[20] Final Statement of the 30th CBCI General Body Meeting The Church's Role for a Better India: http://cbci.in/statements.aspx

The Bishops also emphasized the priority in the Church of Social Justice. They continue,

"Economic development has brought about increasing inequities, an ever-widening gap between the rich and the poor with consequent tensions spilling over into violence. We see around us a betrayal of the poor and marginalized, the tribals, dalits and other backward classes, women and other groups who live in dehumanising and oppressive poverty. We witness rampant exploitation of children. There is disappointment with those in public life for whom ethical concerns matter little."[21]

Persecution

Perhaps the most immediately grave is the physical violence suffered by many Catholics in India. In recent years, Catholic faithful and clergy have been threatened and attacked by mobs. Churches are repeatedly vandalized and many sacrileges are committed on holy sites. "These churches are thriving even as Christians suffer persecution in Hindu-Nationalist parts of India," says Archbishop Veglio.[22] The persecution that is faced by many Christians is unrelenting, consistent, and tragically, often dead

Yet, Bishop Albert D'Souza of Agra notes that, historically, Christianity was welcomed and tolerated by Hindus.[23] These communities for centuries lived in peace side-by-side. The conflicts that did emerge were primarily political, and only religious by coincidence. Across the divisions of cast, class, and religion, Christianity crosses these boundaries through social

---

[21] Final Statement of the 30th CBCI General Body Meeting The Church's Role for a Better India: http://cbci.in/statements.aspx

[22] http://www.thehindu.com/news/the-india-cables/article1715617.ece

[23] Catholic Focus Youtube.

infrastructure, such as schools and hospitals. Opponents to Christianity, use this point as a means of attack, saying Christians are polluting non-Christians indirectly through this outreach.[24] Some find this exposure to be threatening and use it as justification for persecution.

Population Control

Even if Catholics are free from physical persecution in some regions, the dangers arise in other forms. In the Christian center of Kerala, there are assaults against the family by means of population control. Legislators are attempting to introduce a two-child policy for each family. The punishment for those who do not follow the law will be heavy fines, and the resulting children will be denied basic rights and state benefits, which in essence would deny them their personhood.[25] Further, if passed, the "Women's Code Bill" will provide free contraceptives and free abortions in state hospitals. The Church has responded to these threats with commitments to financially compensate for large families.

Limited Resources

The Church of India is thriving, but is constrained by a lack of resources. The deterioration of the economic situation for many has left basic human needs unmet, in many cases, to the point of desperation. As Bishop Monis remarks, "We are starting from scratch with everything, in fact. We need churches, parish and social centers, schools... in short, everything."[26] The Catholics of India request the assistance of the universal

---

[24] Catholic Focus Youtube.

[25] "Families under attack in Kerala." *Catholic Insight* Feb. 2012: 21. *General OneFile*. Web. 13 Sep. 2012.

[26] http://catholiclane.com/good-and-bad-news-from-catholics-in-india/

church in these endeavors. Speaking for their best interests, the Bishops stated:

"As leaders of the Church in India, we re-affirm our commitment to build up a Better India. We realize that we cannot achieve our goal in isolation. We invite all sections of the Church, priests, religious men and women, lay faithful and all men and women of goodwill to be fully involved in this noble endeavor. In the realization of a Better India, the role of the lay faithful is of decisive significance. In particular we appeal to our youth, with their dynamism and vibrancy, to be involved in this task. We count on our brothers and sisters in the Christian Churches and communities to work with us in a collaborative effort. And we can never forget that it is not just by our efforts that we build up a Better India. As a Church, we want to pray for the realization of this goal." [27]

Future of the Church

Despite these enormous challenges, Bishop D'Souza insists the Church is full of growth and life. Citing the areas where Catholics are leading the way in a divided society, compared to non-Christians, their strengths are in tolerance of those of other faiths, in their commitment to service, and in their ability to go beyond societal boundaries; these qualities make Indian Catholics stand out against their fellow countrymen who sincerely search for the truth.[28] Ever hopeful, the Bishop noted that the future of the Church in India is based on the building up of interfaith dialogue, which is

---

[27] Final Statement of the 30th CBCI General Body Meeting The Church's Role for a Better India: http://cbci.in/statements.aspx

[28] Youtube video.

cultivated within the schools.[29] Further, he also believes there is hopefulness in the fact that faith is deeply ingrained in the psyche of all Indians, not only Christians, which serves as a potential catalyst for a deeper faith in Jesus Christ.

In 1999, The Holy Father, Pope John Paul II, during his trip to New Delhi gave a powerful message to the faithful, an exhortation entitled *Ecclesia in Asia*. The Holy Father predicted that,

> "With the Church throughout the world, the Church in Asia will cross the threshold of the Third Christian Millennium marvelling [sic] at all that God has worked from those beginnings until now, and strong in the knowledge that "just as in the first millennium the Cross was planted on the soil of Europe, and in the second on that of the Americas and Africa, we can pray that in the Third Christian Millennium *a great harvest of faith* will be reaped in this vast and vital continent."[30]

HELPFUL LINKS

- Census data with Population % of Religious Observance http://censusindia.gov.in/Census_Data_2001/India_at_glance/relig ion.aspx
- Wikipedia http://en.wikipedia.org/wiki/Christianity_in_India
- Ancient Christians in India (with video) http://www.pbs.org/wnet/religionandethics/episodes/april-24-2009/ancient-christians-in-india/2754/
- Youtube video from Catholic Focus on the Catholic Church in India http://www.youtube.com/watch?v=C6SlR98ZZBo

---

[29] Youtube video.

[30] Ecclesia in Asia, para. 1.

- Post-Synodal Apostolic Exhortation *Ecclesia in Asia*
  http://www.vatican.va/holy_father/john_paul_ii/apost_exhortation
  s/documents/hf_jp-ii_exh_06111999_ecclesia-in-asia_en.html
- Official Website, Our Lady of Good Health, Marian Shrine
  http://www.vailankannishrine.org
- Devotion to Monti Sahibin, or Our Lady of the Mount
  http://www.mangalorean.com/news.php?newstype=broadcast&bro
  adcastid=144539

Ireland

With the American childhood tales of leprechauns and pots of gold, annual St. Patrick's Day celebrations, and the historically large influx of Irish immigrants, it can be said that in America today, generally speaking, there is a certain popular acquaintance with Irish customs. Beyond these cultural norms, however, this familiarity ends. Yet, there is much to discover about Ireland and its long relationship with the Catholic faith. While this work is not an exhaustive or comprehensive account, it does seek to shed light on foundational elements of the culture and society of Ireland, particularly with regard to the Roman Catholic Church, and to provide a basis upon which to understand common experiences of a contemporary Catholic in Ireland. The Ireland of today is different from the Ireland of last century. With political, economic, and social changes, the aftermath affects the religious life of the everyday Irish Catholic. Whereas the major challenge was once religious persecution, today, through the influence of a growing secularism, religious indifference is considered by the Church one of the greatest threats.

DEMOGRAPHICS

When considering the trends of the Irish Church, to include factors such as the number seminarians, Mass attendance, family practice, one can arrive at some disappointing conclusions.

Particularly evident is the fact that in some areas, church attendance is very low. Weekly Mass attendance has dropped to around 40 percent, and even lower in urban areas like Dublin.[1] In other ways, there is room to be pleased. Despite the low figures of attendance, Irish Catholics are generous to the church even in hard times. For example, the International Eucharistic Congress in Dublin in 2012 was financed above all by the voluntary contributions of ordinary Catholics.[2]

Whereas donations are strong, other areas of participation are noticeably low. Without the influx of younger generation church-goers, the strong backbone of good Catholics in Ireland is an aging group.[3] Archbishop Diarmuid Martin of Dublin, when reflecting on the demographics of the Church in Ireland commented that,

> [A] significant fact is that the number of those under 6
> years of age is higher than of those over 70.

---

[1] David T. Buckley, "Celtic Crossroads: Ireland's New Model of Church-State Relations," *Commonweal* 138, no. 17 (26 Sept. 2011), *available at* https://www.commonwealmagazine.org/celtic-crossroads.

[2] Diarmuid Martin, "A Post-Catholic Ireland?" *America Magazine* (20 May 2013), *available at* http://americamagazine.org/issue/post-catholic-ireland.

[3] *Id.*

> Demographers estimate that the population of the island of Ireland will once again reach the eight million of pre-famine Ireland and that 50 percent of that population will live on a narrow strip of land along the east coast of Ireland from Gorey to Dundalk, most of which will be within the territory of the Archdiocese of Dublin. Will that emerging demographic reality still be "Catholic Ireland"?[4]

Given the large number of young children, and the fact that these young children are not participating in Catholic religious formation, it is a reasonable to suggest that this large nascent population in a once historically dominant Catholic area will perhaps be more multicultural and representative of other faiths, mostly through the migration of people of other ethnicities and religious backgrounds. This is not simply far-fetched speculation, but a probable indication of future realties.

Many argue that Ireland is simply on the express route to post-Catholic Europe.[5] As such, there is a growing belief that the future of the Catholic Church in Ireland is not a promising one. Outside the Church there is no shortage of attacks and criticism, but what is more notable is that this is also true from inside the Church. Scholar David Buckley noted that "The Irish press generally praised Taoiseach Kenny's anti-Vatican outburst, and the World Atheist Convention held its global convocation in Dublin this June, with Irish Senator Ivana Bacik warning of 'creeping fundamentalists' in

---

[4] *Id.*

[5] Buckley.

Irish life. For all these reasons, papal historian George Weigel recently called Ireland 'the most stridently anti-Catholic country in the Western world.'"[6] That is quite the claim for a country once considered as one of the most Catholic.

The strategies of how the Church is to move forward are included in a later section, but the basic theme is to find middle-ground. Buckley continued,

> At its best, the Irish approach to church-state relations is well equipped to chart a middle path between religious rule and assertive secularism. That path would require the state to treat all religious communities equally without driving religion from public life—in the process encouraging religious participation in education and health care, and influence on public policy in such areas as criminal justice, housing, and foreign aid. Catholic officials would exercise influence through persuasion, not coercion, and in conjunction with partners of other faith communities.[7]

This method relies upon dialogue and seeks to build up in areas where there have been challenges. It is not destined to be an easy way forward, but many are actively seeking to reverse the current trends.

EARLY HISTORY

Understanding where the Irish Church came from is helpful in

---

[6] *Id.*

[7] Buckley.

appreciating the context of the present day. The following historical account is by no means complete and all-encompassing. Considering the long history of Christianity in Ireland, this brief description will only capture a few key elements of a long, rich story that spans well over a thousand years. A central figure in the establishment of Christianity in Ireland is famously, Patrick, a popular Catholic saint who is esteemed in the United States as well. His arrival in Ireland takes place within the background of a people who were frequently subject to attack from foreign invaders. The most significant of these was the invasion of the Gaels from Gaul in the first century B.C. The Gaels treated the existing population in much the same way as they were to be treated by later invaders: "they killed some, deposed others and compelled the rest to pay tribute."[8] By the time St. Patrick, a Roman citizen from Britain, arrived in the fifth century A.D., although still only the dominant minority, the Gaels had imposed their language and legal system on the country.[9] Yet, the Catholic faith took root in the hearts of many faithful at this time, growing at a steady pace, in part due to the establishment of a local hierarchy, but in large part due to the work of religious orders. Though a traditional Episcopal system was established, the early Irish Church was dominated by a network of monastic centers through great rival foundations.[10] These religious orders would greatly contribute in the establishment of Christianity as a dominant religion.

From the ninth to the eleventh centuries Ireland experienced

---

[8] R.D. Edwards, "Ireland, The Catholic Church in," *New Catholic Encyclopedia*, 2nd ed., vol. 7 (Detroit: Gale, 2003), 553.

[9] *Id.*

[10] *Id.*

other invasions but they were not successful in achieving conquest.[11] These good prospects, however, did not last. In 1172 Henry II, with an invasion army of Normans, Norman-Welsh and Flemish soldiers, subjected the Irish rulers to his control.[12] This English control would last for centuries. Amidst the changes of the 16th century, particularly King Henry VIII proclaiming himself "King of Ireland" and the Protestant Reformation, the Irish staunchly maintained its political and religious distinctions. It is of note that although firm roots of the Reformation were established in England, Scotland, and Wales, it is not so of Ireland. [13] One can note the strong preference even from this time that lasted into modern Ireland.

Ireland's Catholicism, it may be argued, proved politically invaluable to the nation as well. According to W.D. Cooke, "Ireland, in the course of the long nineteenth century, was a significant part of the new political reality born in 1801, but certain aspects of its government and culture made it completely distinct not only from the metropolitan norm but from other areas of the recently constructed United Kingdom."[14] Historian Oliver Rafferty added, "*Of all the features that made Ireland different, none was more important than Catholicism...* Catholicism's dominance in Ireland and its function in shaping Irish culture and mores ensured that whatever hybrid identity emerged as the country played its role on the stage of British history in the nineteenth century, the Roman

---

[11] W. Dennis D. Cooke, "The Religious Dimension in the Northern Ireland Problem," *Lexington Theological Quarterly* 16, no. 3 (1981), 85.

[12] *Id.*

[13] *Id.*

[14] *Id.*

Catholic faith would be essential to it."[15] The government and the Church thrived under these terms of mutual respect and support.

History of Contemporary Society

As explained by Edwards, the Republic of Ireland (Eire) encompasses five-sixths of the island of Ireland. Under English control for centuries, the island was split into two political divisions during the early 20th century, and the Republic of Ireland achieved its political independence in 1949. The six counties in the north of the island were established as Northern Ireland in 1920 and are now a part of the United Kingdom and Northern Ireland.[16]

The Irish Free State was set up in 1922 to be a completely secular state, but its leaders saw the Church as an Irish institution that distinguished them from the English. [17]The new government maintained loyalty to the nation's Catholic majority, which is clear in the drafting of its 1938 constitution, which also permitted external association with the king of Great Britain. The New Catholic Encyclopedia noted that "The constitution admitted that civil authority comes from God, the form of government being decided by the people. It maintained the parliamentary system set up under the Irish Free State Act, recognized the special position of the Catholic Church as the Church of the majority of the people and established religious toleration for Anglicans, Presbyterians and other

---

[15] Oliver P. Raffery, "The Catholic Church, Ireland and the British Empire, 1800–1921," *Historical Research* 84, no. 224 (2011), 288.

[16] Edwards, 553.

[17] *Id.*

denominations.[18] The association and even preference of the Catholic Church in this legal document is undeniable. The Catholic Archbishop Charles McQuaid of Dublin even helped to draft the constitution prohibiting divorce and abortion.[19] Even in rhetoric, Irish politicians have often used Catholic symbolism to convey their political messages, such as the Easter Rebellion of 1916 (planned on that day to suggest national rebirth) and The Good Friday Agreement of 1998 (set for that day to represent reconciliation.)[20] The new government held the Catholic Church in high esteem and so did popular opinion.

This popular sentiment, however, would begin to slowly dissipate. Not only did the secular rule of law change, with the new Irish government in place, but the focus of the Irish Church also evolved in the 20th century. The Second Vatican Council served as a major touchstone for the development of the Church's focus. As with other countries, the local Church of today was influenced heavily by the efforts of the Council. Ecumenical themes involving cooperation, and an increase in missionary activity took root among Irish Catholics in the immediate postconciliar years.

The close relationship between the state and the Catholic Church was also evident on the local level in the school system. For most of the century, the Church controlled state-supported schools, which

---

[18] *Id.*, 565

[19] Amy Hackney Blackwell & Ryan Hackney, *The Everything Irish History Heritage Book: From Brian Bore and St. Patrick to Sinn Fein and the Troubles, All You Need to Know about the Emerald Isle* (Avon, MA: Adams Media, 2004), 119.

[20] *Id.*

meant that almost all children were educated by priests, monks, and nuns.[21] By mid 20th century, reform also arrived for the schools. Also around this time, the schools were undergoing radical changes to provide access to higher quality schools, which entailed combining secondary and vocational schools into "comprehensive schools" that taught the humanities, sciences and technical subjects.[22] The Encyclopedia describes that,

> In 1966 the state assumed the total cost of secondary school administration in return for the abolition of fees, and by the end of the decade most Church-run schools elected to enter the "state scheme" on this basis. Despite the state's involvement, the religious remained at the heart of the system. In 1973 the Church leadership endorsed the state initiatives, and encouraged the continued cooperation and mergers between local schools. In 2000 the Ministry of Education continued to fund all schools, regardless of religious affiliation. The reform of education continued with much analysis and a sometimes heated exchange of viewpoints on the content of the curriculum, on class sizes, on the career prospects for lay teachers in Church schools. [23]

The point of education and the structure of the schools is one of on-going debate in Ireland, like other aspects of contemporary society. Frequent discussions on the relationship between Church

---

[21] *Id.*, 118.

[22] Edwards, 566.

[23] *Id.*, 566–67.

and State are commonplace in civil discourse. Despite the Republic's historical association with the Catholic Church, there are regular challenges to this relationship in the public square.

CULTURE

Just as Irish politics has been linked with the Catholic identity, popular cultural expressions also reflect this close relationship. As authors Hackney and Blackwell wrote, "It went without saying that a post-famine Irish person was also Catholic; the two were almost synonymous. Emigrant Irish took this cultural trait with them, and Irish all over the world were assumed to be devout Catholics. This religious identity merged into the Irish national identity."[24] Some of the Irish Catholic experience is similar to American traditions, such as in Marian devotions, while others are distinctive. Like Americans, Irish often have crosses or religious pictures of the pope, Sacred Heart, or a favorite saint in their homes. [25] But there are many long-held and cherished traditions that are unknown to many outside Ireland.

What makes Irish spirituality special are these many sacred practices and holy sites that are particular to the country. While most western Catholics will know the story of St. Patrick, or may have heard of the Marian apparitions in Knock, they probably do not know what takes place at *Croagh Patrick*, nor is it likely they can tell you the story of St. Brigid of Fochord. Even the familiar festivities surrounding Christmas and Easter have their own style, such as in

---

[24] Blackwell & Hackney, 117.

[25] *Id.*, 118.

the Christmas Day Swim. The most famous of these swims, which take place all over the country, is at the Forty Foot Rock, just south of Dublin. On Christmas Day hundreds of people can be seen jumping off the rock into the Irish Sea wearing only their bathing suits, often, in order to raise money for charities.[26]

At Christmas Eve, as in the United States and other countries, there is a popular midnight Mass. This event is a huge social gathering where family, friends and neighbors who may not have seen each other all year come together and celebrate with carols, live music, and more. And it's the only time all year when mass is held at midnight.[27] Another Christmas-time tradition is the Horse Racing on St. Stephen's Day, which falls on the day after Christmas. In Germany, horse races are held in honor of St. Stephen's love for the ponies, but in Ireland, it's more of a social gathering and a chance to get out of the house. The races in Leopardstown, South Dublin attract almost 20,000 every year.[28] It is also a little known fact that a popular Christmas tradition in America today is one that has Irish roots. Thomas Paul Thigpen writes,

Long ago when the,

Catholic faith was suppressed in Ireland by the British Authorities, the Irish faithful developed a Christmas Eve custom that served as a secret code. Priests were outlawed

---

[26] Michael Thompson, "Top Ten Irish Christmas Traditions," Examiner.com (19 Dec. 2012), *available at*
http://www.examiner.com/article/top-ten-irish-christmas-traditions.
[27] *Id.*
[28] *Id.*

and had to travel in disguise. The opportunity to attend Mass was rare, and the chance to take part in a Christmas Mass was rarer still. So these households set burning candles in their windows and left their doors unlocked as a signal to any priest who might be passing through the neighborhood in secret. The lights were a sign that he was welcome to enter and to hold a Mass in their home. It was a privilege that Irish Catholic families prayed for all year long. Irish immigrants brought this custom to America and today, Christian homes of all kinds have lights burning in their windows at Christmas.[29]

This tradition is important, both culturally and historically, and although it is practiced in America for simple decoration, it is more meaningful when understanding the fierce persecution that the symbol of the candle represents.

Irish Catholic culture today has gained other traditions due to its history. Irish Catholicism has an extraordinary number of links to its Celtic and medieval past. According to the National Catholic Reporter, "Irish culture has always had a large complement of religion in it. Traces of Druidism and nature worship are probably still there. St. Patrick contributed the solid core. The rest is a mishmash of superstition, pietism, a sugary sentimentalism, a streak

---

[29] Thomas Paul Thigpen, *Building Catholic Family Traditions* (Huntington, IN: Our Sunday Visitor, 1999), 36.

of Puritanism, and a bleak authoritarianism borrowed from Victorian England."[30]

Some religious holidays have direct links to pagan festivals; for example, the annual pilgrimage to *Croagh Patrick* originated in the Celtic festival of *Lughnasa*.[31] This pilgrimage offers opportunity for many to offer sacrifice and penance, in which Irish and non-Irish alike both participate. The annual pilgrimage up *Croagh Patrick*, considered the holiest mountain in Ireland, draws hordes of the faithful to this steep, stony mountain in the bogs of County Mayo, where they crawl up the hill on their hands on knees.[32] The Pilgrimage is in honor of Saint Patrick, since it was on the summit of the mountain that Saint Patrick fasted for forty days in 441 AD and the custom has been faithfully handed down from generation to generation.[33] Before St. Patrick, the pilgrimage to this mountain was done for other reasons. The website for the holy site's visitor center states that "the tradition of pilgrimage to this holy mountain stretches back over 5,000 years from the Stone Age to the present day without interruption. Its religious significance dates back to the time of the pagans, when people are thought to have gathered here to

---

[30] Arthur Jones, "Ireland's Struggle to Become a 'Mature Society,'" *National Catholic Reporter* 47, no. 26 (14 Oct. 2011), 14–15.

[31] Blackwell & Hackney, 117.

[32] *Id.*, 118.

[33] Teach na Miasa Croagh Patrick Visitor Centre at the Foot of the Holy Mountain, *available at* http://www.croagh-patrick.com/visitorcentre/holy-mountain (last visited 7 Sept. 2015).

celebrate the beginning of harvest season."[34] *Croagh Patrick* is a great example of merging local traditions with the Catholic faith.

Aside from St. Patrick, another national patron is St. Brigid, known to the Irish as "Mary of the Gael." Like St. Patrick, devotion to St. Brigid is of ancient origin. According to tradition, Brigid was born at Fochard Muirtheimne, a few miles north of Dundalk about 450 AD, a place that was later known as *Fochard Bríde*.[35] This Christian nun was likely named after a pagan goddess,[36] another example of the Celtic traces of Irish Catholicism. Today pilgrims visit *Fochard Bríde* daily. Public pilgrimages are held every day during the year, a candlelight procession takes place on the Saint's feast day (1 February), a Mass for the Sick is celebrated in early June and there is a national pilgrimage on the first weekend in July. [37]

Last, but certainly not least, is the strong Irish tradition of devotion to Our Lady. The tradition to honor the Blessed Mother developed early on, particularly during the Middle Ages, becoming widespread by the 8th century,[38] and increasing in popularity over time. By the 18th Century, however, as previously discussed, devotional religious objects were forbidden in Ireland. A single-

---

[34] *Id.*

[35] Archdiocese of Armagh, St Brigid's Shrine, Faughart, *available at* http://www.armagharchdiocese.org/2007/11/08/stbrigidsshrinefaughart/ (last visited 7 Sept. 2015).

[36] Saint Brigid: Mary of the Gael, *available at* http://www.ewtn.com/library/MARY/BRIGID.htm.

[37] Archdiocese of Armagh.

[38] Marian Devotion in Ireland, *Irish Catholic, available at* http://www.irishcatholic.ie/article/marian-devotion-ireland#sthash.x2EDP31O.dpuf (last visited 7 Sept. 2015).

decade rosary, known as a *Pádraigín Beag*, which could be hidden in the sleeve, became commonplace and serve as another example of how Marian devotion flourishes in times of persecution and hardship.[39] This time of persecution was characterized by much suffering.

It is within the context that the Irish apparition of Our Lady of Knock came to be. One of the most significant Marian events in Irish history occurred in August 1879 at Knock, Co. Mayo when 15 people witnessed the apparition of the Virgin Mary and other figures.[40] "The Story of Knock began on Thursday evening of the 21st August 1879 when Our Lady, St. Joseph and St. John the Evangelist appeared at the south gable of Knock Parish Church."[41] Beside them and a little to their left was an altar with a cross and the figure of a lamb, around which angels hovered. These apparitions had many similarities as others, both before and after them in other countries around the world. The 15 witnesses were ordinary poor people, and the land was in deep crisis as the famine of 1879 hit hard, bringing fresh terror to a region where the memories of the horrors of 1847 were still raw.[42]

Not only were the lives of those living at the time touched by these miraculous events. The effects of this apparition bore fruit for generations to come. There was a significant increase of Marian groups in Ireland from 1930 to 1960, a time regarded as the 'fullest

---

[39] *Id.*

[40] *Id.*

[41] Irish Tourism, Knock Shrine, *available at* https://www.irishtourism.com/historic-sites-buildings-in-ireland/knock-shrine/1449 (last visited 7 Sept. 2015).

[42] Marian Devotion in Ireland.

flowering' of 'Irish Devotional Revolution', begun in the 19th Century.[43] As examples in other countries have also shown, persecution often has the positive impact of increased religious devotion. Today Knock Shrine is an international place of pilgrimage and prayer where over one and a half million pilgrims come every year and ranks among the world's major Marian Shrines.[44]

CHALLENGES

In some ways, Ireland has seen significant progress and is a radically different country than it was a century ago. There is much to be thankful for in some areas, such as improvements to standard of life and the nation's economic growth. In the 1980s Ireland was a relatively poor country in European terms, but by the start of the new millennium it had become one of the most affluent.[45] In other areas, particularly regarding social and moral issues, the news has not been as positive. Ireland has gradually been experiencing increasing secularization that has affected all members of society, particularly the youth.

---

[43] Marian Devotion in Ireland.

[44] Susan Tassone, Our Lady of Knock Had Largely Unknown Connection to Souls in Purgatory, Miracle Hunter, *available at* http://www.miraclehunter.com/marian_apparitions/approved_apparitions/knock/articles/knock_tassone.html (last visited 7 Sept. 2015).

[45] Thomas G. Casey, "Jolted by Affluence," *America* (27 Nov. 206), *available at* http://americamagazine.org/issue/593/article/jolted-affluence.

Poverty

Yet even in areas where there has been improvement, the situation is not ideal. One such area is the growth of Ireland's economy, which even with the wealth that Ireland has been gaining, there remains considerable poverty. Through their Justice and Peace Commission, pastoral letters and other statements, Irish bishops took a leading role in protesting against an economic system that failed to address the problem of poverty in Ireland, pointing to deficiencies in political planning, the greatest of which they identified as an unnecessarily high level of unemployment.[46] The Bishops have taken an active role in advocating economic opportunities for all families, as this is an economic issue, but it is at the same time a moral one. The surge in industry has also affected family life as more time is spent away from family than ever before. Within the scope of economic success rest the challenges of remembering the unemployed and the balance of family life.

Secularization and Clericalism

The overall economic progress that has been developing in Ireland in recent decades is not without a cost, however, to the social landscape. Ireland is today picking up the pieces economically and paying the price socially.[47] This development some might say is very recent, but there is good reason to believe that it has been gradually

---

[46] Edwards, 567.

[47] Martin.

building up over some time. Archbishop Diarmuid Martin of Dublin described this point as follows:

> "When was asked to return to Dublin, Pope John Paul II asked me why secularization had taken place so rapidly in Ireland. It was one of the rare occasions when I told a pope he was wrong! The roots of change in Ireland were there but were not seen. It is not that Ireland is today in a momentary out-of-the-ordinary period in its history, somehow temporarily adrift from what is really the default position. There is no default position anymore, and there has not been such a position for some time. In many ways the church in Ireland had been trapped in an illusory self-image. The demographic majority the church enjoyed hid many structural weaknesses, and the church became insensitive to such weakness."[48]

In this passage, Martin attributes at least some of the secularization to the structural weakness of the Irish Church. One major structural weakness is the clericalism that has been strong in Ireland. While the days of the dominant or at times domineering role of clergy within what people call the "institutional church" have changed, part of the culture still remains and from time to time reappears in new forms. [49] Historically, this notion is most often seen through insensitivities and tendency to protect members of the clergy

---

[48] *Id.*

[49] *Id.*

from the responsibility of any wrong-doings.

The challenge in combating clericalism is finding a balanced strategy that will yield successful results in transforming this culture without leading to the opposite extreme. Martin continues, "Clericalism will be eliminated only by fostering a deeper sense of the meaning of the church; that understanding of the nature of the church will come not from media strategies or simply by structural reforms, but by genuine renewal in what faith in Jesus Christ is about. If we focus only on structures and power, there is a risk that clericalism might be replaced by neo-clericalism."[50] Many would find the solution to be in a more populist or democratic control of the hierarchy, but this is also not the way. Martin suggests, "The Christian presence in society is not achieved by the imposition of a manifesto or simply by high-profile social criticism. It is more about the witness people give to Christian principles, mediated within the particular responsibilities they carry."[51] The key is fostering a culture in which one wants to do what is right.

Northern Ireland

The conflict in North Ireland is worth mentioning for the impact it had on all Irish Catholics. According to Reverend Eamon Casey, Bishop Emeritus, "The most decisive changes in Ireland have resulted from the effects of the ceasefire and subsequent Good Friday Agreement in Northern Ireland. For years the complex political landscape of Northern Ireland was at the center of the Irish

---

[50] *Id.*

[51] *Id.*

agenda."[52]   Culturally speaking, with a dominantly Catholic population in the Republic as a whole (90% of the population identified as Roman Catholic in 2000[53]) and its Protestant majority neighbor in the North, there were many conflicts. According to the *New Catholic Encyclopedia,*

> The Protestant majority, with political and cultural ties to Great Britain, viewed their Catholics neighbors with suspicion. A local parliament with powers delegated from the British parliament had allowed Northern Ireland to enjoy what was effectively single-party rule until 1972 when that parliament was abolished. In 1968 police violence in responding to activities of a group fighting discrimination against Catholics in housing, employment and electoral practices rekindled hostilities between the two factions. Over the next few years the conflict hardened into deadly guerrilla warfare as the nationalist Irish Republican Army (IRA)—a body illegal in the Republic as well as in the North—directed violent attacks on extremist groups on the loyalist side. Members of the British army, the police and many innocent civilians died in the bombings, shootings and other acts of violence that followed."[54]

---

[52] Casey.

[53] Edwards, 568.

[54] *Id.*

Although there were obvious sympathies, the management of the conflict by the Church was not so straight-forward. Rather, it was complicated by the use of violent tactics of the IRA. In 1994, The Downing Street Declaration, a joint statement outlining a proposed peace process led to an IRA and loyalist cease fire the following year.[55] Finally, and as the commentary continues,

> While hostilities erupted again in 1996, they were reduced to intermittent flare-ups as negotiations continued. On Good Friday, 1998, a peace settlement was reached by the IRA and loyalist factions that would create a 108-seat Assembly in Northern Ireland capable of protecting the political rights of the region's Catholic minority. While voters in both sections of the island approved the proposal, by 2001 it had yet to be implemented. Blessing the agreement, Pope John Paul II saw it as an affirmation that a "new era of hope" had begun for the region.[56]

Social Issues

As secularism has been gradually setting in, various social and moral issues have arisen over time that has challenged the status quo. In Ireland, as elsewhere, the first severe jolt for the postconciliar Church came with the publication of the encyclical *Humanae*

---

[55] *Id.*

[56] *Id.*, 569.

Vitae in 1968.[57] In 1979, the Holy Father, Pope John Paul II made a pastoral visit to Ireland,[58] in which he expressed concern over the growing materialism that seemed to be plaguing society. Others within the Church were encouraged to address this problem. Seeing their Church in jeopardy, lay groups formed to battle parliament's "liberalizing" civil legislation regarding abortion and divorce.[59] Though these groups were initially successful, this work has been regularly challenged by issues regarding abortion, divorce, contraception, and homosexual "marriage." By the mid to late 1990's, abortions were permitted in certain cases, and divorce became legal.[60] Contraception was finally legalized in the 1980s, and, by 1999 a referendum was requested on the legalization of abortion.[61]

The next challenge to the Christian family in Ireland is set to take shape, which already pits the government and the Catholic Church on opposing ends. The Irish government has announced it will hold a referendum in 2015 on the issue of whether same sex couples should be able to marry. According to BBC News, "A spokesman for the government said it would be 'actively supporting' the introduction of civil marriage for same sex couples in the referendum. The move comes 20 years after homosexuality was decriminalized by the state.

---

[57] *Id.*, 568.

[58] Irish Catholic Bishop's Conference, "Commemorating Pope John Paul II's 1979 Pilgrimage to Ireland" (6 Sept. 2009), *available at* http://www.catholicbishops.ie/2009/09/07/commemorating-pope-john-paul-iis-1979-pilgrimage-to-ireland/.

[59] Edwards, 568.

[60] *Id.*

[61] *Id.*

Same-sex couples in the Republic of Ireland have been able to enter a civil partnership since January 2011, but not marriage"[62] The Bishops have already voiced their disagreement and have continued the campaign in defense of traditional marriage. Bishop Denis Nulty of Kildare & Leighlin said the "Catholic Church in Ireland would campaign against the introduction of same sex marriage in the referendum and said 'the Church regards the family based on marriage between a woman and a man as the single most important institution in any society. To change the nature of marriage would be to undermine it as the fundamental building block of our society,' the bishop added."[63] In the coming months and years, the Irish Church will endeavor to find ways to shape the hearts and minds of the faithful as the nation progresses down the path of secularization and addresses these most essential moral questions.

FAITH FORMATION

When 75 percent of Irish Catholics say the Church's teaching on human sexuality has no relevance to them,[64] it is clear that there is much work to do. As generations of Irish Catholics have been

---

[62] "Gay Marriage: Republic of Ireland to Hold 2015 Referendum," BBC News (5 Nov. 2013), *available at* http://www.bbc.co.uk/news/uk-northern-ireland-24825547.

[63] *Id.*

[64] Michael Kelly, "Irish Priestly Vocations in Worrying Decline," Catholic World Report (30 Oct. 2012), *available at* http://www.catholicworldreport.com/Item/1706/irish_priestly_vocations_in_worrying_decline.aspx#.UosbF8Trxow.

straying from the fold, the important work of the clergy and lay people is to put into motion a deep renewal in faith and prayer. The official program "Share the Good News" hosts a first-class national directory for catechesis, but its implementation is slow and it encounters resistance to change. [65] Even those charged with passing on the faith in the parish have been decreasing in number. According to Reverend Casey, "Our school system and our teachers have made an immense contribution to the transmission of the faith. But many teachers no longer practice, and there is a growing danger that because of curriculum pressures, catechesis will be limited to two events—first Communion and confirmation—and stop there."[66] Thus, it is not only limited teachers, but it is also that many are non-practicing. Casey continues,

> Catholic teachers undoubtedly gave an excellent all-round education to Irish youth, but failed to form young people in the faith and never introduced them to a relationship with a personal God. Families too appear not to have transmitted the faith to their children. It is not surprising that young people have quietly abandoned a Catholicism about which they were taught little and of which they experienced even less in their daily lives. Theirs is a loss the church has passively accepted with hardly a whimper.[67]

---

[65] Casey.

[66] *Id.*

[67] *Id.*

It is clear that the fault not only lies with teachers and clergy, but the Irish family also bears some of the responsibility. The duty is not only on the priests and Bishops to set the expectations of society. It also falls to the educators, friends, mentors, and especially the parents.

INTEGRATING PLURALISM

With large influxes of migrants entering Ireland, there is a new challenge to accommodate a diversity of different cultural and religious identities. For Catholic leaders, the new and growing Irish pluralism presents an opportunity, pointing toward a future for Ireland as a multi-religious nation.[68] So far, there is reason to be hopeful as interactions have been generally positive. Yet there are more questions than answers in the years ahead, particularly as the education system is being reformed. The difficulty will arise from going a primarily Catholic vantage point to one that is accommodating other faiths. Buckley notes that

> It is important to emphasize that taking the wishes of minority parents seriously is not anti-Catholic. In a country where the Catholic Church controls over nine in ten primary schools, the challenge of protecting the rights of minorities, including those who identify as nonreligious, is a real one. Smart reformers, like the Irish Human Rights Commission and the Catholic Schools Partnership, are well aware that Ireland will

---

[68] Buckley.

have to address such challenges—or risk litigation by European human-rights bodies. And so Ireland finds itself in the ironic position of needing to protect the consciences of its religious minorities in order to preserve the public presence of Catholicism. [69]

This balance of protecting minority rights while also protecting Catholicism may seem a difficult task, and may even seem unnecessary to some, but with external and internal pressures to do so, it will not be one that is easily ignored.

Sex Abuse

The revelation of a sexual abuse crisis in America shocked the nation and the world. Just a few years later, however, the Irish Church would follow the same lamentable course. For more than two decades, simultaneous tragedies of episcopal malfeasance played out in both the U.S. and Irish churches, as bishops in both countries systematically mishandled allegations of child sexual abuse committed by their priests.[70] Ireland had been suffering a unique set of circumstances at the time the scandal, which magnified the situation further. Casey commented that "The effects of the child abuse scandals have had a demoralizing effect on the entire church in Ireland and continue to do so. In one sense the scandal crisis could not have come at a worse time, in that confidence in the church was well on the wane; and when the scandals broke, their effects were

---

[69] *Id.*

[70] Blackney, 118

devastating."[71]

The official investigation, the Ryan Report, released in 2009 by the Commission to Inquire into Child Abuse[72] is a five-volume catalog of the widespread sexual abuse. When the Report was released, Church officials issued their own responses to the findings. The Holy Father's reaction to the report is noteworthy. Benedict was "deeply disturbed and distressed," the Vatican said, and expressed his "profound regret at the actions of some members of the clergy who have betrayed their solemn promises to God, as well as the trust placed in them by the victims and their families, and by society at large. [73] His words describe well the sentiment shared by many in the Church. When it came to a response, Benedict is also a leader of action, and not just sympathies. According to Professor Nicholas Cafardi,

> "Pope Benedict acted quickly when the Murphy Report was issued. He convened a high-octane summit including Cardinal Sean Brady of Armagh, primate of Ireland; Dublin Archbishop Diarmuid Martin; and five curial cardinals, among them Cardinal Prefect William Levada of the Congregation for the Doctrine of the Faith, and the papal nuncio to Ireland, Archbishop Giuseppe Leanza. No one knows for sure what was said at this summit. But in public,

---

[71] Casey.

[72] Jones, 14–15.

[73] "Pope Outraged and Shamed by Irish Clergy's Abuse," *National Catholic Reporter* 46, no. 5 (Dec. 2009), 4.

> Pope Benedict's words have been blunt… he has said
> he shares "the disdain, the feeling of betrayal and the
> shame of the **Irish** faithful," and promises that "the
> priests who are to blame will pay for it."[74]

In Ireland, many of these clergy did pay. Following talks with the pope and other Vatican officials that Archbishop Martin called for the resignation of those bishops who had failed to protect the young.[75] But still many wonder how it was allowed to happen in the first place. This is a difficult question to answer. Compounding the problem, in both Ireland and America, was a crucial lack of understanding   by   the **church's** canon   lawyers   of   how the **church's** penal law could and should be applied to pedophiles.[76] Finally,   the   report   says,   the   **Irish** bishops--like   their   U.S. counterparts--"did not feel Rome was supporting them in dealing with this issue."[77] What should have been done is open to much debate, but where we are today is another matter. Today Ireland has strong child protection measures in place.The Church has also refined its guidelines and issued new cautions on identifying and swiftly arriving at solutions. Pope Francis has also issued his own advice on preventing this sort of tragedy in the future. Martin writes,

---

[74] Nicholas P. Cafardi, "Fraternal Correction: Lessons from the Irish Sex-Abuse   Crisis,"   *Commonweal*   (8   Mar.   2010),   *available   at* https://www.commonwealmagazine.org/fraternal-correction.

[75] *Id.*

[76] *Id.*

[77] *Id.*

> In the comments Pope Francis made at the
> congregation of the cardinals just before the conclave,
> he spoke about the need for the church to break out
> into what he called the outskirts—the frontiers—of
> human existence. And he added when the church
> does not break out of herself to evangelize, she
> becomes self-referential and so shuts herself in. One
> of the keys to understanding the mismanagement of
> the recent sexual abuse scandals in the Roman
> Catholic Church in Ireland must be precisely the
> measure in which the church in Ireland had become
> self-referential."[78]

Placing the needs of others above the prestige and honor of one's reputations is part of solving this problem. "While we await these changes, however, good priests and laity need to stay alert. We cannot let our bishops go back to business as usual, to the bad old days when an uncritical hierarchy saw evil being done by their fellow bishops and chose to say nothing,[79] Bishop Martin stated, echoing the hope expressed by many others.

SEMINARIANS

Traditionally, those who answered the call to religious life in Ireland were numerous. In recent years, however, the numbers of new religious has significantly declined. In 1990 there were 525

---

[78] Martin.

[79] *Id.*

students studying for the diocesan priesthood in Ireland; in 2013 there were 70.[80] Another statistic shows that in 1984 there were 171 ordinations or religious professions in Ireland; in 2006 there were 22.[81] There are religious congregations that have not had an ordination for 15 years and more and there are dioceses that have currently no seminarians.[82] Clearly, these are all very drastic changes.

Catholic Worldly Report issued the following analysis:

> In Ireland, vocations to the priesthood have remained stubbornly low and continue to drop at a time when decline has been largely halted in the United States and other parts of the western world. This year, the number of Irishmen entering seminary to train for the priesthood hit an all-time low. While Irish bishops have spoken of a vocations crisis for almost two decades, the stark situation came into sharp focus this autumn when just 12 men began studies for Ireland's 26 dioceses. It is the lowest number of new seminarians on record, almost half of last year's class of 22 men. On average, just 50 percent of men who enter Irish seminaries go on to be ordained. Based on this year's entry of 12 men remaining steady—if not

---

[80] Edwards, 566

[81] "Ireland's Priests Will Have almost Disappeared in 20 Years; What then?" Association of Catholic Priests (29 May 2013), *available at* http://www.associationofcatholicpriests.ie/2013/05/irelands-priests-will-have-almost-disappeared-in-20-years-what-then/.

[82] Martin.

declining further, as certainly seems possible—
approximately 180 Irishmen will be ordained diocesan
priests in the next 30 years. At the same time, it is
estimated that 1,684 priests will have either died or
retired from active ministry in that time-frame. These
estimates do not take into account the number of men
who may leave the priesthood or become incapa-
citated before the usual retirement age of 75. This
means that by 2042, approximately 450 priests will
serve in Irish parishes, as opposed to the 1,965
currently working in the country's 26 dioceses. The
number of priests serving in parishes in Ireland is set
to shrink to less than a quarter of the current number
in just 30 years, unless the current dramatic decline in
vocations is arrested.[83]

Traditionally, to have a seminarian in the family was looked upon
very favorably. Families who produced priests were celebrated, and
many parents encouraged their children to seek a religious vocation.
It was a status symbol to have a priests or nun in the family, because
it showed that the family had enough money to pay for religious
education. [84] In present-day Ireland, when religious life has suffered
and economic growth is robust, it is no longer necessarily true that
affluence encourages seminarians. The effects of the vocation crisis
are also felt in both urban and rural areas as well. It is not the case of
a secularized, urban Ireland and a healthy, rural Ireland. The same

---

[83] Kelly.

[84] Blackwell & Hackney, 118.

cultural processes are at work across the country.[85]

There is one seminary in Ireland for the ordination and education of priests, Maynooth College, which has been a historically preeminent institution. According the College's history, "Maynooth College was founded in 1795 as a seminary for the education of priests and by 1850 had become the largest seminary in the world. Over its history it has ordained more than 11,000 priests. Many of these have ministered outside Ireland and it has inspired two major missionary societies, directed to China (1918 - the Columbian Fathers) and to Africa (1932 - Saint Patrick's Missionary Society)."[86] In addition to Maynooth, Irish seminarians may also be found in attendance in Rome at the Pontifical Irish College. Founded in 1628, this is the last of the many Irish Colleges that were once scattered over Europe when it was not possible to educate priests in Ireland.[87] Today the College is home to 60 students, with half coming from Ireland and the others representing many different nations. [88]

As vocations spring from within the life of believing families and communities,[89] and as the faith has diminished in Christian families, it has naturally brought forth reverberations in religious life. As the challenge of forming the modern day Irish faithful is addressed, the decline in vocations will see improvement. "The renewal of the

---

[85] Martin.

[86]   Maynooth   College,   History,   *available*   at http://maynoothcollege.ie/seminary/history/ (last visited 7 Sept. 2015).

[87]   Pontifical   Irish   College,   Rome,   *available*   at http://www.irishcollege.org/college/ (last visited 7 Sept. 2015).

[88] *Id.*

[89] Martin.

church in Ireland and the challenge of creating a new Christian presence in Irish society tomorrow will come from a renewed generation of lay men and women who feel confident to witness to the meaning that their Christian faith brings to their lives."[90] Just as addressing the renewal of the faith is a matter for the secularization of society, it is also one that would answer the problems related to seminarians.

FUTURE

As interconnected as the world is becoming, the future of the Catholic Church in Ireland will not be dependent upon any outsider statistics or reporting. The future course rests with the Irish faithful. Bishop Martin commented that Irish Catholicism has its own unique history and culture and that Renewal in the Irish church will not come from imported plans and programs; it must be home-grown.[91] There have certainly been major drawbacks in recent years, particularly with the allures of materialism and secularization, ushered in by economic success, and the just anger expressed in reaction to the sexual abuse cases that weakened an already fragile Church.

For decades Ireland was looked on as one of the world's most deeply and stably Catholic countries. Today Ireland finds itself, along with other parts of Europe, being classified as "post-Catholic."[92] Despite the enormous tasks that lay ahead, the question that may

---

[90] *Id.*

[91] *Id.*

[92] *Id.*

come to mind is "how to go forward?" Martin suggests, "There is a further and more vital need: that of charting a new path to allow the church once again to have an impact on society and mediate the Christian message into the broad culture of the Ireland of tomorrow. Reform is not just an inner-church reality. A church trapped in inner-church squabbles will never be attractive to others. The church will relinquish many of the institutional roles it has held in Ireland." [93]

Inherent to this discussion is an appeal for widespread collaboration, with the clergy and lay members involved. A solution will likely involve establishing appropriate structures that would reflect the participation of all the baptized and that takes place at parish, diocesan and national levels and address all issues facing our people at this time of crisis. [94] Public and open dialogue on the issues that is fair and honest will help ease any tensions that may exist on difficulties that Ireland faces. As Buckley suggests,

> "In the midst of religious and economic crises, Catholicism may simply drop out of Irish public life, or remain only as a vestigial reminder of earlier times. Yet hope persists that a commitment to addressing economic crisis, promoting internal accountability, and engaging pluralism can salvage the best of

---

[93] *Id.*

[94] Michael Kelly, "Ireland Assembly of Religious and Laypeople Calls for Open Church, Re-Evaluation," *National Catholic Reporter* (8 May 2012), *available at* http://ncronline.org/news/global/ireland-assembly-religious-and-laypeople-calls-open-church-re-evaluation.

church-state relations in Ireland. The three defining features of today's Ireland—economic crisis, abuse cover-ups, and increased pluralism—provide opportunities to put this new church state model into action. [95]

With the various different structures and standards to contend with in 21st century Ireland, the solutions to problems will have to be both unique to the times while still faithful to uphold the truth. As daunting as the task may seem, the time is upon the Irish Church now to seize the moment and emerge stronger and more united. Bishop Martin said it best when he noted, "It is not a time to be lamenting; it is a time to be rising to the challenge with courage and Christian enthusiasm."[96]

---

[95] Buckley.

[96] Martin.

Mexico

Introduction

The Catholic population in Mexico has long been one of the largest in the world. Statistically second after Brazil, Catholic Church membership among Mexico's 110 million people has included the vast majority of the population. As recent as the year 2011, 83.9% of the country[1] have identified in some way as Catholics, even despite trends that reflect a decline in the past several years. Even with the decrease in the percentage of the population considering themselves Catholics, with so populous a country, Mexico remains a stronghold of the faith.[2] These statistics are in part due to Mexico's historically well-established Christian lineage over the span of five centuries. Catholicism was brought over to Mexican civilization with the Spanish explorers and began to take root right away. The majority of the Mexican people are of mixed Spanish and Amerindian descent, but a large percentage of

---

[1] *CNN,* "La Población de Catolicos Aumenta en el Mundo pero no en America," May 28, 2014, at http://mexico.cnn.com/mundo/2014/05/28/la-poblacion-de-catolicos-aumenta-en-el-mundo-pero-no-en-america.

[2] *Pew Forum.* <http://www.pewforum.org/2013/02/13/the-global-catholic-population/>

the population in the south is pure Amerindian.[3] The religious practices of the indigenous civilization were deep-rooted at the time of Christianity's arrival in the country. The nation's numerous cultural monuments and ruins bear witness to a full and vibrant practice of faith that has been carried out and passed on through centuries of generations; the ruins of civilizations such as the Aztec, Zapotec, Mayan, with their pyramids, public buildings and temples, stand side-by-side with the ruins of Catholic churches and convents.[4] From its roots in indigenous religion to its incorporation with Catholicism, there is a diversity of ways the practice of faith is apparent in Mexican society.

Many Amerindians, despite their Catholicism, continued to maintain some traditional beliefs and practices that predated the conquest; syncretistic practices, such as those found among Catholic Mayans, were also common.[5] As in other countries where Catholicism is introduced to a society with a different cultural background, there tend to be adaptations that incorporate aspects of the local lifestyle. This process of inculturation reflected the nation's climate, geography, tradition and also the availability of building materials and skilled masons, and the process was overseen in detail

---

[3] Olmedo, D. *New Catholic Encyclopedia*

Vol. 9. 2nd ed. Detroit: Gale, 2003. p575-586. COPYRIGHT 2003 Gale, COPYRIGHT 2006 Gale, Cengage Learning D. OLMEDO, 575

[4]   Ramsay,   Allan.   "THE   CATHOLIC   CHURCH   IN MEXICO." *Contemporary Review* 290, no. 1689 (Summer2008 2008): 173. *MasterFILE Premier*, EBSCO*host*(accessed February 28, 2014)., 174

[5] Olmedo, 586.

by Spanish friars with consideration to local feeling.[6]   The
dispositions of the local population were expressed in Mexican
Catholicism in a manner that would be suitable to popular belief
while also consistent with Church guidelines. To a Western
Christian, church architecture and decoration might seem
excessively penitential, yet Amerindian traditions and experiences
of suffering were a part of the local spirituality.[7] With these
preferences well-expressed by the early Mexican Church, the
Church was able to capture the hearts and minds of many in those
early days. It is worth noting as well that the Church grew in
number through those who had come from the European continent
as well, and while this statistic represents a sizeable portion, many
Amerindians did convert to the faith in those times.

The Church was able to continue to develop and expand over
the next few centuries, but by the late 20th century, the Catholic
demographic had begun to see the effects of Protestant
missionaries. Both mainstream Protestant and evangelical
communities have multiplied among both urban and rural areas,[8]
yet these figures still represent a minority in Christian practice
among Mexicans. By the early 1990s, a noticeable shift in religious
affiliation could be seen, motivated in part by the evangelical
movement.[9] From 1970 to 1990, Roman Catholic affiliation went
from 96.2% to 89.7%, with the highest Catholic representation in

---

[6] Ramsay, 174.

[7] Ibid, 174.

[8] Olmedo, 586

[9] Merrill, Tim. L., and Ramón Miró, editors. *Mexico: A Country Study.*
Washington: GPO for the Library of Congress, 1996.

the central western states extending from Zacatecas to Michoacán.[10]
At the same time, the Evangelical affiliation grew. It surged from 1.8
percent in 1970 to 4.9 percent in 1990, with the Assemblies of God,
Seventh Day Adventists, the Church of Jesus Christ of Latter Day
Saints (Mormons) and Jehovah's Witnesses experiencing the most
growth.[11] As where the highest Catholic population could be seen in
the central western states, the Protestant growth was especially
strong in the southeast. By 2011, as stated above, only 83.9% of the
population affiliated as Roman Catholic, representing a further
decline. [12] Demographically, the pattern of decline is steady, but
overall, the proportions of the population that are Catholic versus
other Christian are still significantly distinct.

Early History through Modern Day

In its 500-year history in Mexico, the Catholic Church has
experienced a range in support from government and society. The
Roman Catholic Church's role in Mexican history goes back to 1519,
when Hernán Cortés, the Spanish conqueror of New Spain, landed
on the coast of Mexico, accompanied by Roman Catholic clergy.[13]
From the moment these first missionaries came, the Catholic Church

---

[10] Merrill and Miro.

[11] Ibid.

[12] Cabaniss, Margaret. *Crisis Magazine.* "Number of Catholics in
Mexico Declining." 6 April, 2011.

http://www.crisismagazine.com/2011/number-of-catholics-in-mexico-
declining Accessed 25 September, 2014.

[13] Merrill and Miro.

began to take root in this Amerindian nation. Soon after, the first Franciscan, Dominican, and Augustinian friars arrived to begin the work on an organized basis, dividing the mission work between them.[14] In the beginning years, this relationship was strong, and it was in this period of Spanish conquest and its aftermath, that the Church earned its reputation as "friend of the Indians."[15] The government in place was administered by colonial authorities, but it was a relatively stable era in the nation's history. In the seventeenth and eighteenth centuries Mexico, by then fixed in a traditionally colonial pattern of administration, enjoyed a remarkably long period of prosperity.[16] For three centuries the Catholic Church in New Spain (Mexico) had been in close connection with Spain,[17] but it would not always be so.

The turbulence in Spanish colonial life that would ultimately bring about the independence of Mexico began in the early 18th century following the end of the wars of Spanish succession. The victorious Bourbon dynasty, imbued with the doctrines of Enlightenment rationalism, replaced the Habsburg dynasty, whose monarchs had been pious and deferential supporters of the Church. It was with this transition that persecutions of the Church in Mexico began. The monasteries were suppressed, the rights of the clergy were curtailed, and the Jesuits were disbanded and expelled. These attacks on the clergy, who had been the traditional defenders of the poor and

---

[14] Ramsay, 175

[15] Ramsay, 178

[16] Ibid, 179

[17] Merril and Miro.

indigenous peoples of Mexico, provoked bitter responses of protest and even insurrection on the part of the people.

The growing reaction to French Enlightenment influence over Spain and the colonies continued into the early 19th century. The invasion of Spain by Napoleon and his imposition of a French regime there led to the upheaval of all the Spanish colonies from 1808 to 1814, which would begin to sever entirely their relationship with Spain.[18] In Mexico, an eleven-year revolt began under the leadership of Miguel Hidalgo y Costilla, a Catholic priest who rallied his followers under the banner of Our Lady of Guadalupe and led them to believe that they were rising in defense of the Spanish crown against the liberal, anti-Catholic French government.[19]

After Hidalgo was captured and executed, the cause was taken up by a second Catholic priest, José Maria Morelos, whose declaration of independence, entitled "The Sentiments of the Nation," announced that "America" (Mexico) does not "profess or recognize any other religion besides the Catholic one, nor will permit nor tolerate the public or secret use of any other" and "will protect with all of its power and will keep watch over the purity of the faith and its dogmas and the conservation of its regular bodies."[20] One year later, Morelos' Constitution of Apatzingán contained similar provisions, excluding

---

[18] Ibid.

[19] "¡Mueran los gachupines!, lo que en realidad dijo Miguel Hidalgo," *24 Horas,* January 8, 2016, at http://www.24-horas.mx/mueran-los-gachupines-lo-que-en-realidad-dijo-miguel-hidalgo/

[20] *Sentimientos de la Nación,* November 21, 1813, at http://www.ordenjuridico.gob.mx/Constitucion/1813.pdf.

from citizenship anyone not professing the Catholic faith or guilty of heresy.[21]

After the death of Morelos in 1815, the revolutionaries continued to fight for the same objectives until 1821, when a new liberal constitution was introduced in Spain that alarmed both conservative creoles and the Mexican Catholic bishops. The colonies' creole general, Augustín de Iturbide, negotiated a truce with the rebels and declared Mexico's independence based on the "three guarantees," which were ultimately represented in the three colors of Mexico's flag: the white representing the purity of the Catholic religion (the only one to be tolerated), the green representing the independence of the country, and the red representing the unity of common blood of the now-independent Mexicans.[22]

In the years following, with the sometimes brutal fight for independence that began in 1810, the Church struggled to maintain its status while finding a new place for itself in the independent life of Mexico.[23] The colonial government and the Mexican Church had long built strong ties, so this transition proved to be most unsettling. Although the preservation and protection of the Catholic faith had been one of the principal demands of the independence movement, friction began between Church and state soon after independence. The pope repeatedly urged Mexico to return to unity with Spain. The

---

[21] *Constitution de Apatzingan,* October 22, 1814, at http://www.diputados.gob.mx/biblioteca/bibdig/const_mex/const-apat.pdf.

[22] "México tu bandera es la más bonito del mundo," at www.telesecundaria.gob.mx/anterior_semanas/MEXICO_BANDERA_05_MAR.html

[23] Ibid.

Catholic bishops wished to be loosed from obligations that had tied it to the state under Spanish rule, while the government sought to release itself from obligations to the Church. The conflict was exacerbated by the U.S.'s minister to Mexico, Joel Roberts Poinsett, a descendant of French Huguenots who established York Rite masonry in the country to undermine the influence of the Catholic religion and promote U.S. economic and political influence in the country. Aligned against Poinsett and the York Rite was the Scottish Rite lodge, which tended to defend the country's traditional religious and political institutions and sought to prevent the supremacy of the U.S. over Mexico.[24]

After Mexican independence, Church-state relations would never be quite the same. What would ensue, in the history of this relationship following independence, would involve a series of efforts on the part of the government to curtail the church's influence.[25] Yet, even as Mexico fought for independence and established its own government, the Catholic faith of many of the Amerindians was retained in this new period of sovereignty. At independence, Mexico was considered homogeneously Catholic and the Church was credited with fashioning the Mexican character, with the population at this time estimated at 6,121,426, of which more than half were Amerindians.[26] Not all developments were encouraging, however. Independent Mexico did see negative changes in its Church as well. The war caused the number of priests and religious to

---

[24] Gilbert M. Joseph, ed. *The Mexico reader: history, culture, politics* (Durham: Duke University Press, 2002), 11-14.

[25] Ibid.

[26] Olmedo, 575.

decrease; seminaries to close; missionary reinforcements from Europe to be discontinued; and many lives of faithful claimed by violence. [27] Further, the Mexican Church lost on a significant source of income. While Catholicism became the state religion when independence was proclaimed in 1821, the financial support formerly gained through its relationship with the Spanish Crown was now lost, which over the first 40 years caused a succession of related crises. [28] A series of laws were enacted that removed the Church's permission to own property and other privileges. The first major secular legislation was on July 12, 1857, when the government confiscated all church properties, suppressed all religious orders, and empowered the state governors to designate what buildings could be used for religious services. [29] Mexico's first religious civil war was fought between 1857 and 1860 in reaction to the legislation. [30] This period was not a stable one for the Church. It also led to a further weakened national unity and decades' long unrest. The Church found itself in a weak position by the time the Mexican Revolution broke out in 1909, a time that ushered in a long period of anarchy. [31]   Sadly, however, the darkest period to date was yet to come.

The next decade would see the height of hostility between the government and the Church, with the administration of President Plutarco Calles. Calles went on to carry out severe anti-Catholic laws that would alienate the Church from its people in an unprecedented

---

[27] Ibid, 575-576

[28] Ibid, 575

[29] Merril and Miro.

[30] Ibid.

[31] Ramsay, 181

Missionary Priests in the Homeland

way. He believed that only the government should have the freedom to form the minds of its citizens and insisted that the church was poisoning the minds of the people.[32] In order to carry out these guidelines, he prohibited much of the clergy from carrying out their ministry, which led to many regions of Mexico without a single Mass celebrated for a long period of time.[33] In a country that has developed a significant Catholic community, these changes were vigorously rejected. The underlying social backdrop of anarchy and unrest led another revolution from 1911-1920 and a new constitution in 1917, both were directly hostile to the Church.[34] The constitution of 1917 highlighted and institutionalized many of the nineteenth-century secular reforms; chief among the restrictions were: lack of legal standing of ecclesiastical marriages, the enabling of state governments to determine the number of clergy permitted to operate within their boundaries, and the prohibition of ministers to criticize the government, [35] among many others. It is within the context of these harsh realities that the most violent period known as the *Cristero Rebellion* occurred.

The *Cristero Rebellion* of 1926-29 was a time in which the anti-Catholic persecution in Mexico reached its height. To consider some

---

[32] *Catholic World Report.* "The Story, Martyrs, and Lessons of the Cristero War."1 June 2012.

<http://www.catholicworldreport.com/Item/1396/the_story_martyrs_and_lessons_of_the_cristero_war.aspx#.UxA0 0_ldXHw> Accessed 20 September, 2015.

[33] Ibid.

[34] Olmedo, 575

[35] Merril and Miro.

of the unreasonably harsh and unrealistic demands impose on the Church at this time: in one area (*Sonora*), the governor ordered all churches closed, officials in the state of Tabasco required priests to marry if they were to officiate at mass, and the Chihuahua government allowed only one priest to minister to the entire statewide Roman Catholic population.[36] In such a short span of time, many Catholics were persecuted and killed. In all, approximately 250,000 people were died of war-related injury or disease in this three-year period.[37] Thankfully, that is not how this chapter ends. As the saying goes, "the blood of the martyrs is the seed of the faithful," this intense time of suffering deeply affected the Church in Mexico, with many instances of renewal and examples of martyrdom. There are a total of thirty-five martyrs who have been canonized and fifteen who have been beatified in recent years, the most famous among them being: Blessed Miguel Agustin Pro, S.J. – Executed on November 23, 1927, Blessed Jose Sanchez del Rio – A fifteen-year-old Cristero executed on February 10, 1928, and Blessed Anacleto Gonzalez Flores – Great leader of peaceful resistance – Executed April 1, 1927.[38] Attempts to suppress the faith may have reached alarming levels, but Catholicism in Mexico was strengthened like never before through the heroic virtue of countless individuals.

The violence of this era was put to an end largely due to the Church's intervention, both from within Mexico and abroad. The involvement of the United States in this affair proved to be a most

---

[36] Ibid.

[37] *Interview with historian Jean Meyer by Matthew Cullinan Hoffman for the National Catholic Register, unpublished complete version.*

[38] *Catholic World Report.*

helpful aid in bringing the crisis to a close, but the Mexican Bishops and the Holy See were also involved in the peace negotiations. The end of this persecution finally came about under the pressure of U.S. Ambassador Dwight Morrow, with the help of the U.S. Knights of Columbus.[39]   The Knights commenced on a public relations campaign to educate the American public and to raise funds for aid. In August 1926, they established a fund that raised over a million dollars to offer relief services for those exiled from Mexico, to provide for exiled seminarians to continue their priestly formation, and to educate the American public about the true situation.[40] According to Catholic World Report, "The Order printed and distributed five million pamphlets about the war and two million copies of the Pastoral Letter of the Catholic Episcopate of the United States on the Religious Situation in Mexico. The U.S. Knights also sponsored over 700 free lectures and reached millions by radio."[41] The conflict finally reached a peaceful resolution under the administration of Manuel Ávila Camacho (1940-46).[42]   The position of the Catholic Church vis-à-vis the state in subsequent decades was considerably more neutral. The new government offered non-enforcement of the discriminatory legal provisions in exchange for the Church's assistance in achieving social peace.[43] Though there was no outright discrimination and more stability, it was not a complete reversal in practice and it would only be a temporary agreement.

---

[39] Ibid.

[40] Ibid.

[41] Ibid.

[42] Merrill and Miro.

[43] Ibid.

There were still some political freedoms restricted through the constitution, but by the early 1980s the tide was beginning to change. The Church would no longer accept the status quo and demanded the overturn of the anticlerical provisions, insisting to have the right to have a more visible role in national affairs.[44] The Church would quickly take the public stage and for the first time in decades have the platform to address national concerns. The Church also began to take a larger role in criticizing elements of Mexican society that were unjust. One of the first injustices the Mexican bishops highlighted was political corruption and they released a Global Pastoral Plan for 1980-1982, which contained a highly critical assessment of the Mexican political system.[45] The Church had begun to exercise authority in public spheres that had long been silenced. Formal ties with the Vatican resumed in 1991, which included formal representation of Mexico to the Vatican State.[46] By 1992, the church-state relationship had experienced a new all-time high when a proposal to remove all restrictions on the Church was approved by the federal legislature,[47] by which churches were recognized as legal entities and once again permitted to own property, foreign clergy and ministers were again allowed in the country, and Mexican clerics were granted the right to vote, to criticize the government, and were exempted from taxes.[48] On a legal basis, the Mexican Church stands much better today than it did last century, having re-gained much of

---

[44] Ibid.

[45] Ibid.

[46] Ramsay, 182.

[47] Merrill. and Miro.

[48] Ramsay, 182.

the political rights it had lost during its anti-clerical periods of government. Though the Church in Mexico has regained much of the damage and limitations imposed upon it over the course of the past century, there still remains a degree of tension between local governments and parishes at the local level in some areas at times. Even with legal victories that lifted restrictions on religious freedom, many still sense at least some distrust of the Church by government officials. While there isn't open persecution anymore, some consider is as an "aversion," represented by biased teaching regarding the Cristero War in public schools.[49]

As trying as they are, the challenges to overcome any lingering discriminatory measures from this era is no longer the chief preoccupation and goal of the Church in Mexico. The contemporary political battles are fought less often against the state, than against social trends of the Mexican people influenced by a growing secularism. As Mexico began to establish itself as a stable, economically viable country free from war, it began to confront issues common to many other modern nations through new legislation.[50] Political battles that plague other nations, such as corruption, economic instability, the legalization of abortion and other social movements contrary to the faith are considered the new arena where the Bishops have turned their efforts. The crisis is not only from outside the Church, but stems from the hearts and minds

---

[49] *BeliefNet.* "Mexican Roman Catholics Celebrate 27 New Saints." <http://www.beliefnet.com/News/2000/05/Mexican-Roman-Catholics-Celebrate-27-New-Saints.aspx#xe35l95WIIWKjlyC.99> Accessed 23 September, 2015.

[50] Olmedo, 586.

of the faithful themselves.

Current Challenges

With the focus turned towards the threats from within society and away from governmental anti-clericalism, the challenges are perhaps no less significant. Whereas the persecution against the Church unified the faithful, many of threats from within society have divided members of the Church. The growing acceptance within society to accept immoral stances on social issues such as abortion and gay marriage have been challenging the Church under the contemporary social climate. The Mexican church has achieved political and social gains while overcoming painful setbacks that include legalized abortion and gay marriage in the capital of the most **Catholic** country in the Spanish-speaking world; it is also a nation grappling with a rampant drug war that has spread fear into once-tranquil regions.[51] The Bishops' Conference supported the constitutional reform that established "non-discrimination" for homosexuals and ensured that homosexual "marriage" would be imposed by the Supreme Court. Even with varying degrees of Church support throughout different Presidential administrations, the

---

[51] Gomez Licon, Adriana and Michael Wasserstein. "Pope Visits Hearts of Conservative Catholic Mexico," *Associated Press, Boston.Com*, 22 March   2012. <http://www.boston.com/news/world/latinamerica/articles/2012/03/22/po pe_visits_heart_of_conservative_catholic_mexico/   >   Accessed   25 September 2015.

Church remains a consistent and vocal presence and a moral compass many can turn towards in uncertain times.

The Mexican Church faces the same problems as many other nations, those of outward conformism and inner agnosticism, declining congregations, shortage of vocations and the indifferent quality of many candidates for the priesthood.[52] Different shortages in the Church have made it difficult to counter-act some of the challenges that have been arising. For example, the death of priests in rural areas has consequences in the increasing numbers of unbaptized children and young couples cohabitating outside marriage.[53] The rise in Evangelical Protestantism has also led to unease in the strongly Catholic country. Coming largely from the United States, the evangelist missions are young, enthusiastic and prepared to put up with considerable hardship and they occupy remote areas from which the Church itself has been forced by lack of priests to withdraw. [54] The solution to many of these problems concern the spiritual well-being of the nation's many Catholics and the need to resist that which is contrary to the faith.

Economic Instability and Violence

The drug war in Mexico is not just a matter of criminal activity that can be found in any part of the world. It is particularly pronounced with far-reaching effects and devastating levels of violence. **Mexico** has been traumatized by the deaths of more than

---

[52] Ramsay, 184.

[53] Ibid.

[54] Ibid.

47,000 people in drug-related violence in less than six years,[55] and large areas of the country are under the effective control of one or more of the notorious cartels, gangs, and militias. To give a comparison with another well-known war, in 14 years of war in Iraq and Afghanistan, roughly 8,300 total lives have been lost for all Coalition partners combined.[56] The scale of the war on drugs in Mexico cannot be under-emphasized. Few weeks go by without the media reporting some massacre of innocents, and police and government officials are regularly targeted.[57] To some, there is hardly any hope for progress after decades of broken promises of leaders and failed outcomes of good initiatives. Inflated by globalization through the ease of the passage of goods, it is considered so pervasive and prevalent in Mexico and for so long that it might be described as sanctioned by time and thus ineradicable.[58] The solution to the war on drugs and related struggles is indeed complex and the situation requires that the crisis be approached from multiple angles. The educational emergency in **Mexico**, broken families, corruption and inefficiency in the distribution of the nation's resources, injustices in international trade that mean fewer jobs, and those poor-paying, for **Mexican** youth, all these contribute to organized crime and to common crime.[59] If only this were a

---

[55] Gomez Licon and Wasserstein.

[56] http://icasualties.org/

[57] Gomez Licon and Wasserstein.

[58] Ramsay, 184.

[59] Anderson, Antonio. "Bullets and Beatitudes." *First Things: A Monthly Journal Of Religion & Public Life* no. 233 (May 2013): 19.*MainFile*, EBSCO*host* (accessed March 5, 2014).

problem that could be solved by the signing of a governmental resolution or the collective will of the Mexican bishops. The pandemic is much more complex, however, and involves various societal and economic efforts.

Yet, the Church stands at the forefront of the charge, advocating for the end of drug trade and the violence inherent in the industry. Many brave religious leaders have actively sought to end this saga at great peril to their own lives. In addition to widespread extortion attempts by gangs, church officials have said clergy have received threatening notes and telephone calls after sermons against drug use and trafficking.[60] Not enough can be said about the valiant efforts of many great priests to this end. For example, fearless activism for peace and human rights made Mexican legendary Bishop Jose Raul Vera Lopez a candidate for Nobel Peace Prize.[61] This praise is tempered with a caveat. Although the bishop has shown courage in confronting kidnappers and drug lords, he is also involved in directing organizations that advocate abortion and homosexual perversion as "rights."[62] The threat from extortionists is also a serious problem. In the country's capital alone, more than 10 priests have been threatened with extortion, said the Reverend Hugo Valdemar

---

[60] Romo, Rafael and Catherine E. Shoichet. "Archbishop: Mexican cartel threatened Catholic Seminary." *CNN.* 4 December, 2013.< http://www.cnn.com/2013/12/03/world/americas/mexico-cartel-catholic-seminary-extortion/ >

[61] Gomez Licon and Wasserstein.

[62] Matthew Cullinan Hoffman. "Catholic Diocese Sponsors Homosexual Youth Group that Accepts Sodomy, Cross-Dressing." CatholicExchange. (accessed February 2, 2021).

Romero, a spokesman for the archdiocese.[63] According to Romero, none of these extortionists have been paid, even with attempts as high up at the major seminary of the Archdiocese of Mexico City. A further related challenge is with the more isolated cases of corruption in the local churches, where drug money might be accepted for good causes, such as in the rebuilding of buildings and in support of social welfare projects. While some may think of it as a good that would not perhaps otherwise come, the Church still rejects this sort of association. This concession compromises their ability to speak out against crime, mayhem and terrorism. [64] All around, between the real threat of violence and extortion to the corruption-related temptations of local Churches, the war on drugs has wide-reaching impact for all Catholics of Mexico.

Spiritual Crises

The drug industry in Mexico sheds some light on another problematic area: the way some on the "margins" of society have practiced variations of Catholicism that are fundamentally flawed and contrary to the faith. Although many million Mexicans are proud to consider themselves Catholic, there is a popular tendency to practice faulty variations of Catholicism, some more mild and while others more extreme.

---

[63] Romo and Shoichet.

[64] Jenkins, Philip. 2011. "Mexico's crisis of faith." *Christian Century* 128, no. 6: 53. *ATLA   Religion   Database   with   ATLA Serials*, EBSCO*host* (accessed February 28, 2014).

Several new religious devotions have grabbed hold of Mexico in the last twenty years, largely to innovated saints at the margins of the Roman Catholic Church, few of them officially sanctioned,[65] the most well-known among these "saints" is *Santa Muerte*, Saint Death. Figured as the Grim Reaper, she has garnered significant attention from scholars in Mexico and the United States as patron saint of drug dealers, transgender sex workers and police officers—professions requiring routine risk of life.[66] Other novel devotions within recent years are numerous for various struggles of those who find themselves on the "margins of society" due to poverty, hopelessness, and crime. Those who are on the other end of the economic spectrum and find themselves in a position of affluence have turned away from the faith as well, and towards magic. Many of these problems are not specifically Mexican and are also experienced in other parts of the world, but the solution here will require a response that takes into account the cultural and religious sensibilities of the Mexican people.

Spirituality

Due to the range of cultural influences, Catholic spirituality in Mexico is diverse, perhaps more so than other Catholic countries. It ranges from those who support traditional folk religious practices, to

---

[65] Hughes, Jennifer Scheper. 2012. "The Niño Jesús Doctor: novelty and innovation in Mexican religion." *Nova Religio* 16, no. 2: 4-28. *ATLA Religion Database with ATLASerials*, EBSCO*host* (accessed February 28, 2014), p. 4.

[66] Hughes, 5.

those who adhere to the theology of liberation, and from charismatic renewal prayer groups to the conservative Opus Dei movement.[67] Lay groups and associations are also well-organized, representing these different groups. The largest and best known include Mexican Catholic Action, Knights of Columbus, Christian Study Courses, Christian Family Movement, and many smaller, private organizations.[68] There may be a variety of groups with different charisms, but they all share a common basis in Catholic faith.

More broadly speaking, when one thinks of Mexican Catholic spirituality, there are certain devotions and traditions that come to mind, some popular even outside of Mexico. The image that comes to mind perhaps first and foremost is that of Our Lady of Guadalupe. The Virgin of Guadalupe is well-known throughout the entire region and she bears the title as the "patroness of all the Americas."[69] The origin of the devotion to the Virgin of Guadalupe traces back to December 1531, when the Blessed Mother appeared on three occasions to a Christian Indian woodcutter named Juan Diego on the hill of Tepeyac, six kilometers north of Mexico City's main plaza.[70] She spoke to him in the local tribal language and told him to inform the local Bishop of her desire to have a church built in her honor on that spot.[71] It was only after the third request, upon the miraculous appearance of the image of the Virgin on the cloak of Juan Diego,

---

[67] Merrill and Miro.

[68] Merrill and Miro.

[69] Anderson, Carl A. "Our Catholic Hemisphere." *America* 196, no. 20 (June 4, 2007): 12. *MainFile*, EBSCO*host* (accessed March 6, 2014)., 13

[70] Merrill and Miro.

[71] Ibid.

that the Bishop acknowledged the miracle and agreed to build a shrine.[72] Today the original cloak with the miraculous image hangs above the altar of the new Basilica at the foot of Tepeyac hill. [73] To Mexicans, the message of Our Lady of Guadalupe is not simply just another message of love and peace for the whole world but holds a specific and important meaning for the people of Mexico. According to anthropologist Eric R. Wolf, "the Guadalupe symbol links family, politics, and religion; the colonial past and the independent present; and the Indian and the Mexican. It reflects the salient social relationships of Mexican life and embodies the emotions they generate."[74]   For others, the Virgin of Guadalupe represents the reconciliation of two opposing worlds, in the fusion of two religions, two traditions, and cultures.[75] Devotion to Our Lady of Guadalupe remains strong even as other aspects of Mexican society have changed. The UNAM national opinion poll found, for example, that nine out of ten Mexicans continued to ask intercessions from the Virgin or a saint.[76] Pope John Paul II referred to Mexicans as Guadalupanos, devoted to their own cult of Our Lady of Guadalupe.[77] Even though other aspects of religious devotion may change, the love of our Lady is as vibrant as ever.

Another tradition of Mexican religious culture that has become popularized even outside of Mexico in other Latin American

---

[72] Ibid.

[73] Ibid.

[74] Ibid.

[75] Ibid.

[76] Ibid.

[77] Ramsay, 184

countries is the *Dia de los Muertos*, the Day of the Dead, celebrating each year on November 1ˢᵗ the lives of the deceased with food, drink, and parties, and recognizing death as a natural part of the human experience, a continuum with birth, childhood, and growing up to become a contributing member of the community.[78] Instead of treating death with solemnity and sorrow, this tradition seeks to lift the spirits through lively mementos of the lives of those who have gone before.

Every year before Christmas, another popular practice is celebrated in Mexico. *Las Posadas* is 400 year old celebration commemorates Mary and Joseph's difficult journey from Nazareth to Bethlehem in search of a warm place to stay the night.[79] According to *American Catholic,*

"Beginning on December 16 and ending nine days later, on December 24, *Las Posadas* commemorates the nine months of Mary's pregnancy. Each night, one family agrees to house the pilgrims. And so it begins: At dusk, a procession of the faithful takes to the streets with children often dressed as angels and shepherds...The group representing the Holy Family stands outside a series of houses, singing songs, asking for lodging. They are refused time and again until the group reaches the designated house. Finally, the travelers are permitted to enter. Prayer and

---

[78] http://education.nationalgeographic.com/media/dia-de-los-muertos/ > Accessed 29 September, 2015.

[79] Heffron, Christopher. "Las Posadas: A Mexican Christmas Tradition." *American Catholic.* 26 December, 2011. http://www.americancatholic.org/news/report.aspx?id=3711

song continue in the home, and festive foods are shared... The tradition continues each evening with a different house as the chosen Posadas. The last night—Christmas Eve—usually features a midnight Mass. The nine days of *Las Posadas* is more than just a feel-good tradition: It deepens faith and strengthens ties within the community at a holy time. Just as Mary and Joseph faced the cold weather—and even colder innkeepers that night—participants brave the elements in bringing their love for the Christ Child to their streets. *Las Posadas* isn't about being somber and still during Christmas: It's about pilgrims and a pilgrimage, rousing song, prayer and deep faith—all of it in motion. [80]

There are certainly many other aspects of Mexican Catholic spirituality and this one description is not all-encompassing, but these main elements of Catholic culture in Mexico are well-known and universally celebrated throughout the region.

Mexico's extensive history with the Catholic Church is evidenced in the number and diversity of individuals who have led virtuous lives in different eras. Many of these people are honored and given special recognition in popular culture. In recent years, the Mexican Catholic Church has had an increase in canonized saints, a trend that has been bolstering the faith of the local Church. Mexico's only saint for some time was San Felipe de Jesus (canonized in 1862), a Mexican monk who was crucified in Nagasaki, Japan, when his ship stopped over there in a storm. [81] In 2000, there was a canonization of the 25 marytrs of the *Cristero* Rebellion. The best known of the 25

---

[80] Heffron.

[81] *BeliefNet.*

martyrs is Father Cristobal Magallanes, who reputedly pardoned his killers as he died by firing squad May 25, 1927[82] Also being canonized were the founders of two religious organizations: Maria de Jesus Sacramentado Venegas of the Congregation of the Sacred Heart and Jose Yermo y Parres of the Congregation of the Servants of the Sacred Heart of Jesus and of the Poor.[83] The first Amerindian saint of the Americas, Juan Diego, a popular figure known through the miracle of Our Lady of Guadalupe, was canonized in 2002. Continuing to emphasize the importance of the contributions of local indigenous believers, Pope John Paul II highlighted the lives of Blesseds Juan Bautista and Jacinto de los Angeles who were martyrs from the conflict-torn southern Mexican state of Oaxaca. "With this beatification, the church emphasizes the mission to proclaim the gospel to all peoples," the pope said. Referring to the two, he said their elevation by the church should "encourage indigenous peoples today to appreciate their culture and languages, and above all their dignity as children of God."[84] These canonizations highlight in a public way for all the Church to appreciate the contributions of the members of the indigenous culture who have exceptionally lived out the faith.

Other main spiritual leaders in Mexico who were recently canonized were Saint Rafael Guízar Valencia and Mother Lupita.

---

[82] Ibid.

[83] Ibid.

[84] Jeffrey, Paul. "Pope hails indigenous, but critics unimpressed." *Christian Century* 119, no. 17 (August 14, 2002): 16. *Biography Reference Bank (H.W. Wilson)*, EBSCO*host* (accessed March 6, 2014).

Saint Rafael Guízar Valencia (canonized in 2006 by Pope Benedict XVI) was a Catholic bishop (and Knight of Columbus) who cared for the wounded, sick, and dying in Mexico's 1910-20 Revolution.[85] Pope Francis canonized in 2013 Maria Guadalupe Garcia Zavala, a Mexican who dedicated herself to nursing the sick, and helped Catholics avoid persecution during a government crackdown of the faith in the 1920s. Also known as Mother Lupita, she hid the Guadalajara archbishop for more than a year after fearful local Catholic families refused to shelter him.[86] Mother Lupita was co-foundress of the Congregation of the Handmaids of St Margaret Mary (Alacoque) and the Poor. Today, the Congregation has 22 foundations and is present in five different Nations: Mexico, Peru, Iceland, Greece and Italy.[87] All of these saints enrich the tapestry of the faith by their unique contributions and stories and are a source of great pride to the Mexican people.

---

[85]   *Catholic   Online.*   "St.   Rafael   Guizar   Valencia."   < http://www.catholic.org/saints/saint.php?saint_id=7638 >

[86] "Catholics get hundreds of new saints with pope's first canonization ceremony at Vatican," *Fox News.* 12 May 2013.

< http://www.foxnews.com/world/2013/05/12/catholics-get-hundreds-new-saints-with-pope-first-canonization-ceremony/ >

[87] "Mexico to Have a New Saint - "Mother Lupita" García Zavala,"

*Hispanically-speaking   News.   12   February,   2013.   < http://www.hispanicallyspeakingnews.com/latino-daily-news/details/mexicos-maria-guadalupe-garcia-zavala-to-be-canonized-in-may-says-pope-bene/22062/ >

Seminaries

In Mexico, there is a long tradition of priestly formation and seminaries, which goes back to the times of the Council of Trent, with the foundation of the College "San Pedro" in Guadalajara in 1570. [88] Now there are over 60 seminaries scattered throughout the country. Most of these were formed as regular seminaries to provide priests to local dioceses, but there are some with special emphases, such as for Missionary efforts or seminaries for Americans preparing for the priesthood. In addition, outside of Mexico, priests can pursue post-graduate study at the Pontifical Mexican College in Rome, Italy. The mission of this program is to keep alive the bond between Mexico and the Magisterium.[89]   In Mexico City, the Hispanic Seminary of Our Lady of Guadalupe provides the United States with Spanish-speaking priests who are American citizens or residents. After their studies, the seminarians return to the United States[90] to carry out their work of their respective ministries. Through this annual exchange, many American priests are able to benefit from learning more about Mexican culture and spirituality, while

---

[88] Pope John Paul II, *Meeting with the Seminarians of Mexico, Address of His Holiness John Paul II,* Major Seminary of Guadalajara, 30 January 1979,

<

http://www.vatican.va/holy_father/john_paul_ii/speeches/1979/january/documents/hf_jp-ii_spe_19790130_messico-guadalajara-seminaristi_en.html

>

[89] Ibid.

[90] Hispanic Seminary of our Lady of Guadalupe. Archdiocese of Mexico. http://www.seminariohispano.org.mx/english/

improving their Spanish language skills, and may forge a greater partnership with the Church in Mexico.

Historically, the Knights of Columbus have played a significant role with seminarians in Mexico and the United States. During the *Cristero* struggle, American Catholics opened their arms to those displaced by violence when up to a million Mexican Catholic refugees fled north and seminaries were built so Mexicans could study for the priesthood in the States.[91] More recently, the Catholic Legal Immigration Network of the U.S. Conference of Catholic Bishops have contributed in this area of serving the needs of Mexican immigrants in the United States.[92] Today there continue to be plenty of examples of partnership between the Mexican and United States' local Churches and organizations in supporting one another.

Future Outlook

The troubles that ail the Mexican people today are indeed complex and will require comprehensive solutions. To this end, the Mexican Church has its work cut out. But in this effort, they ought not to act alone. Catholics on both sides of the border must promote a Catholic solution to the problems of poverty and economic and educational opportunities for the poor of Mexico.[93] All nations are better connected than ever before through increasing globalization; therefore, before long, our neighbors' struggles become our very own. In reality, what happens between the United States and Mexico

---

[91] Anderson, 14.

[92] Ibid.

[93] Ibid.

will shape the future of this hemisphere.[94] When it is possible to support one another, it will build up the Church in the whole region, and in turn, the world. As was seen with the involvement of the Knights of Columbus, for example, during the period of intense persecution during the *Cristero* war, there is always a potential to have an impact through the support of one another. There is never a situation too bleak, or a crime too severe, to be beyond the reach of transformative change.

The true battle for peace and stability in Mexico is not in the government halls or through the promises of elected officials, but it is in the heart and mind of each member of society. As the **Mexican** bishops have said, "The fundamental root of violence is in the orientation of the heart of every human. Evil is not in what surrounds us, but in the heart, 'from whence come evil designs' (Matt. 15:19). There is no sinner without a future, just as there is no saint without a past."[95] By striving to reach the hearts of the faithful in Mexico, the Bishops are seeking to put an end to the violence that reaches every part of society. The Church looks to promote the saving message of Jesus Christ in the forefront of these conflicts. As one Mexican priest said, "Christ's shocking gospel love is also the cure. Jesus shocks the world with his witness and teaching against violence. He is no pacifist; he doesn't stick a daisy in the muzzle of your rifle. No, he spatters you with his blood. He does not teach us to run from violence; he teaches us to confront violence by standing firm and offering our other cheek."[96] To some, to combat violence

---

[94] Ibid.

[95] Ibid.

[96] Ibid, 19.

with love might seem weak and ineffective in bringing about change in Mexico, but it is the proven path to building up the Church. If the 25 Mexican martyrs prove anything to society today, it is that in the face of instability and violence, there is the capacity for tremendous good. Civil society may at times fall short, but the Mexican Church, on the path of bringing forth the Gospel, will continue to permeate every area of society, and it is the seed of faith that will bring forth the true fruits of peace and goodwill.

Helpful links

Official Shrine website, Basilica of Our Lady of Guadalupe (Spanish)

http://basilica.mxv.mx/web1/-home/index.html

Basilica of Guadalupe (English site)

http://www.sancta.org/basilica.html

Conferencia del Episcopado Mexicano/ Conference of Mexican Bishops (Spanish)

http://www.cem.org.mx/

Pontifical Mexican College of Rome

http://www.colmexroma.it/

Pontifical University of Mexico (Spanish)

http://www.pontificia.edu.mx/

Hispanic Seminary of Our Lady of Guadalupe, seminary for US Spanish speaking Seminarians

http://www.seminariohispano.org.mx/english/

Diocesan Seminary of Guadalajara

http://www.semguad.org.mx/

Knight of Columbus, Mexican Martyrs booklet

http://www.kofc.org/un/en/resources/communications/martyrs_
booklet.pdf

Legionaries of Christ
http://www.legionariesofchrist.org/eng/index.phtml?height=768&widt
h=1366&sw=1&sw2=

Meeting with the Seminarians of Mexico, Pope John Paul II, 1979
http://www.vatican.va/holy_father/john_paul_ii/speeches/1979/january
/documents/hf_jp-ii_spe_19790130_messico-guadalajara-
seminaristi_en.html

Rome Reports: Saint Lupita Remembered for Simplicity and
Devotion to Poor and Sick
https://www.youtube.com/watch?v=gQddrsKfQT0

Nigeria

INTRODUCTION

Nigeria is a country in West Africa and the most populous of the African continent.[1] Unlike the United States, which is known for its strength in diversity and for its religious communities that generally live in peace alongside one another, the adherents of the two main religions in Nigeria—Muslims and Christians—are generally divided. While these tensions do not completely define the religious landscape, any discussion of contemporary religious life in Nigeria would be remiss without a mention of these differences. In some areas, there is a relative peace, but this is not the norm for the whole country. For example, Muslims and Christians live together without tension in the western part of Southern Nigeria;[2] yet in the North, interreligious conflict sadly is quite prevalent.

---

[1] "Nigeria, The Catholic Church in," *New Catholic Encyclopedia,* 2nd ed., vol. 10 (Detroit: Gale, 2003), 392.

[2] Jude C. Aguwa, "Christianity and Nigerian Indigenous Culture," *Religion, History, And Politics in Nigeria: Essays in Honor of Ogbu U. Kalu,* ed. Chima J. Korieh & G. Ugo Nwokeji (Lanham, MD: University Press of America, 2005), 13.

DEMOGRAPHICS

Overall, the total population is fairly evenly split between Christians and Muslims, with the Muslims largely inhabiting the north, and the Christians forming an important minority in the south and west. Among the region's many tribes, the Igbo are predominately Catholic.[3] As a basis of comparison, the Nigerian Christian population is nearly the same size as the total population of Germany, of whom, 20 million are Catholic and 60 million Protestant.[4] Clearly, Nigerian Christians are a sizeable contingent with great influence and a force to be reckoned with on the African continent and in Christendom as a whole.

The Catholic Church holds the biggest single demographic block among the Christian denominations and, benefitting from a part of a long established, worldwide network of Christian theological scholarship, is considered to be head and shoulders above the rest in the development of theological infrastructure.[5] This organization is supported by the network of social institutions, such as hospitals and schools throughout the country.

The precise break-down of Christian population demographics is

---

[3] "Nigeria, The Catholic Church in," 392.

[4] Pew Research Center, "Global Christianity—A Report on the Size and Distribution of the World's Christian Population" (19 Dec. 2011), *available at* http://www.pewforum.org/christian/global-christianity.

[5] Chukwudi Anthony Njoku, "Economy, Politics, and the Theological Enterprise in Nigeria," in *Religion, History, And Politics in Nigeria: Essays in Honor of Ogbu U. Kalu,* ed. Chima J. Korieh & G. Ugo Nwokeji (Lanham, MD: University Press of America, 2005), 148.

unknown, given the controversial aspect of this competitive evangelization. For this reason, the national census has not asked questions about religion since 1963,[6] and these figures are best estimates only. Even among Christians, there is much dispute for how many members comprise each denomination, with different denominations vying for prominence, which some refer to as *denominationalism.* Denominationalism is one of the worst divisive elements in Africa, with some even at times turning to violence.[7] Fortunately, many of these Christian groups have renounced their fighting and turned to organizations that instead focus on Christian unity and solidarity. These joint organizations come together in areas of common interest, such as Christian councils, refugee relief, Biblical translations,[8] and the like. Though they stem from disagreement, these joint ventures have gone past what divides them from one another toward the greater good of solidarity, marking a positive step forward.

CHRISTIAN HISTORY

According to Kenyan scholar of African religions John Mbiti, "Christianity in Africa is so old that it can rightly be described as an indigenous, traditional and African religion."[9] While it can be claimed that Africa encountered Christianity well before it encountered Islam, it is only true for certain parts primarily in the

---

[6] Pew Research Center.

[7] Mbiti, 227.

[8] Mbiti, 227.

[9] Mbiti, 223.

northern Africa. In Nigeria and the greater West African region, traditional African religions were prevalent until the introduction of Islam, which quickly spread through the country.

In the Nigerian North, the seeds of Arabic culture and Islamic religion were sown as early as the eleventh century.[10] Christianity did not first arrive until sometime later in the 15th century through **Augustinian and Capuchin monks from Portugal.**[11] Attempts to introduce Christianity in Nigeria that had occurred prior to the nineteenth century had failed woefully.[12] **In the nineteenth century after the abolition of the slave trade industry, Christianity would return and, this time, take root.**

In 1842, the first Christian church (Methodist) arrived in Western Nigeria,[13] followed by several other Protestant denominations in the ensuing years. The Catholic mission came to Lagos, the capital city, by 1863, followed by other Christian churches in the Eastern portion of the nation. By 1888, Christianity had gained a stronghold in Southern Nigeria.[14] It should be noted that while the major works of evangelism in Eastern Nigeria were carried out at the early stage by foreign missions, the planting of Christianity in Yorubaland was largely conducted by Yorubas themselves, the freed

---

[10] Aguwa, "Christianity and Nigerian Indigenous Culture," 13.

[11]

http://www.catholicdioceseoyo.org/index.php?option=com_content&view=article&id=80:historical-hints&catid=36:articles

[12] Aguwa, "Christianity and Nigerian Indigenous Culture," 14.

[13] *Id.*, 13.

[14] *Id.*

slaves from Sierra Leone.[15]

At this time, the North had come under the control of an Islamic Empire, and hence, the spread of Christianity suffered when attempts were made to enter these territories. Unlike in the South, there were political obstacles to evangelize in the North because permission to do so had to be granted by Islamic clerics before any evangelical work could be undertaken.[16] Any evangelization that could occur would require extreme caution.

Though Christianity could not easily permeate this northern society, it was transmitted in other ways. **The spread of Christianity that was impeded by political constraints was made possible through immigration of Southern Christians Nigerians who established churches and schools.**[17] The fact that Catholic schools were operating in this area is not one at all to be underestimated. Father Joseph Shanahan of the Holy Ghost Fathers was convinced that "those who hold the schools hold the country, hold its religion, hold its future." It was the quality of education that attracted the local population into joining the schools, which ultimately led to some of them becoming missionaries and clergy themselves. By 1915, the Holy Ghost Fathers and the Catholic Missionary Society could count almost 20,000 pupils in their tutelage,[18] a significant percentage.

These Christians were laying roots in their new home in the Nigerian North and they were not seeking to leave, becoming a

---

[15] Sadiq, 654.

[16] Aguwa, "Christianity and Nigerian Indigenous Culture," 13.

[17] Sodiq, 647.

[18] "Catholic Humanitarian Aid and the NigeriaBiafra Civil War," in *Religion, History, And Politics in Nigeria*, 160.

steady fixture of Christianity in a region that until this point had no traces of it other than passersby. This period, from the introduction to Christianity to Nigeria up until Nigerian independence, beginning in 1960, is marked mostly by peaceful relations.

Christian Missionary education would continue to thrive in the east for decades, but soon, a new challenge began to arise. The tiny region had far more educated workers than jobs, and by the 1960s, approximately 1.5 million administrative and technical jobs in the Northern Province went to largely Christian-educated Igbos, a point that greatly upset their Muslim counterparts.[19] This dispute, though more centered on resources than religion, enflamed the already sensitive situation. By the time of the war of independence, the field was ripe for Christian-Muslim conflict.

POST INDEPENDENCE TO PRESENT DAY

A change in governmental regime meant a change from the status quo. Christians pressed for the separation of the state from the church, while Muslims insisted on the application of Islamic law.[20] Jealousy and hatred toward the educationally and technically advanced Igbo[21] led to the crimes of September 29, 1966, when thousands of Igbo men, women, and children were killed. Estimates of the number of deaths due to violence at the time range from 5,000

---

[19] *Id.*

[20] Sodiq, Yushau. "Can Muslims and Christians Live Together Peacefully in Nigeria? *Sodiq, Yushau Muslim World* 99, no. 4 (2009) 647.

[21] "Catholic Humanitarian Aid and the NigeriaBiafra Civil War," in *Religion, History, And Politics in Nigeria*, 160.

to 50,000, while the number of refugees ranges from 700,000 to 2,000,000.[22] Even with the considerable violence that had already occurred, hostilities continue to escalate further. By 1980, Islamic revival movements emerged in the face of growing Christianity, but the war was battle was far from over.[23]

Since Nigeria's political climate greatly affects the ability of its Catholics and Christians overall to practice their faith, there can be no discussion of what it means to be a Catholic in Nigeria without referencing the threats that Catholics face. What started in small degrees in the decades following Christianity's arrival in the country was dramatically escalated in the years leading up to war of independence, and has only been worse following it.

After the war for independence began, the new government chose not to impose any religion, however it did allow the freedom for states within Nigeria to adopt the Islamic Sharia law if they so desired.[24] This is indeed the route that many chose to take, and today Sharia law still remains in effect in many provinces. Under the strict imposition of such laws, alcohol was banned, only people with beards would be awarded government contracts, Islam became a required subject in public schools, and men and women were not allowed to travel together on public transportation.[25] The punishment for failure to comply was often as severe as the requirement itself. Violations of law garnered such harsh punishments as public stoning and

---

[22] *Id.*

[23] *Id.,* 164.

[24] "Nigeria, The Catholic Church in," 394.

[25] *Id.*

amputation.[26] Governance by Sharia law principally was confined to predominantly Muslim states. But by early 2000, there was a push to expand Sharia into northern territories with higher Christian populations, such as Kaduna state, leading protest and reprisals, churches and mosques destroyed, and thousands dead.[27]

The daunting challenge posed by the inhibition of political freedoms for Nigerian Catholics is not the only obstacle that they face. A majority of Nigerian families also face the harsh realities that accompany poverty. In their plenary assembly in March of 2012, the Nigerian bishops insisted that "the nation's political leaders have failed to live up to people's expectations" and called for a restructuring of the economy to meet people's needs.[28] Basic human needs inherent to survival are not being universally met and it causes a great strain to the Nigerian Church. There is an ancient Igbo saying based upon this predicament that "you can not sing Alleluia on an empty stomach."[29] Church ministers that do not address the needs of the people is not one that stays relevant. Igbos will always welcome a Gospel that addresses their suffering in the current Nigerian economic order, a Gospel that extols the positive beliefs and practices of our ancestors.[30]

Some in Nigeria, and in Africa as a whole, view traditional Christian denominations, such as Roman Catholicism and

---

[26] *Id.*

[27] *Id.*

[28] "Signs of the Times," *America* (29 March 2004), available at http://americamagazine.org/issue/479/news/signs-times.

[29] Heille, 53.

[30] Heille, 54.

Anglicanism to be representative of colonialism, and therefore contrary to the plight of the native African. In the village as well as in the towns, one aspect of this type of Christianity is that it is superficial, blended with western culture and materialism and still estranged to the depths of African societies.[31] This view challenges Catholics to demonstrate the authenticity Catholicism truly offers to the Nigerian. Since the 1960s, the development of African theology has become evident and has gained great momentum.[32] In the succeeding decades, the African Church has adapted greatly in its application of Christianity to the challenges unique to Nigerians. This theology attempts to understand and interpret the Christian faith according to the Bible and within the total African context, taking into consideration both Nigerian cultural heritage and Nigeria's contemporary situation.[33]

To undertake the enormous task of guiding this evolution in theology, experts in the field of theology must be encouraged and promoted. While this area also has witnessed tremendous growth and output, it does not come without a cost. The education and formation of scholars and theologians place some financial strain on the Church in Nigeria. The Catholic Church in Nigeria lacks the funds to accommodate its large number of seminarians. There is a shortage of qualified personnel and money for training.[34] African

---

[31] [John] Mbiti, 232.

[32] Mbiti, 226.

[33] Mbiti, 226.

[34] "Nigerian Cardinal: Spiritually Hungry World Needs Holy Priests," Christian Telegraph, *available at* http://www.christiantelegraph.com/issue10926.html (last visited 7 Sept. 2015).

prelates have sought financial help from abroad without success, despite the fact that educating seminarians in Nigeria is relatively inexpensive (just $1,000 per year).[35] While many foreign donors eagerly provide funds to relieve physical poverty, few are willing to fund provision of spiritual needs.

In addition to religious strife in the northern states and poverty, health is a great concern. The death toll resulting from the spread of AIDS within Nigeria's population remains high. In addition, the overabundance of abortions and contraception present significant challenges.[36] Women in particular are bombarded with condoms and all forms of abortifacients under the guise of "liberation."[37] Governmental religious persecution, economic struggles both in society at large and in the formation of priests, as well as the threat posed by abortion and contraceptives are the primary challenges faced by Nigerian Catholics today.

TERRORISM

The Islamic terrorist group Boko Haram has murdered more than 2,800 people in Nigeria since they began attacks in 2009, according to Human Rights Watch.[38] The group's standing list of

---

[35] *Id.*

[36] "Nigeria, The Catholic Church in," 394.

[37] Catholic anchor

[38] Mike Pflanz, "Nigerian Catholic Church Hit in Suicide Attack," *Telegraph* (28 Oct. 2012), *available at* http://www.telegraph.co.uk/news/worldnews/africaandindianocean/nigeria/9639071/Nigerian-Catholic-church-hit-in-suicide-attack.html.

demands includes implementing Sharia law in all of Nigeria. Nigeria's main Christian body has said the attacks on churches suggest a "systematic religious cleansing."[39] Boko Haram deliberately attacks churches at opportune moments, such as during services and on holidays.

The terrorist threat of Boko Haram will not be resolved over night or without the support of the rest of the world. In the United States, Nigerian Christians have decided to come alongside their brethren in Nigeria, fighting back with the creation of the Christian Association of Nigerian Americans (CANAN)—an organization committed to raising awareness about what its members call "'pre-genocide' conditions in their homeland."[40] If their own government is unwilling or unable to defend these basic human rights, the rest of the world will have to take a greater stand in the coming months and years.

Speaking at the Vatican, Pope Benedict said: "I am following with deep concern the news from Nigeria, where terrorist attacks are continuing, especially against Christians." He urged Nigerians "to cooperate in the construction of a peaceful and reconciled society in

---

[39] Human Rights Watch, "Nigeria: Boko Haram Attacks Likely Crimes Against Humanity

Security Force Abuses Help Fuel Spiraling Violence" (11 Oct. 2012), *available at* https://www.hrw.org/news/2012/10/11/nigeria-boko-haram-attacks-likely-crimes-against-humanity.

[40] J.C. Derrick, "Standing with the Brethren," *World* (15 Dec. 2012), *available at* http://www.worldmag.com/2012/11/standing_with_the_brethren.

which the right to freely express faith is guaranteed."[41]

CULTURE AND SPIRITUALITY

Despite the difficulties stemming from adherence to the faith, Christianity is thriving in the Nigeria. Nigerian Christianity is still relatively young, but the Catholic faith is deeply entrenched now in society, with common devotions as in other parts of the world. It is hard not to see signs of Christian ideals in the service of African Christians, including the large number of African catechists, evangelists, laymen, elders, nuns, deacons, pastors, ministers, priests, bishops, archbishops, and cardinals who make up the formal contingent of the ecclesiastical officials. These at least symbolize the concrete and serious presence of Christianity in Africa and its acceptance by African peoples.[42] The number of Nigerian Christians supporting the work of the Church affirms the lasting impact Christianity will have in the country.

Values of Nigerian culture are comfortably expressed in the Nigerian Christian experience. Even in the face of religious violence, the fabric of Nigerian society elevates the role of community, kinship, and harmony. Nigerian cultural preference for the community's well being and the trade routes linking the northern and southern towns are two areas that help bring Muslims and Christians together.

---

[41] "Nigeria Violence: Pope Benedict XVI Calls for Peace," *BBC News* (20 June 2012), *available at* bbc http://www.bbc.co.uk/news/world-africa-18517418.

[42] Mbiti, 233.

> It can be said of the various ethnic Nigerian cultures,
> that they nurture social, economic, political, linguistic,
> and religious institutions with great bias for
> promoting life, security and harmony among human
> beings, as well as peace with the gods.... The Nigerian
> society is the course of key cultural values.... It all
> begins in the family of kins which provides the
> individual a firm and indispensable anchor. The idea
> of community, village or town – *umuna* (Igbo) or *ilu*
> (Yoruba) is based on the kinship system.[43]

In contrast with the individual-centric focus of U.S. culture, African societies tend to place primary focus on the benefit of the community. The community is highly prioritized and tends to subsume individual goals and choices.[44] Jude Aguwa notes that, "[t]hese practices are expressions of the deeper understanding of being one's brother or sister's keeper."[45]

In particular, the Igbo culture reflects a profound sense of sacred that existed before its exposure to Christianity. Among the Igbo people there is a distinct recognition of a Supreme Being—beneficent in character—who is above every other spirit, good or evil. He is believed to control all things in heaven and on earth, and dispenses rewards and punishments according to merit.[46] This reverence of the

---

[43] Jude C. Aguwa, "Christianity and Nigerian Indigenous Culture," in *Religion, History, And Politics in Nigeria*, 15.

[44] *Id.*, 16.

[45] *Id.*

[46] Heille, 46.

Supreme Being made for an easy transition. Considering Christianity and Islam are also communitarian, it is no wonder that these faiths thrive in Nigeria.

Similarly, the Igbo way of defining people in terms of the families to which they belong comports with the Christian idea of the community of saints.[47] The Igbo believe that since ancestors play pivotal role in the lives of their earthly progenies, ancestors are considered "organic members of the community of the living."[48] Veneration is not simply limited to a prayer of thanksgiving for these family members, though this is also part of it, but consists of actual rituals.

> The rituals, both sacrifices and prayers, allow the devotees to obtain purification of ritual defilement arising from broken taboos and other offenses, and to appease the deities and patron spirits in order to ensure their protection against evil spirits. In prayer, for instance, the people accomplish a variety of actions, including begging, thanksgiving, conversing, telling reporting, unburdening the heart by opening up to God, consulting with God, calling on God, or crying out to God. Praying therefore is a constant part of the daily experiences of people.[49]

This ritual and veneration play into the larger values of Nigerian

---

[47] Heille, 50.

[48] Aguwa, "Christianity and Nigerian Indigenous Culture," 17.

[49] *Id.*, 17.

culture, which include long life, many children, good health, and prosperity at work.[50]

POPULAR DEVOTION

Nigerians are very similar to Roman Rite Catholics in America in many ways, one of them being the devotion to the Blessed Virgin Mary. The Rosary in particular occupies a special place in their spirituality, second only to the Holy Mass.[51] As devotion to Mary and the Rosary grew in Nigeria, so did Marian-oriented organizations. The Legion of Mary, the Mary League, and the Christian Mothers Organizations were the primary vehicles for this devotion.[52] On a national level, devotion to Mary is recognized by the country's dedication to our Lady as Queen of Nigeria and by its status as a national feast on the October 1.[53] The government of Nigeria has shown official support of Christianity in other ways as well. Every year, the government gives financial aid to Christians visiting the Holy Land and New Testament sites in Greece and Rome, just as it pays for Muslims to make the "haj," or pilgrimage to Mecca, Saudi Arabia.[54]

---

[50] *Id.*

[51] Chigere, 507.

[52] Aguwa, "Christianity and Nigerian Indigenous Culture," 16.

[53] Chigere, 507.

[54] Cindy Wooden, "In Rome, Nigerians See Social Benefits from Spiritual Pilgrimages," Catholic News Service (24 Sept. 2012), *available at* http://www.catholicnews.com/services/englishnews/2012/in-rome-nigerians-see-social-benefits-from-spiritual-pilgrimages.cfm.

SPIRITUAL LEADERS

The vitality of Christianity in Nigeria is evinced by the quality and the devotion paid to its spiritual leaders. Though relatively young as a Christian nation, Nigeria already has world-renown leaders—primarily Fr Cyprian Michael Iwene Tansi and Cardinal Francis Arinze. It is widely believed that Tansi will be Nigerian's first Catholic saint.[55] Beatified in 1998 by Pope John Paul II, Tansi has been proclaimed as a model of priestly zeal and prayer.[56] If his beatification drew one million people, some walking 50 or 60 miles to the ceremony,[57] one can only imagine how jubilant the Church of Nigeria will be when he is officially canonized.

Cardinal Arinze, the President of the Pontifical Council for Interreligious Dialogue, may be more recognizable within the western world, as he was once believed to be a strong contender for the papacy. According to the *Washington Post*,

---

[55] John Damian Adizie, "Nigerians Celebrate the Feast of Blessed Cyprian Michael Iwene Tansi," *Nigerian Observer* (24 Jan. 2014), *available at*
http://www.nigerianobservernews.com/24012014/24012014/features/featur es4.html#.Ve0EcrTIbFI.

[56] Official Site for the Cause of Canonization of the Servant of God Blessed Cyprian Michael Tansi, Biography of Blessed Tansi, http://blessedtansi.com/html/blessedtansi_biography.html (last visited 6 Sept. 2015).

[57] "The Pope in Nigeria," *Economist* (26 May 1998), *available at* http://www.economist.com/node/158866.

The church leadership became more Nigerian with the rise of Tansi and, later, Arinze, who was born to the Ibo faith and converted to Catholicism at age 9. He became archbishop in 1967, at the start of the war in the state of Biafra, in which the Ibo and other southeastern tribes sought independence from an authoritarian government. After the end of that war in 1970, the victorious federal government expelled the foreign-born priests for supposedly supporting the rebel cause.[58]

Cardinal Arinze provides the overall Church with important lessons on how to deal with others from different faiths, because he has seen firsthand the destructive effects of religious conflict. In the words of Fr. Matthew Hassan Kukah, secretary-general of the Catholic Bishops' Conference of Nigeria, Arinze has especially "helped to soften the Catholic church's approach to Islam."[59] In his view, Muslims and Christians should stop the specter of religious violence and engage n interreligious relations and solidarity to foster justice and peace in areas of ecology, promotion of the concern of the

---

[58] Craig Timberg, "Nigeria's Spiritual Rainmaker Is Eyed at Vatican: Old-Line Papal Candidate Fostered Church's Growth" (17 Apr. 2005), *available at* http://www.washingtonpost.com/wp-dyn/articles/A59514-2005Apr16.html.

[59] Patricia Lefevre, "For Muslims and Christians, Survival Depends on Dialogue," *National Catholic Reporter* (10 May 1996), 5.

women and education of youth.[60] These adjustments in society would reap tremendous benefits if only both sides are willing to engage in this positive way.

OUTLOOK

One journalist asks, "Can Nigeria's millions of Christians, living side by side with an almost equal number of Muslims, effect harmonious interfaith relations that will be a model for the rest of the world?" That question may not be answered for years. Bishop Sunday Mbang, head of the Methodist church in Nigeria, says "there is no alternative to dialogue and that dialogue is crucial if both religions are to survive."[61]

Nigerian spiritual leader, Archbishop of Jos, Most Rev. Ignatius Kaigama, stressed "the importance of reconciliation and forgiveness in totality as a prelude to everlasting peace and peaceful coexistence."[62] The future road is uncertain if amends are not made and true forgiveness is not granted. Without these elements, any dialogue will bear no fruit. The Archbishop also advocated for a public confession and apology for all the atrocities of the country

---

[60] Interreligious Relations and Solidarity: Contextualizing the Vision of Francis Cardinal Arinze for Religious Education in Nigera, Matthew C. Ugwoji, Fordham University Dissertation, 2008.

[61] Lefevre, "For Muslims and Christians, Survival," 5.

[62] Catholic Bishops' Conference of Nigeria, "Catholic Bishops, Faithful Publicly Pray and Seek Forgiveness for Sins of Civil War and Other Atrocities Against Humanity in Nigeria," *available at* http://www.cbcn-ng.org/newsdetail.php?tab=115 (last visited 6 Sept. 2015).

which have resulted in the deaths of many innocent Nigerians, as a result of tribal, ethnic, religious and political crises, particularly since the time of the Nigerian Civil War, which officially came to an end in 1971." On this point, the Catholic Bishops Conference President is in full agreement.[63]

These aspirations may seem futile to some, but all is not bleak. Violence is occurring against Christians, but the view of Christians as a weak minority on the verge of extinction in Nigeria is a false one. Another positive side effect of the devastating reality of war is the increase in vocations to the priesthood. "With the departure of the missionaries and the end of the civil war, priestly vocations 'mysteriously shot up,' Anthony Olubunmi Cardinal Okogie, Archbishop Emeritus of Lagos explained, observing: 'It is said that the blood of martyrs is the seed of Christians."[64] Even as war and Protestantism slow priestly vocations elsewhere in Africa, Nigerian seminaries are "bursting at the seams."[65]

"In the beginning, the Europeans and Americans brought the faith to us," Cardinal Okogie said. "Now in our time of plenty and their own lean time, we are returning the favor. It is a debt that we owe and we intend to continue to pay as long as the Lord continues to bless us with vocations and our services as sought by those who need it."[66] This increase in priests from Nigeria is a blessing to the greater church, as they are sent to carry out their vocation on foreign shores. The vocations "boom," Cardinal Okogie said "is a moment of

---

[63] *Id.*

[64] "Nigerian Cardinal: Spiritually Hungry World Needs Holy Priests."

[65] *Id.*

[66] *Id.*

grace that we must seize and use to maximum effect for the benefit of the church in Nigeria and beyond."[67]

Steady growth, theological development, cultural assimilation, demonstrations of Christian unity, and strong leadership are all positive attributes of the Nigerian Church. The way forward will surely not be easy, but it is one that promises to bear much fruit.

---

[67] *Id.*

Philippines

DEMOGRAPHICS

Among neighboring countries in Asia, the island nation of the Philippines stands apart for its high Catholic population. According to the Conference of Catholic Bishops of the Philippines, this country boasts the third highest national figures of Catholics in the world, after Brazil and Mexico.[1] With so many Catholic constituents (82%), there is not a question that the influence of Christianity and the Catholic Church is strong, from politics to culture to society at large.

Other religious affiliations include: various Protestant (5.4%), Islam (4.6%) Philippine Independent Church (2.6%) *Iglesia ni Kristo* (Church of Christ) (2.3%) and others (2.2%), as of 2005.[2] Though these last two groups are considered independent Christian communities, with followers roughly equal to Protestant denominations, they stand out on their own. It is commonly held that these two independent churches were established as a result of differences with the Roman Catholic Church,[3] sharing some similarities, but with key stark differences. These groups have seen

---

[1] Bishop Gilbert Garcia, The Missionary Challenge of the Philippines, *available at* https://youtu.be/VZTy6SRCjPU (CBCP Media Office, June 2007).

[2] Patricio N. Abinales & Donna J. Amoroso, *State and Society in the Philippines* (Lanham, MD: Rowman & Littlefield, 2005), 12.

[3] *Id.*

growth in recent decades, along with evangelical Protestant churches, but the overwhelming majority remains Catholic.

HISTORY

For a region of the world that has seen considerably few Christians, such a dominantly Catholic nation might be considered quite the anomaly. Apart from the small nation of East Timor, the Philippines is the only Christian nation in Asia.[4] The history of how this reality came to be began in the 16th century with the Spanish expeditions. "Although the Portuguese explorer Ferdinand Magellan (c.1480-1521) raised a cross at Cebu when he landed with the first Spanish expedition in 1521, the conversion of the Filipinos did not begin until 1565, when Miguel Lopez de Legaspi conquered the Philippine Archipelago for the Spanish crown."[5] These moments set the course that the nation would continue upon for centuries to come, altering all aspects of Filipino life. To practice one's faith in Christianity became main component of what it meant to be a good citizen.

In the Philippines under Spanish rule the state and the Catholic Church were closely interconnected. With that said, the development of the faith has to be discussed in light of the Spanish rule. The important role of the church originated from an exclusively Spanish

---

[4] *World and Its Peoples: Malaysia, Singapore, Brunei, and the Philippines* (Tarrytown, NY: Marshall Cavendish, 2008), 1256.

[5] *Id.*

institution, *the patronato real*, or the royal patronage,[6] whereby the pope had granted to the Spanish kings the permission to spread the Catholic faith among the native peoples, to support the church financially, and the privilege of appointing suitable personages in ecclesiastical positions.[7] From the arrival of Christianity, the state established a clear relationship with the Church that would serve as a background for events in years to come. Religious orders also settled in the Philippines before long. Accompanying the first groups of conquistadors were members of the main religious orders: the Augustinians, Franciscans, Jesuits, Dominicans, and Recollects.[8] These groups, among others, have established roots in Filipino society where they have thrived.

As a result of state policies that were sympathetic to the Catholic Church and other factors, conversions were numerous and grew by significant measure. Though some may argue that some of these changes were against the will of an oppressed people, there were elements inherent in Filipino culture that made for a particular openness to receive the faith. Many aspects of Catholicism, such as holy water and the veneration of saints, appealed to the Filipinos, though prominent example also had a degree of influence, with the conversion of the native elite encouraging their followers to accept Christianity.[9] Whatever the reason that drew an individual to the Church, it is incontestable that the Church grew quickly and surely.

---

[6] Ooi Keat Gin (ed.), *Southeast Asia: A Historical Encyclopedia, from Angkor Wat to East Timor* (Santa Barbara, CA: ABC-CLIO, 2004), 1077.

[7] *Id.*

[8] *Id.*

[9] *Id.*, 1129.

As Filipinos fought for national independence, instead of abandoning the religion of their colonizers, their Catholic identity remained a strong facet of Filipino culture. Dr. Jose Rizal, national hero during the time of independence from Spain, is considered "the first Filipino" and stands out foremost in the nation's history. Rizal had a revolutionary spirit with a Catholic sensibility who strove to create a secular, national community.[10] Jose Rizal was a patriot, poet, novelist, scholar and artist. Through his writings he galvanized the Filipino people into a nation that resisted continued colonization by Spain, although he himself emphasized the difficult tasks of preparation and education, the essential conditions, as he saw them, for personal freedom and national independence.[11] It is by the example of those such as Dr. Jose Rizal, that the Philippine identity has been refined and enhanced, and this identity is a solidly Catholic one.

CHURCH ORGANIZATION

Through decades of growth and popular leadership, the Catholic Church became the institution it is today in the Philippines. In Manila alone there are over 1,700 Catholic parishes, perhaps one of the densest concentrations in the world.[12] Influence is due to size of

---

[10] John Nery, *Revolutionary Spirit: Jose Rizal in Southeast Asia* (Singapore: Institute of Southeast Asian Studies, 2011), xviii.

[11] *Id.*

[12] Rodolfo Severino & Lorraine Carlos Salazar (eds), *Whither the Philippines in the 21st Century?* (Singapore: Institute of Southeast Asian Studies, 2007), 104.

the populace, but the Catholic Church also controls several organizations and satellite groups. through its mainstream organizations. According to Rodolfo Severino,

> Two of the most prominent Church-controlled organizations that have been historically politically influential are the Catholic Bishops Conference of the Philippines (CBCP) and the Association of Major Religious Superiors in the Philippines (AMRSP). These two are viewed as "critical observers" of Philippines politics. The Catholic Church opinion is voiced through the position statements and pastoral letters issued by the CBCP and AMRSP on a wide range of issues—human rights violations, population policy, land disputes, constitutional change, environmental degradation—that are disseminated directly to the faithful mostly through Sunday homilies.[13]

CBCP includes over 80 ecclesiastical jurisdictions, including 16 archdiocese, 56 diocese, 7 vicariates, 5 prelatures, and 1 military ordinariate. AMRSP represents 195 Catholic congregations for religious women and 93 for men, the more prominent being the Dominicans, the Franciscans, the Benedictines, the Jesuits, the Augustinians, the Salesians, the Lasallians and the Marists.[14]

The size of the body also helps to sustain its force. An immense

---

[13] *Id.,* 105.

[14] *Id.,* 106.

number of parishes, schools, charity networks, media as tools to enable the Church to reach out to its members in every barrio and town of the Philippines.[15] According to Severino,

> Given its pervasiveness in everyday Filipino life, the Catholic Church has consistently earned the trust of Filipinos relative to other institutions. A nationwide survey conducted in 1998 revealed that Filipinos expressed greater confidence in both the church and the schools that in political institutions like the courts and Congress. It is no surprise then that Filipinos have continued to look to the Church for moral guidance and credibility on a wide range of issues.[16]

The prominence of the Church has touched all aspects of life. Politically, initiatives that oppose Church teaching historically do not fare well. This statement has long been true for Filipinos, however, recently in late 2012 and early 2013 controversial political measures that affect family life have grown in popularity and even earned the approval of the government.

SPIRITUALITY AND CULTURE

As discussed, the Filipino culture was already predisposed to accepting a rich Catholicism with related traditions shared with their pre-Christian roots. That is not to say liturgical expression in the

---

[15] *Id.*, 104.

[16] *Id.*, 104–05.

Philippines matches that which is found in Rome or New York City. Catholicism in the Philippines contains similarities, but also some distinctions. According to a Catholic Encyclopedia, "From the start Filipinos nurtured their own brand of Catholicism."[17] While it is understandable that when two cultures meet that neither one completely absorbs the other, there is a significant residual trace of tribal customs that preceded Philippine Christianity. One guide to the Philippines notes that,

> Elements of tribal belief absorbed into Catholicism have resulted in a form of "folk Catholicism" that manifests itself in various homespun observances—a folk healer might use Catholic liturgy mixed with native rituals, or suited entrepreneurs might be seen scattering rice around their premises to ensure their ventures are profitable. And the infamous reenactments of the Crucifixion held near San Fermando, Pampanga, every year are frowned upon by the official church. Even the Chinese minority has been influential in colouring Filipino Catholicism with the beliefs and practices of Buddhism, Confucianism and Taoism; many Catholic Filipinos believe in the balance of *yin* and *yang*, and that time is cyclical in nature.[18]

---

[17] Frank K. Flinn, "Philippines," *Encyclopedia of World Religions: Encyclopedia of Catholicism* (New York: Facts On File, 2007), 69.

[18] David Dalton & Stephen Keeling, *The Rough Guide to the Philippines*, 3rd ed. (Rough Guides, 2011), 436.

With the introduction of a religion in a new country, it is no surprise that many traditional practices continue to take place, particularly in more rural areas. The challenge for the clergy has been to find an appropriate expression of these dearly held practices and if this is not possible, then they are prohibited. One such example in the Philippines might be the figure of the female priestess. While there are still women "priestesses" in the Philippines, they are outside of the Church. The Roman Catholic Church seeks to reinvigorate more orthodox beliefs and practices among the rural poor but suffers a shortage of priests.[19] In the countryside it is more difficult to have the broadest reach and as a result there is more room for these types of difficulties. This point is one that is commonly made in criticism of the Catholic faith in the Philippines. Despite these facts, Mass attendance is considered the norm, which is not always true for Western Catholic societies.

With differences such as these, it may seem to the outsider that there is not much in common with the Filipino Catholic, however, that is far from the truth. The devotions found in Manila, for example, could be just as easily discovered on the streets of Los Angeles. Filipinos enjoy religious fiestas, processions, and devotion to the saints, especially the Santo Niño, or the Christ Child. Likewise they treasure sacramentals such as relics, the use of holy water, and the wearing of medals.[20] This description is one that could depict Catholics of practically any nation, a reflection of the universality of the Catholic Church.

---

[19] *World and Its Peoples*, 1256.

[20] Flinn, 69.

Among all of these cultural treasures, the *fiesta* stands out as a day of communitarian solidarity. Celebrated on the special day of the patron saint of a town or *barangay*, the fiesta is a time for general feasting. The fiesta always includes a Mass, and the biggest events include a parade, dance, basketball tournament, cockfights, and other contests, and perhaps a carnival, in addition to visiting and feasting.[21] The priority of community building is an admirable one, with love and service of neighbor in the forefront.

Lent and Christmas are manifested in rich expression in the Philippines as in other countries. During the Lenten season, most communities do a reading of the Passion narrative and a performance of a popular Passion play. [22] The celebration of Christmas is also steeped in tradition. The *Simbang Gabi* is a prominent during Advent. This tradition includes nine-day Masses in honor of the Blessed Virgin Mary and in preparation for the commemoration of the birth of our Savior.[23] Christmas in the Philippines is not too different from Christmas in the United States. Filipino Catholic families decorate their homes for Christmas with colorful lights, garlands and native décor, and even oftentimes Christmas trees. But the most important reminder of this season is the "Belen" (Creche), which is placed in a prominent place in the

---

[21] *Philippines: Country Study Guide* (Washington, DC: International Business Publications, 2011), 103.

[22] *Id.*, 104.

[23] Diocese of Pasig, Pastoral Notes on the Celebration of the Simbang Gabi, *available at* http://dioceseofpasig.org/blog/pastoral-notes-on-the-celebration-of-the-simbang-gabi/ (last visited 6 Sept. 2015).

Christian home.[24] Another similarity, particularly with Hispanic-Americans is the *noche buena* tradition of a big family feast after attending the Mass on Christmas Eve.

POPULAR ORGANIZATIONS

Following Vatican II, there was a growth in non-government organizations, people's organizations and other movements.[25] Many in the church perceived Vatican II as an opportunity for change, a call that particularly resounded in some communities. The past few decades witnessed how Evangelical churches flourished in the country, with the Catholic Charismatic groups showing the most striking growth; two of the biggest of these is *El Shaddai Prayer Movement* and the *Couples for Christ* – together claim to have three million registered members each.[26] With a charisma and style that seem to appeal to the religious imagination of the Filipinos, these movements continue to gain momentum.

The *El Shaddai* movement has figured prominently as one of the most important and significant power blocs in Philippine politics today, particularly during elections.[27] As seen with the historical relationship between the government and the Church, what this organization advocates tends to bear more weight and consideration by policymakers, who realize the reach and pull an organization of its size has in society. The *Couples for Christ* has as its mission a

---

[24] *Id.*

[25] Severino & Salazar, 108.

[26] *Id.*

[27] *Id.*, 109.

commitment to the renewal and strengthening of Christian family life. It is popularly known as *Gawad Kalinga* (to give care), a multi-sectoral partnership project engaged in activities that aim to build integrated, holistic, and sustainable communities starting with depressed areas throughout the Philippines, and to rebuild the nation through faith and patriotism.[28]

POLITICAL

With the sheer size of the Filipino church, the fact that politics are affected by its teachings and directives is not necessarily newsworthy. There are around 2,000 Roman Catholic schools, attended by a total of 1.6 million Filipinos; Church schools have a reputation for providing a high standard of education, and the church also runs a number of universities as well as hospitals and other facilities.[29] The credibility of the Church is enhanced through tradition and faith, but also in a much lesser way, by the success and prestigious reputation of its institutions.

As in other countries, the local Church in the Philippines is managed by a body of clergy, the Conference of Bishops. The permanent council of Catholic Bishops Conference is influential, and the council and head of the church in the Philippines are sometimes accused of meddling in politics by some politicians.[30] The complex history leads to sensitivities surrounding the relationship with Church and state, but despite these objections, the Church maintains

---

[28] *Id.*

[29] *World and Its Peoples*, 1256.

[30] *Id.*

considerable influence in the direction of the nation's laws. Rodolfo Severino writes,

> With its resources, credibility, and renewed awareness combined, the Catholic Church in the Philippines can easily reach out to its members and mobilize them almost instantaneously, when necessary. It has demonstrated this in regime changes—making or unmaking leaders—for the past two decades. It has also used its influence to shape state policies, political opinion, and decisions on matters of national interest.[31]

Just because the Church has the authority to influence does not mean, however, that has unlimited ability granted by the government to intervene. This point remains a controversial one, with many even still criticizing that the Church for its involvements, which led to the Second Plenary Council of the Philippines (PCP-II) in 1991. PCP-II is an important agreement that the church and state were to be considered "autonomous and independent" but the Catholic Church would assume the position of "critical solidarity" vis-à-vis the government, which meant it would continue to judiciously analyze the actions of the state without undermining its power.[32]

This reminder of the independence of the two groups served as an important moment in the relationship, but it also led to the establishment of the Parish Pastoral Council for Responsible voting (PPCRV). This initiative, initially in the Archdiocese of Manila and

---

[31] Severino & Salazar, 111.

[32] *Id.,* 112

immediately after this, in all seventy six Catholic dioceses in the country, was to help the electorate assess the worthiness of the political candidates and conduct voter education campaigns throughout the country in time for the 1992 presidential elections.[33] Educating people on voter education is an area of common ground, and this project seems to be a fruitful product of this relationship. Knowing that the majority of voters are members of religious institutions who attend church gatherings regularly, the Commission on Elections, the government body charged with the responsibility of conducting clear and orderly elections, also asked the church for assistance in disseminating voter education materials.[34] These voting initiatives are still in existence today and the different presentations given number in the thousands.

SPIRITUAL LEADERS

Cardinal Sin is remembered as a Catholic and national hero. Cardinal Jaime Sin (1928-2005), archbishop of Manila for nearly three decades until his retirement in 2003, played a leading role in helping to topple the dictatorship of President Ferdinand Marcos (1917-1989, in office 1965-1986) and the corrupt regime of President Joseph Estrada (born 1937; in office 1998-2001).[35] At a time when reform-minded clergy in other developing countries were targets of assassination, Cardinal Sin tirelessly used his pulpit first as bishop, then archbishop, to attack Mr. Marcos' martial law, corruption and

---

[33] *Id.*

[34] *Id.*

[35] *World and Its Peoples,* 1256.

policies that oppressed the poor.[36] He is fondly remembered for raising the plight of the poor in lesser developed countries in a way that was reverberated to world leaders. His efforts to combat political injustice were also monumental. Under Cardinal Sin and his successor, the influence of the church has shaped many government decisions, for example slowing the introduction of birth control policies.[37] His influence has remained until today when there is ongoing deliberation over these controversial policies and he remains an important figure in resisting immoral laws.

The Philippines is also honored with having two officially recognized Catholic saints. The first is St. Lorenzo Ruiz, who was martyred in the year 1637. Lorenzo Ruiz was a layman who worked as a calligrapher for the Dominican parish of Binondo, Manila.[38] He was persecuted for his beliefs by his Japanese captors and ultimately put to death. After Saint Lorenzo Ruiz, St. Pedro Calungsod was the second Filipino declared a saint by the Roman Catholic Church, on 21st, October 2012. St. Pedro Calungsod, a young catechist who was martryed in 1672 while joining Spanish Jesuit Missionaries in Guam, was canonized to become the country's second saint last October 21[39]

---

[36] Michelle O'Donnell, "Cardinal Jaime Sin, a Campion of the Poor in the Philippines, Is Dead at 76," *New York Times* (21 June 2005), *available at* http://www.nytimes.com/2005/06/21/obituaries/21sin.html

[37] *World and Its Peoples*, 1256.

[38] San Lorenzo Ruiz de Manila Parish, Life Story of St. Lorenzo Ruiz, available at http://sanlorenzoruizparish.webs.com/st-lorenzo-ruiz (last visited 6 Sept. 2015).

[39] "Filipino Catholics Celebrate Saint's Canonization," Inquirer.net (30 Nov. 2012), *available at* http://newsinfo.inquirer.net/315879/filipino-catholics-celebrate-saints-canonization.

His recent canonization was met with overwhelming support and enthusiasm by the Filipino faithful. Nearly a million Filipino Roman Catholics gathered in central Cebu City to celebrate the canonization of the country's second saint, 17th-century teen martyr Pedro Calungsod.[40] President Benigo Aquino III was among those in attendance. As he is a popular figure in Filipino society, Church leaders are using his popularity as an opportunity to preach the Gospel to open hearts. Cardinal Ricardo Vidal urged the faithful to emulate Calungsod's love for Christ and sacrifice for his fellow men.[41]

CHALLENGES AND FUTURE OUTLOOK

The Church in the Philippines has its own struggles to face over the coming years; some of them are deeply rooted in centuries of struggle, and some are more recent. Whether they are as a result of poverty, lack of access to priests, or the type of threats that come from the pen of legislation and the efforts of policymakers, the obstacles are plentiful. The following describes some of these challenges that lie ahead for Filipino Catholics.

The problem of poverty is one that the Philippines shares in common with many other nations, Catholic and non-Catholic. The prevalence of this hardship, however, does not make the suffering any less real for the people of the Philippines in this situation. In the

---

[40] "Throngs of Catholic Devotees Gather for Thanksgiving Mass for New Philippine Saint," Fox News (30 Nov. 2012), *available at* http://www.foxnews.com/world/2012/11/30/throngs-catholic-devotees-gather-for-thanksgiving-mass-for-new-philippine-saint/

[41] *Id.*

Philippines poverty is not only widespread, it has also become intergenerational.[42] If one is born to a poor family, the cycle tends to continue. Poverty also has implications beyond one's own roof, as being poor in the Philippines tends to mean one's actions and opinions will not have a place in the course of governmental action. Some believe it as an injustice that deprives the majority of Filipinos, including its indigenous or religious minorities, from a greater sharing in responsibility and in decision-making about the good the nation should hold and promote in common.[43] The poor of the Philippines face difficulties in managing for their own well-being and having appropriate representation in civil institutions. Fortunately, efforts such as the voters' education initiative seek to reconcile these difficulties. But more is yet to be done.

The poor of the Philippines, many of whom live in the rural countryside, may also have challenges having access to Catholic priests. The CBCP cited in 2004 that there is a serious shortage of priests in the Philippines, and at least 25,000 are needed to serve some 68 million Filipino Catholics.[44] Parish priests are interspersed throughout all of the Philippines, but there are areas where the distance to travel is quite great. Even in the big cities, where there are many priests, there is a shortage because of the demands of

---

[42] Cartagenas, Aloysius Lopez, "Religion and Politics in the Philippines: The Public Role of the Roman Catholic Church in the Democratization of the Filipino Polity, *Political Theology* 11, no. 6 (2010), 848.

[43] *Id.*

[44] Helen Flores, "RP Facing Acute Priest Shortage," *Philippine Star* (13 Apr. 2009), *available at* http://www.philstar.com/news-feature/456848/rp-facing-acute-priest-shortage.

population density. According to the CBCP, the ideal ratio should be one priest per 2,000 parishioners, but in Manila, the ratio is approximately 1 priest to 20,0000 parishioners.[45] In many cases, the parish churches are filled beyond capacity.

Yet others are optimistic in the outlook for future priests and missionary activity in the Western world. Pasig Bishop Mylo Hubert Vergara during the celebration of the 5th Directors for Vocation in the Philippines-National Capital Region, said "Philippines is considered the seedbed of vocation in Asia."[46] He also cites the vocation crisis in Europe and the Americas, saying that the Filipino Church is committed to sending priests to alleviate some of these burdens. "That is why we are sending them missionaries that can help them in strengthening back the vocation that they currently need," Vergara said.

Though the Catholic population is higher in the Philippines than in the U.S., the number of priests per parish is not at all equivalent. In the U.S., the population of Catholics is approximately 66.3 million and there are approximately 38, 964 priests.[47] In the Philippines, the population is roughly 71.5 million[48] yet there are approximately

---

[45] *Id.*

[46] "PHL Has No Crisis in Vocations, Says Bishop," CBCP News (14 Nov. 2012), *available at* http://www.cbcpnews.com/cbcpnews/?p=7798.

[47] Statistics by Country by Catholic Population (17 Nov. 2005), http://www.catholic-hierarchy.org/country/sc1.html.

[48] Republic of the Philippines, Philippine Statistics Authority, 2010 Census of PH, *available at* https://psa.gov.ph/tags/2010-census-ph.

7,406 priests. [49] The difference, however, comes with how many priests are available per parish. In the United States there are 1.6 diocesan priests per parish, and 18 percent of parishes are either administered by a nonresident priest or entrusted to someone who is not a priest.[50] In the Philippines, though there are many people per parish, there are more priests per parish, usually at least 2 priests, including a resident priest. There is also less than 1 percent of their parishes without a resident priest. [51] Further analysis is required for any conclusions to be drawn, but these figures shed some light on the present conditions in these two countries.

Beyond vocations and the availability of priests, there are other challenges the Filipino Church has to face that have developed over the past several decades, with respect to changing attitudes within culture and society. There have been serious threats to moral life in Filipino society, with advances made towards widespread access to contraceptives and abortion. The demand for access to civil divorce is also challenging to family life. Both are battles that are very fresh and ongoing in the Philippines.

After 14 years of long debate about the reproductive rights, a new law was signed by the President in December 2012 that promotes

---

[49] Cardinals: Countries Compared, NationMaster, *available at* http://www.nationmaster.com/graph/rel_cat_tot_pri-religion-catholic-total-priests (last visited 7 Sept. 2015).

[50] Mark Gray, "Facing a Future with Fewer Catholic Priests" (16 June 2010),   *available*   *at* https://www.osv.com/OSVNewsweekly/ByIssue/Article/TabId/735/ArtMI D/13636/ArticleID/4248/Facing-a-future-with-fewer-Catholic-priests.aspx.

[51] *Id.*

contraception and sex education in schools.[52] This law was scheduled to take effect January 2013 and offers contraceptives to even the poorest Filipinos. Opponents of the measure—also known as the reproductive-health, or RH, bill—say it will divide the deeply religious country and pave the way for divorce legislation, which is also opposed by the church.[53] Though the law has been signed and has taken affect, this is surely not the end of the discussion. Church leadership is also taking a stand and mounting a counterattack. Bishop Gabriel Reyes, chairman of the CBCP's Commission on Family and Life has stated, "The constitution states that the government should protect the family and marriage. The RH bill is against the goodness of family and the stability of marriage."[54]

The tide has changed in a dramatic way in the Philippines, but the future promises to hold continued challenges for the Catholic faithful. A divorce measure would further divide the nation and greatly change the social landscape of the country. The Philippines is the only Catholic-majority country besides the Vatican not to allow divorce; however, since the 1970s, shifting social attitudes have spurred other Catholic-majority countries to legalize divorce, including Italy, Ireland, and those in Latin America.[55] With hope, the RH bill being signed does not indicate the forward path that the

---

[52] Rhea Sandique-Carlos, "Philippines Adopts Contraception Law," *Wall Street Journal* (29 Dec. 2012), *available at* http://online.wsj.com/article/SB10001424127887324669104578208891390006944.html.

[53] *Id.*

[54] *Id.*

[55] *Id.*

Philippines will take, but if the trend continues, significant changes are in store for Filipino Catholic Church and persecution may be a natural consequence of these challenges, as has been the case when other countries allow laws that violate the national conscience. Catholics of the Philippines have significant difficulties on the road that lies before them, but with the size of its Catholic population, the strong voice of its moral leaders, its rich history, and the examples of their Saints, there is plenty to believe in.

It is said that a canonization does not come at a chance moment in time. The words of Pope John Paul II at the canonization ceremony of St. Lorenzo Ruiz in 1987 were telling and even perhaps prophetic of the future that was before them as Filipino Catholics. The Holy Father said,

> The Lord gives us saints at the right time and God waited 350 years to give us this saint…It is the heroism which he demonstrated as a lay witness to the faith… which is very important in today's world. The witness of San Lorenzo is the testimony we need of courage without measure to show us that it is possible. Faith and life for Lorenzo was synonymous and inseparable. Life without faith would have been without value…he proved that sanctity and heroism are there for anybody and the final victory is made to size for each one of us.[56]

---

[56] Pope John Paul II, Homily on the Canonization of San Lorenzo Ruiz, *quoted at* San Lorenzo Ruiz de Manila Parish, Life Story of St. Lorenzo Ruiz, http://www.chapelofsanlorenzoruiz.org/life.html (last visited 7 Sept. 2015).

Poland

With estimates ranging from 93 to 98% of the total population, Poland consistently ranks as one of the "most Catholic" countries in the world. Despite growing secularism in the country as it assimilates more and more with the rest of the European continent, Catholics are still the most influential group in the country, with faith-based values pervading all parts of the national discourse from elections to school boards and beyond. Based on one recent estimate, Catholics make up at least 93.5% of the population, Orthodox Christian, 1.3%, non-religious, 4%, and all other (including Jehovah's Witness and Muslim) accounting for the last 1.2%.[1]

By this representation, one might assume that every parish is packed full at every Mass, but these figures are self-described Catholics, and do not take into account how often they attend religious services. When a person in Poland takes up the Catholic affiliation, he/she may be referencing any number of reasons, including the traditional or cultural. For example, Poles often evoke Catholicism to describe who they are, whether "European" or "Western," and who they are not, such as Orthodox/Russian,

---

[1]Pawel Zalecki, "Poland," in *Worldmark Encyclopedia of Religious Practices*, vol. 3, *Countries: M-Z*, ed. Thomas Riggs (Detroit: Gale, 2006), 223–29.

Protestant/German, Jewish, or "Eastern."[2] Their Catholic identity is important when differentiating themselves from others ethnic groups. This difference is particularly meaningful, within the context of the historical partitioning by neighboring nations. While language may tie the Poles to other Slavs, religion gives them a mark of distinction which they are quick to cite whenever lumped together with "Eastern Europe." [3] In this sense, being a Polish Catholic has nationalistic implications as well. In addition to its border on the west with Germany, it is bordered on the north by the Baltic Sea and Russia and on the south by the Czech Republic and Slovakia.[4] Most of the people in the country are Polish, but minorities include Ukrainians, Germans, and Belarusians.[5]

The Catholic Church in Poland is made up of several entities. The largest by far is the Roman Catholic Church, but the other three Catholic rites are the Byzantine-Ukrainian, Byzantine-Slavic, and Armenian. The three are in formal union with Roman Catholic Church.[6]

According to the *Worldmark Encyclopedia of Religious Practices,*

---

[2] Brian Porter, "The Catholic Nation: Religion, Identity, and the Narratives of Polish History, *Slavic and Eastern European Journal* 45, no. 2 (2001), 289.

[3] *Id.*

[4] Zalecki, 223.

[5] *Id.*

[6] *Id.*

The Polish Autocephalous Orthodox Church is the second-largest registered religious group, with about half a million laypersons. Protestantism, the third largest branch of Christianity in Poland, is divided into a dozen or so denominations, including the Augsburg-Evangelical (Lutheran) Church, the United Pentecostal Church, and the Seventh-day Adventist Church. There is a sizeable number of Jehovah's Witnesses in Poland and relatively small numbers of Muslims, Jews, and practitioners of Eastern religions, such as Buddhism and Hinduism.[7]

These ethnically diverse demographics are reflective of a nation that has been at the crossroads between two distinct cultures, historically speaking, "the East" and "the West."

HISTORY

Indisputably, religion has been highly significant in Polish history. The Catholic Church is the largest religious organization in Poland and has been closely connected to both the statehood and culture of the country for more than a thousand years.[8] When Pope John Paul II visited his homeland in 1979, he proclaimed that "without Christ it is impossible to understand the history of Poland"[9] Truly, any reflection on Polish history would be remiss if it did not highlight its Catholic national identity. As one author eloquently

---

[7] *Id.*

[8] *Id.*

[9] Porter, 290.

states, "The formation of Polish culture was produced by a synthesis with Christianity, adopted from the West in the tenth century, the percolation of the renaissance, the enlightenment, and romanticism;' it is almost universally accepted in English as well as polish language texts that Catholicism in Poland is a question of national identity."[10] With more than a millennium of development throughout different movements and types of governance, Christianity has endured many seasons from favorability to persecution. This work is not an exhaustive historical summary, but highlights four periods in particular that were formative for the Polish Church of today, beginning with an early period of the settlement of the Polish state. The three periods that follow are important to Polish Christian history because they saw the greatest institutional threat to religious practice, but with each period of persecution, the Christian community became strengthened.

Early History

An understanding of the deep foundations of Christianity from the nation's inception is important for the context of Polish history. According to one scholar, "The Christianization of Poland began in 966, when the Polish dukes received baptism from the Bohemian monarchy. This enabled the dukes to make connections with Christian rulers and protected the country against German hegemony. The date is widely recognized as the beginning of the Polish state."[11] Though Christianity began to spread in this way, the

---

[10] *Id.*, 289.

[11] Zalecki, 223.

first missionary activity is believed to be as a result of Methodius, the Apostle of the Slavs, in Moravia. [12]

As the faith took root in the country, it began to spread in civil society. The monastic and cathedral schools, which were the vehicles for all education and culture, the cathedral chapters, the development of parish organizations, and the spread of the religious orders, such as the Benedictines, Cistercians, Premonstratensians, Franciscans, Dominicans, Carmelites, Augustinians, Hospitallers, and Templars, all contributed to the solid establishment and growth of Christianity.[13] The Church and the Polish state indeed seemed to grow side-by-side. The creation of state structures was connected with the spread of Christianity and the establishment of an ecclesiastical administrative network in the Polish territories.[14] As the nation grew more and more successful, Christian life flourished. In fact, over time, this relationship would grow to the extent that just being a Catholic Pole was symbolic of national unity.

Partitioned Poland (1795-1918)

By the end of the 18th century, Prussia, Russia, and Austria had partitioned Poland. This division was a hindrance to the ecclesial organization of the Roman Catholic Church there. With this occupation, the Orthodox faith was emphasized by the Russians and

---

[12] B. Stasiewiski & Z. Zielinski, "Poland, The Catholic Church in," *New Catholic Encyclopedia,* 2nd ed., vol. 11 (Detroit: Gale, 2003), 438.

[13] *Id.,* 439.

[14] Churches in Poland, Polish Language Blog (7 Nov. 2014), *available at* http://blogs.transparent.com/polish/churches-in-poland/.

the Protestant faith by Prussian and Austrians. The natural result of this partition led to the promotion of national unity, which included the safeguarding of Roman Catholicism. The Roman Catholic Church emerged as the guardian angel of all things Polish, and from then on, being Catholic meant being Polish.[15] After this period ended, the Republic of Poland regained its status, and the Church started the process of rebuilding.

Second World War (1939-1945)

Before World War II, Catholic Poland was thriving. There were about 2,000 monastic foundations, 1,600 priests, 4,500 lay brothers, and 17,000 sisters.[16] In addition, the numerous pilgrimages to the shrines of the Blessed Virgin at Częstochowa, Piekary, and Ostra Brama in Vilna and the increasing participation in the foreign missions and in religious congresses bore witness to a flourishing religious life.[17] By 1939, however, the realities of the Catholic faithful began to greatly change.

According to the *New Catholic Encyclopedia*, the German-Soviet Pact and the German Polish campaign of September 1939 created a new political situation for the Church.[18] The incorporation of the eastern Polish territory into the Soviet Union entailed the prohibition

---

[15] Jan Puhl, "The Catholic Church in Poland: The Battle for Souls," *Spiegel* (8 Jan. 2007), *available at* http://www.spiegel.de/international/spiegel/the-catholic-church-in-poland-the-battle-for-souls-a-458358.html.

[16] Stasiewiski & Zielinski, 449.

[17] *Id.*

[18] *Id.*

of religious propaganda, persecutions, and deportations of clergy and laity.[19] Spiritual activity was hindered, but it was more than an attack on religion, it was also an attack on Polish customs. The German occupation officials were bent on depriving the Church of being a protective shield for all that was characteristic in Polish life and culture.[20] By the end of the war, the future was once again promising. The threat of persecution was no longer there and one was free and even encouraged to practice one's faith again. There was also an effort to heal the wounds, both material and mental, caused by the atrocities of the war. This brief period of stability would very soon after, however, give way to a new form of threat.

Communist Rule (1945-1989)

Almost as soon as the war ended, a communist contingent proclaimed a provisional government,[21] ushering in a new and important period in Polish history. The first years under this new administration was filled with brutal oppression, but in 1956 reformers in the Communist party put an end to the worst abuses and established an informal truce with the Episcopate on the condition that the clergy would stay out of politics and recognize the

---

[19] *Id.*

[20] *Id.*, 450.

[21] Michael T. Kaufman, "40 Years of Communism in Poland: Stalin's House on a Soft Foundation," *New York Times* (18 Aug. 1989), *available at* http://www.nytimes.com/1989/08/18/world/40-years-of-communism-in-poland-stalin-s-house-on-a-soft-foundation.html.

legitimacy of Communist rule.[22] While this arrangement was an improvement, and a moderate religious life could be maintained with significant limitations, this relative peace was not upheld. On both ends, there were deviations that became increasingly frequent over time. The clergy remained vehemently anti Communist, critical of governmental policies, and Communists created obstacles by means of surveillance of clergy, delaying construction of churches, and publicly undermining bishops.[23] Without the ability of either side to gain the upper hand, both Communists and Church hierarchy lived for some time in an unstable peace

Nevertheless, over time, the Church built up resources and made gains. According to the New Catholic Encyclopedia, In 1965, the Church was seeking to overcome these threats,

> through a concentration of her forces. Her interior development was evidenced by the sound training of numerous seminarians in the major seminaries (4,000 seminarians in 1965); by the further development of the Catholic University of Lublin and of the Catholic Academy in Bielany near Warsaw; by appropriate methods of pastoral care; by the zealous activity of numerous religious orders and congregations; by courageous argumentation against dialectic and practical materialism; by the publication of several theological journals of high standing, as, for example, the

---

[22] Introduction, Catholic Church in Poland, Making the History of 1989, *available at* http://chnm.gmu.edu/1989/exhibits/roman-catholic-church/introduction (last accessed 7 Sept. 2015).

[23] *Id.*

Ateneum kapłańskie (Włocławek), the Collectanea theologica (Warsaw), and the Homo Dei (Warsaw); by cooperation in the Ecumenical Movement; by close contact with Rome as the center of the Church; and by the implementation of the decrees and suggestions of Vatican Council II. There was a flourishing religious life that was evidenced by zealous attendance at divine worship, the reception of the Sacraments, the intense devotion to the Blessed Virgin, and the restoration of old churches and erection of new ones.

By the 1970's, Catholics and Communist dissidents began forming alliances. It became more and more common for dissidents (even non-Catholics) to hold meetings in Church basements, where the state authorities usually would not venture to go.[24] This unlikely relationship was harnessed by popular leaders, which gave the Solidarity Movement its foundation. Many parishes became sanctuaries for a wide variety of anti-Communist activists, and important members of the hierarchy (most famously, Cardinal Karol Wojtyła) began to embrace the rhetoric of "democracy" and "human rights."[25] While the Church made efforts to avoid becoming politicized, the strength of the Church, and therefore, its influence on society was growing.

Despite the suffering and violence, persecution helped to strengthen the Polish Church in the 20th century. One of the landmark movements of recent history was the Solidarity movement that sought to unify opposition to communist governance. The fact

---

[24] Introduction, Catholic Church in Poland.

[25] *Id.*

that this pivotal point in this nation's history highlights the influence of Christianity is telling about the importance attributed to personal faith in Poland. The following is the 1981 proclamation of this movement:

> Because it was Christianity that brought us into our wider motherland, Europe; because for a thousand years Christianity has in a large degree been shaping the content of our culture; since in the most tragic moments of our nation it was the church that was our main support; since our ethics are predominantly Christian, since finally, Catholicism is the living faith of the majority of Poles, we deem it necessary that an honest and comprehensive presentation of the role of the Church in the history of Poland and of the world have an adequate place in national education.[26]

These words helped to swell the tide of popular opinion, ushering forward the ideals of the solidarity movement, which would lead to the fall of communism and with it, the ending of institutional persecution of Christianity in Poland.

On this journey to emancipation, Cardinal Wojtyła becoming elected as Pope in 1978 served as a tremendous milestone. Pope John Paul II staged a eight-day pilgrimage to his homeland that drew in approximately thirteen million people—one third of the entire Polish population.[27] Public events and pilgrimages of this sort would aid

---

[26] Porter, 290

[27] Introduction, Catholic Church in Poland.

tremendously in gaining momentum of solidarity. Under the auspices of these large, faith-filled gatherings, Poles en masse started to become empowered. For the first time, many did not see the barriers of division and oppression. For the first time, many felt free.

The 1980's saw a considerable shift in the direction of religious life, particularly concerning parish functions. This development is seen both in the growth of small groups and religious movements in a parish, in establishing parish councils, and in the parish engagement in local and national activities.[28] As the decade drew to a close, the Church was viewed as the primary venue for anti-Communist activism. Mass attendance too reached new heights. By the end of the '80's, the Communist regime was prepared to make concessions. Bishops were asked to take part in the Round Table Talks of 1989 as mediators, and not party to the debate. [29] These proved successful, with new Communist leadership conceding to the forces of solidarity and democratization, reaching the end of an era.

CHALLENGES

In some ways, the transition from communist control to democratization has been difficult for Poland. The year 1989 brought fundamental social and political changes in East-Central Europe, including the establishment of the Third Polish Republic. Poland, along with other countries, entered on the path of economic and

---

[28] Elżbieta Firlit, "Societal Activity of the Polish Parish—Continuity and Change," *Religious Studies and Theology* 27, no. 1 (2008), 85–113.

[29] Introduction, Catholic Church in Poland.

political development, becoming once more a democratic country.[30] The effects of this process are still being seen, but many continue to speculate about the challenges that remain ahead.

With this type of transition, the role of the Church in society has been regularly examined. *The Worldmark Encyclopedia of Religious Practices* states that

> After the fall of the Communist government in 1989, Poles strongly approved of the church's involvement in sociopolitical matters. In the early 1990s, however, the church began to present political and social pressures and demands. For example, in the parliamentary elections of 1991 the church declared its neutrality, but it soon started its own moral and political campaign. This resulted in a change in social attitudes toward the church.[31]

The big question for Polish intellectuals in the post-communist era is church-state relations: How high and how permeable should the wall between church and state be in Poland?[32] Some Poles do not accept the church's interference in political affairs. Those who defend the church's political involvement, however, view it as a necessary consequence of pulling the church into the realities of social life.[33] Further, they contend that the values on which a successful

---

[30] Marianski, 27

[31] Zalecki, 227.

[32] Steele.

[33] Zalecki, 227

democratic society rests do not come from democracy itself; rather, these values come from traditional sources, and in Poland, those are Christian sources.[34] On the other hand, others hope for a total separation of church and state. This contention is based on the belief that democracy in Europe is founded on moral principles contained in national and international charters that guarantee respect for human rights.[35]

This dialogue has affected the way social issues are perceived. Abortion is perhaps the most heavily contested of issues where faith-based values are used in defense of abortion restriction. Among other European nations, Poland's laws are among the most restrictive. Its current law allows for abortion in three cases: rape, if the mother's health is at grave risk, or if the fetus suffers from a disease or malformation.[36] These would be more rare occurrences.

Popular opinion in opposition to abortion, however, was not always the norm. In fact, during the communist period, access to abortion was easy. After democratized Poland was able to restrict access, there has been a growing number who oppose it, reflecting the influence Catholic values have had since the 1990's. Further, one of Poland's mainstream opinion poll agencies reported that those who viewed abortion as acceptable went down dramatically from 65

---

[34] Steele.

[35] *Id.*

[36] Estefanie Aguirre, "Lawyers Say Poland Shocked over Abortion Fine," Catholic News Agency (5 Nov. 2012), *available at* http://www.catholicnewsagency.com/news/lawyers-say-poland-shocked-over-abortion-fine/.

percent in 1993 to 9 percent in 2011.[37] Poland's staunch pro-life stance exists in stark contrast to most other European Union member nations.

The dwindling religious practice of Poles is also a cause for concern. *Reuters* news service reported, "In this, Poland is following the same pattern as countries like Spain and Italy, which grew less religious as they grew richer. Since 2005 the proportion of Poles who pray every day has fallen from 56 percent to 38 percent, according to pollster CBOS. Though still high by European standards, the numbers who take part in a religious service at least once a week fell over the same period from 58 percent of Poles to 52 percent.[38] This rate is troubling, and shows Poles may one day reach similar levels as its European counterparts. The same report, however, is still optimistic, noting that, "despite the profound changes under way in Polish society, Catholicism still runs deep."[39]

As in the case of abortion rights, there is also a pressure to conform to standards of the European Union. As one observer commented, "The EU pressed to change our strict rules against abortion, euthanasia, birth control and same-sex marriages," he said. "The propaganda is to make Poland modern like the western countries if you would like to be rich and prosperous. They do not mention the authority of Blessed John Paul II or Pope Benedict and

---

[37] *Id.*

[38] Christian Lowe, "Catholicism and Sex Shops: The Struggle for Poland's Soul," Reuters (17 Oct. 2012), *available at* http://www.reuters.com/article/2012/10/17/us-poland-religion-idUSBRE89G09320121017.

[39] *Id.*

their social teaching supporting family and marriage institutions."[40] In a society where there is a diversity of media sources and opinions, it may be that, in the mainstream marketplace, the voice of the faithful is not spoken, much less heard. This is a challenge the Church and lay organizations face, to remain prominent in the public square.

Remaining engaged in discussions, such as the one on abortion, in-vitro fertilization, homosexuality, etc, will help the Church keep a pulse on the nation as society has been transitioning from one values system to another. The repercussions of this transition have the potential to be significant. There are basically two schools of thought about the future of the Church in Poland. According to one change scenario, there will be a rapid decline in the importance of the Church, yet, according to another, the role of the Church will be subject to multi-directional changes, not excluding the possibility of the strengthening of its importance in certain areas of daily life. [41] Clearly the Church is actively seeking to strengthen itself and maximize its influence, but the future direction will be based on elements both within and beyond the direct church control. The Church must determine anew the social role appropriate for it in the new socio-cultural context.[42] Herein lies the challenge for Church leadership.

---

[40] Matysek.

[41] Janusz Marianski, "The Roman Catholic Church in Poland and Civil Society: Contradiction or Complementarity," *Religious Studies and Theology* 27, no. 1 (2008), 30.

[42] *Id.*

CULTURE AND SPIRITUALITY

After the Polish systemic breakthrough of June 1989, a new context has been created that has radically changed how the central microstructure, the parish, functions. [43] This change in turn has helped to emphasize the fullness of Polish Catholic Spirituality. Elżbieta Firlit noted that,

> The number of Catholic associations alone has erupted, manifesting various causes and devotions. Since the beginning of the 1990s there has been a trend towards registration of various Catholic associations working in such areas as culture, politics, economy, social welfare, sports and recreation, prevention and re-socialization as well as many associations within particular professions, e.g. Association of Polish Catholic Pharmacists, Association of Polish Catholic Lawyers, Catholic Association of Polish Doctors....[44]

The Polish Catholic culture that has found its expression in a myriad of ways are all centered on a collection of popular devotions, from feast days to holy sites. Like Catholics in other countries, there is a special regard for major feasts such as Christmas and Easter, as well as the saints and the Blessed Virgin Mary. Unlike other European countries, many of these feasts are also national holidays,

---

[43] Firlit, 85–113.

[44] *Id.*

such as Easter Monday, Corpus Christi, Assumption of the Virgin Mary, All Saints' Day, and Saint Stephen's Day). [45]

Other mainstream Polish population traditions are: sharing of *oplatek* (Christmas wafer), blessing of food in church, blessing of a candle on Candlemas Day and lighting it at the bedside of a dying person, blessing of palms and herbs in church, and taking part in a Corpus Christi procession.[46] In addition, Poles celebrate their "name days" or their "imieniny," which is based upon the calendar of the saints. [47] This celebration is more popular than one's own birthday.

A distinctive characteristic of Polish Catholicism is the devotees' strong attachment to holy sites.[48] At the forefront of holy sites is the Marian shrine of *Jasna Góra*. This shrine is located in the city of Czestochowa in Southern Poland. It is recognized as the spiritual heart of the country and is treated as the national shrine. As one priest, Father Simon Stefanowicz, who serves at the shrine has said, "*Jasna Gora*" or "*Bright Mountain*" stands as a beacon of faith – even in the face of secularization.[49] This shrine is made popular because it houses the holy icon, "*the Black Madonna.*" This icon is a "painting

---

[45] Zalecki, 226.

[46] *Id.*

[47] Philip Earl Steele, "Still the World's Most Catholic Country," CatholicCulture.org, *available* *at* http://www.catholicculture.org/culture/library/view.cfm?recnum=4033 (last visited 7 Sept. 2015).

[48] Zalecki, 226.

[49] George P. Matysek, Jr., "Special Report: Deep-Rooted Polish Faith Faces Secular Challenge," *Catholic Review* [Baltimore] (19 July 2011), *available* *at* http://catholicreview.org/article/life/special-report-deep-rooted-polish-faith-faces-secular-challenge.

of the Madonna and Christ Child which legend states was painted by St. Luke the Evangelist. St. Luke is believed to have used a tabletop from a table built by the carpenter Jesus. It was while Luke was painting Mary that she told him about the events in the life of Jesus that he eventually used in his gospel," according to EWTN Library.[50] It is commonly held belief that this icon miraculously endured many troubled times, still relatively unscathed, from theft to fire. To this day, it is known for having brought forth miracles in the form of healings. *Jasna Gora* is also special because it is there that one may find hanging to the right of the icon, the stole of Pope John Paul II, ripped with bullet holes – worn on the day he survived a 1981 assassination attempt.[51]

Despite the pilgrims, shrines, official feast days, and patron saints, Poland faces the threat of secularism, amidst the richness of its spirituality. While freedom and democracy made possible a degree of practice and expression that was impossible before, there have been new threats that have also arisen. In addition to all of the faith-based associations and groups, over 300 sects moved into Poland and even satanic worshipers. Even the press is shared by negative influence, to include negative and immoral publications criticizing everybody and everything.[52] With the benefits of the availability of faith-based literature, have come the consequences of negative counter messages.

POPULAR LEADERS

---

[50] Bryan J. Walsh, "The Black Madonna of Poland—Our Lady of Czestochowa and Jasna Gora, *available at* http://www.ewtn.com/library/MARY/BLACKMA.htm (last accessed 7 Sept. 2015).

[51] Matysek.

[52] *Id.*

When reflecting upon the popular figures of the Polish Church, many come to mind, but perhaps the most internationally renowned is Pope John Paul II, whose cause for canonization has been cleared just eight years after his death. The *Worldmark Encyclopedia of Religious Practices* comments on his important works, "The archbishop of Kraków, Karol Józef Wojtyla and as pope, continued to apply the decisions of Vatican II and placed special emphasis on Marian devotion. He opposed the imposition of martial law in Poland (1981) and supported—prior to the collapse of Communism—the Solidarity movement, a labor union that was an important element of Polish civic society."[53] Due in part to his influence, Poland was elevated on the world stage in a positive way. In the following years, the church enjoyed huge influence in Poland thanks to John Paul's authority and his role in inspiring the Solidarity movement that helped topple communism in 1989.[54] Beyond Poland, he is beloved by many, particularly young people, who got to know him through the World Youth Day pilgrimages that he started.

Catholics around the world have also been introduced to another Polish saint, Maria Faustina:

> St Faustina's name is forever linked to the annual feast
> of the Divine Mercy (celebrated on the Second Sunday

---

[53] Zalecki, 225.

[54] "Cardinal Jozef Glemp, Longtime Leader of Poland's Roman Catholic Church, Dies at 83," Fox News (23 Jan. 2013), *available at* http://www.foxnews.com/world/2013/01/23/cardinal-jozef-glemp-longtime-leader-poland-roman-catholic-church-dies-at-83/.

of Easter), the divine mercy chaplet and the divine
mercy prayer recited each day by many people at 3
p.m... In addition to carrying out her work faithfully,
generously serving the needs of the sisters and the
local people, she also had a deep interior life. This
included receiving revelations from the Lord Jesus,
messages that she recorded in her diary at the request
of Christ and of her confessors.[55]

St. Maximilian Kolbe is another native Pole who became
internationally well-known, but for other reasons. Having lived
during Nazi persecution, while imprisoned in the Auschwitz
concentration camp, he sacrificially offered his own life in
substitution for that of a father of a family during the Holocaust.
Many clergy were lost during this time, up to 25% of Catholic priests,
as well as many leading laymen.[56] He is honored today in the
universal church along with the many Polish Catholic priests and
laypersons who were lost during this tragic period.

Others who are not as internationally well-known but were
instrumental in the growth and development of the Polish Church
include Cardinal August Hlond (1881-1948) who played a significant
role in creating the framework of a free Polish state, as well as Price
Adam Sapieha (1867-1951),who cooperated with the Polish
government in exile and stood up for persecuted members of society

---

[55] St. Maria Faustina Kowalska, Saint of the Day, *available at*
http://www.americancatholic.org/Features/Saints/saint.aspx?id=1931 (last
accessed 7 Sept. 2015).

[56] Stasiewiski & Zielinski, 450.

during the Communist era.[57] Another bishop who later became cardinal was Stefan Wyszynski.

> Bishop Stefan Wyszynski (1901–81) was nominated primate of Poland in 1948. He was a skillful politician and was able to negotiate with the Communists. Under his administration the church founded seminaries, church courts, charities, sacral buildings, and convents. He was raised to the rank of cardinal in 1952. Wyszynski was imprisoned in 1953, following his condemnation of the Communist government. He was freed in 1956, but relations remained tense.[58]

He is most known for encouraging popular devotion. Firlit notes,

> Wyszynski understood how much these practices meant to the average Pole. Even during Stalin's lifetime, Poles by the millions dared to make pilgrimages to their beloved Jasna Góra. In the year following World War II, for instance, more than four million Poles — a sixth of the population — visited the monastery... The fruits of Wyszynski's wisdom can be seen everywhere in daily Polish life.[59]

Polish religious life would not be what it is today without the sacrificial works of these men and women.

---

[57] Zalecki, 225.

[58] *Id.*

[59] Steele.

Religious Life and Seminaries

As parish life has grown since 1989, so have the number of parishes and the scope of the parish priest. As of 2005, there were 10, 163 parishes, compared with 8,905 at fall of communism.[60] Of these parishes, the majority are in the countryside. Relatively, the biggest number of parishes is rural, next city parishes and country town-rural parishes follow, 64.5%, 20.5% and 15.0% respectively.[61]

The parish priests play a key role in the parish in Poland. The importance of their position can be seen not only in the way the parish is managed and basic religious functions are performed, but also in animating and realizing social activities of the parish. Based on the data published by the Holy See (April 26, 2006) on account of the May pilgrimage to Poland of Pope Benedict XVI, 28,546 priests worked in Roman Catholic parishes in Poland.[62] Therefore, on average there are around three priests per parish (2.8).[63]

Despite the increase in the number of parishes, there are fewer priests and fewer people going to Mass. "Much, much more people used to go to church and attend Mass during the Communist time," said Marta Reimfuss, a parishioner of Ss. Peter and Paul in Krakow and an English-speaking tour guide. "They were praying for independence – for freedom. I must admit that it's changed because we have more and more freedom, so we can decide if we go to church

---

[60] Firlit, 85–113.

[61] *Id.*

[62] *Id.*

[63] *Id.*

or not."[64] In a time when the church helped unite the Polish faithful against a common enemy, Mass attendance was at an all-time high.

The effects of secularism have also taken a toll on Polish priestly vocations in recent years. In 2009 for the first time, the number of students in the country's diocesan seminaries dipped below 4,000.[65] This figure is disconcerting, but overall, the number of priests per parish is still higher than other countries. Although there had been 32 fewer seminarians beginning first year formation in diocesan seminaries in 2009 as had in 2008, by contrast, the *U.S. Conference of Catholic Bishops* reports 5,247 seminarians in the United States, but the total US population is eight times as large as Poland's 38.1 million.[66] In other words, there may have been fewer seminarians, but there are still a decent number of seminarians based upon the total population. Similarly, the number of women joining religious communities has also dropped. In 2009, a year when 28 convents closed, 300 women entered pre-novitiate programs – down from 723 a decade ago.[67]

Despite these statistics, there are signs of thriving religious life all around. Even the Churches of Krakow are a testament to beauty of religious life even in the aftermath of persecution. The baroque splendors of many of Krakow's churches survived the destruction of war, and several of them are easily equal to the churches of Rome.[68]

---

[64] Matysek.

[65] *Id.*

[66] *Id.*

[67] *Id.*

[68] Alexander Lucie-Smith, "Poland Is Still the Land of the Blessed," *Catholic Herald* (5 July 2012), *available at* http://www.catholicherald.co.uk/

Poles also show signs of still being greatly influenced by the example of Pope John Paul II. Papal statues and banners can be found in big cities and small towns, and there's even a memorial plaque high in the Tatra Mountains, where the pope loved to ski as a young man.[69] As one hopeful Polish priest reflects,

> Just as the pope helped inspire the Solidarity movement and emboldened the faith of the Polish people with his call to 'be not afraid,' he continues to inspire today. Father Stefanowicz said that's especially true for young people. They give the priest hope for the future. Many young people come to the church and to the sacraments," he said. "They like to participate in walking pilgrimages and all kind of religious retreats and spiritual oases following the example of Blessed John Paul II.[70]

Poles for generations to come will surely be blessed by the treasures of Polish Christianity, from the devotion to Pope John Paul II and other great saints and leaders, to the sacred religious traditions upon which the nation was founded and has further developed and strengthened throughout the centuries.

FUTURE OUTLOOK

---

commentandblogs/2012/07/05/poland-is-still-the-land-of-blessed-john-paul-ii/.

[69] *Id.*

[70] *Id.*

Amidst the challenges, the Church in Poland shows no signs of diminishing its resolve to challenge all Poles to be committed to the Gospel message and the sacraments of the Church. The following encompass some major values that the Church wishes to protect:

> the dignity of the human person, the sacredness of human life, the central role of the marriage-based family, the importance of education, legal protection of individuals and groups, co-operation of all for the benefit of the common good, work understood as a personal and social good, political power conceived of as service subordinated to reason, law and human rights, and a vision of social and community relations based on authentic culture and the ethics of solidarity.[71]

These goals reflect Church priorities in light of present-day societal struggles. Yet, despite its aspirations and resolute dedication to stay relevant, some who may have a more pessimistic view might consider the Catholic Church to be disconnected and outdated. With the levels of those who are practicing Catholics dwindling in recent decades after the fall of communism, one might, after all, find reason to be discouraged.

Further, many who follow the plight of the Polish Church wonder how the nation will resist following in the footsteps of fellow developed European nations. Leading elements within the clergy, as well as broad segments of Poland's laity, however, would like to believe that Poland is poised to enter Europe as an example of

---

[71] Marianski, 27.

Christianity's vitality and viability in an otherwise postmodern, post-Christian culture.[72] This, however, remains uncertain.

Even in the face of disconcerting signs, there is still cause for optimism. Rather than considering the Catholic Church as irrelevant today in the wake of a growing economy and societal influences and pressures, there is good reason to believe that it is not the case. The parish has become an area where the old and the new social order, tradition and modernity, the need to adapt to changing conditions and the need to preserve its basic, fundamental functions meet.[73] Instead of being the area where there are divisions, it is more so considered to be an area of common ground.

As Warsaw professor and author, Philip Earl Steele commented, "No doubt millions in Poland would be inclined to agree with Rev. Dariusz Oko, who recently remarked that 'despite all, the Church is still the most beautiful, the most healthy, and the most idealistic thing we have.' One might add that it's also the most Polish thing they have."[74] In a similar vein, as one Polish priest noted, "After all, the Catholic Church has been a fixture in Poland since 966, producing more than 156 saints and blesseds. It's not going away. We are and will continue to be victorious in Christian tradition and heritage." [75] May voices of hope and reason, such as these, prevail.

---

[72] Steele.

[73] Firlit

[74] Steele.

[75] Matysek.

Vietnam

INTRODUCTION

Christianity in Vietnam has seen both substantial set-backs and tremendous growth in its nearly 500 years of history. Despite political setbacks and the effects of communist control, the Catholic Church continues to grow and Vietnam is considered the 3rd largest Catholic representation in all of Asia. Beyond Vietnamese borders, the United States also has a significant Vietnamese Catholic contingent and many Vietnamese priests now call America home and serve American communities. These ethnic Vietnamese communities are thriving in a land where many of them have experienced religious freedom for the first time in their lives. But amidst this gratefulness, there is a bittersweet remembrance of the harsh realities of Christian life in their home country, where many faithful continue to experience persecution and discrimination, despite improvements in recent decades.

DEMOGRAPHICS

Extending south from China in a long, narrow S-curve, Vietnam is a tropical country occupying the east coast of the

Indochinese Peninsula. [1]Vietnam is a mixture of cultures from surrounding indigenous communities from the North and islands from the South that migrated into the land over the course of generations. The largest group is the ethnic Vietnamese (*Kinh*), who comprise over 85 percent of the population.[2] Today these people constitute the bulk of the Vietnamese population, with Chinese, Cambodians, and Montagnards being the largest minority groups.[3] For several centuries China governed the region, and as such, Chinese culture and religion strongly influenced the Vietnamese throughout this period. Today the trace of these Chinese ties is still evident with respect to Vietnamese culture.

Vietnam also has the third-largest population in Southeast Asia, with 84.4 million citizens,[4] the majority of whom live in the countryside. Of these approximate 84 million citizens, a minority of them are Catholic, but the exact total estimate is a subject of dispute. The government places Roman Catholics at around 5.3 million, while Catholic leaders go as high as 8 million, which would be nearly 10 percent of the population.[5] In a communist nation that has not been

---

[1] *Roland Bruce St John, "Vietnam," in Worldmark Encyclopedia of Religious Practices, vol. 3, Countries: M–Z, ed. Thomas Riggs (Detroit: Gale, 2006), 562.*

[2] "Vietnam," in *Countries and Their Cultures*, vol. 4, ed. Carol R. Ember & Melvin Ember (New York: Macmillan Reference USA, 2001), 2415.

[3] St John, "Vietnam," 562.

[4] Mark Galli, "A New Day in Vietnam: How a Little NGO Is Helping Christians Gain More Freedom in a Country Still Plagued by Human Rights Abuses," *Christianity Today* 51, no. 5 (May 2007), 27.

[5] *Id.*, 29.

consistently fair or just to its Christian constituents, it is understandable that accuracy in record keeping has been a challenge.

With that said, even the government admits that the church is growing rapidly, as it has been for decades.[6] Particularly since government has taken steps to be more cooperative with the Church in recent years, it has been slightly easier to practice ones Christian faith in Vietnam. "The rapid spread of Christianity in the last two decades, especially among ethnic minorities in the Northwest and Central Highlands, has alarmed Vietnamese government officials."[7] In some areas, the reaction to this growth is harsher than other areas, but overall there is more or less a trend to make progress towards religious freedoms, though a necessary caveat is the great degree of uncertainty attached to this commitment. "Vietnam is a country in transition and seeks strong ties with the U.S. for economic and geopolitical reasons," and seems to have made the calculated decision to act in ways to further develop its prosperity.[8]

HISTORICAL BACKGROUND OF CHRISTIANITY IN VIETNAM

Catholics have a long history in Vietnam, going back to the 1500s when the first Franciscans missionaries arrived.[9] According to New Catholic Encyclopedia,

---

[6] *Id.*

[7] Institute for Global Engagement, Vietnam, available at https://globalengage.org/relational-diplomacy/countries/vietnam (last accessed 7 Sept. 2015).

[8] *Id.*

[9] Galli, 28.

Full-scale missionary activity commenced with the arrival of another contingent of Jesuits in 1624. Leading this contingent was Alexander de Rhodes, SJ (1593–1660), known as the "apostle of Vietnam." De Rhodes made his way to Hà Nội in 1627, where he encountered extraordinary success, baptizing the king's sister and about 6,700 Vietnamese in three years. In 1630, he was expelled and the first Christian (unnamed) was beheaded for the faith. De Rhodes returned to Vietnam in 1639, reporting that there were now 100,000 Vietnamese Catholics. The influx of new missionaries from the Paris Foreign Mission Society led to a period of swift growth.[10]

Christianity may not have been embraced with open arms by everyone in Vietnam, but those who did embrace it often did so enthusiastically. The amount of Christians multiplied at high numbers early on, and only six years after the arrival of De Rhodes, the first Christian was martyred. Clearly, one converted in Vietnam not to gain prominence in society or because it is popular, because being a Christian in 17th century Vietnam could cause one to pay the ultimate price.

Despite these real drawbacks, Christianity grew. Though there have been periods of relative tranquility under different rulers, the Church in Vietnam has known more trials and tribulations than peace. It would be over two centuries after the first Catholic missionary set foot in Vietnam that there would be some governmental protection for Catholics. Roman Catholicism persisted

---

[10] St John, 300.

in the face of recurrent, often severe persecutions until religious freedom for all Christians was finally guaranteed by treaties with the French regime in the late nineteenth century.[11] As in other Asian countries under colonial rule, Christianity was encouraged. Under colonial rule Catholicism established a solid position within Vietnamese society as the French authorities encouraged its propagation as a balance to Buddhism as well as a vehicle to promote Western culture.[12]

But this protected status would not remain. Vietnamese history as described by the Conference of Bishops of Vietnam is as follows:

> In the beginning, although Catholicism was considered Western religion, it was received in tranquility, even with the curiosity. But then, from the misunderstanding that those who followed western religions would deny their traditional customs as well as not be loyal to the Royal Court any more, the authority promulgated decrees banning Catholicism. The persecutions have broken out with innumerable arrests, imprisonments and killings throughout four centuries, under three dynasties. A lot of Vietnamese Catholics have shed their blood so as to witness their faith. There were about 130,000 people to die as martyrs by a variety of tortures and sufferings.

For generations of Vietnamese families, this brutality was severe and unrelenting. Yet Church history from the time of the very first

---

[11] St John, 566–67.

[12] *Id.*

Christians has showed that where persecution exists, the faith flourishes. As early Church Father Tertullian notably said, "the blood of the martyrs is the seeds of Christians."[13] Throughout the 17th and 18th centuries there were sporadic, but heavy persecutions, in which hundreds of thousands of Christians lost their lives. During the 19th century, a total of almost 300,000 Christians suffered for their faith.[14] In the face of this suffering, many courageously chose to make a stand. These examples of bravery are inspirational. For example, many priests continued their ministries in secret, knowing that at any time if they were captured, death would almost certainly follow.

The official count of all of those who suffered through this time will never be known. Any records that existed were subsequently destroyed. The figures that are known from one period in the 20th century are from beautifications that occurred. A total of 117 martyrs, comprising 96 Vietnamese, 11 Spanish Dominicans, and 10 French members of the Paris Foreign Mission Society, were beatified on four different occasions (64 on May 27,1900, 8 on April 20, 1906, 20 s on May 2, 1909 and 25 on April 29, 1951).[15] Of these 117, 8 were bishops, 50 priests (15 Dominicans, 8 members of the Paris Foreign Mission Society, 27 seculars), 1 seminarian, and 58 lay people (9 Dominican tertiaries and 17 catechists). On June 19, 1988, Pope John Paul II canonized these "117 Martyrs of Vietnam."[16] These martyrs, once only special to Vietnamese Catholics, many whom lived by their example, are now celebrated by the universal Church. Their model of

---

[13] CBCV, History of the Catholic Church in Vietnam.

[14] St John, 501–02.

[15] *Id.*

[16] *Id.*

bravery speaks to those who suffer persecution in any place and in any time.

VIETNAM WAR AND THE AFTERMATH FOR VIETNAMESE CATHOLICS

The Church in the North

In the wake of the political situation in Vietnam, and the isolation the Church in the North experienced from 1954-1975, religious life drastically changed for Vietnamese Christians. Cut off from the Church in the south and the Church of Rome for over 2 decades, persecuted by the Communist government, and devastated by the departure of more than half a million laity and clergy in the 1954 exodus, the Church in the north barely survived with only slightly more than half of the Catholic population remaining.[17] These members fled in search for a new home, if only at least temporary, where they could live in peace.

Private property was also susceptible to seizure by the government, including property belonging to the Catholic Church. After 1954 the Communist government confiscated the Church's social and cultural institutions, and confined the clergy and religious to strictly religious activities.[18] There would be no public ministry that did not first require governmental authorization. Priests could not freely offer the sacraments. In the aftermath of the Communist victory over the south in 1975, there was another massive exodus, with more than 1.5 million Vietnamese fleeing to foreign countries,

---

[17] *Id.*

[18] *Id.*

especially to the United States.[19] In northern Vietnam in 1975, there were few hopeful prospects for the Catholic faithful.

After 1986, however, there were finally some official changes that would impact Church life in the North, when the government began a policy of liberalization.[20] With reforms ushered in by the Second Vatican Council, the liturgy began to be adapted to the Vietnamese culture.

> Of special note are new translations of the Liturgy of the Hours and the Roman Missal (the new version has been in use throughout the country since 1992). Deserving the highest praise is a modern translation of the New Testament with scholarly introduction and notes, the fruit of 20 years of labor by a team of 14 translators. Thirty thousand copies of this 1,299-page volume, published in August 1994, were sold out immediately. The translation of the Old Testament has also been completed.[21]

With religious literature and liturgical books being published in revised translations, Vietnamese authorities were more open to tolerating them. Bibles, catechisms, and liturgical books no longer needed to be smuggled to the north at great personal risk as "counterrevolutionary propaganda."[22] These positive developments did not automatically usher in a new era of freedom, but they were

---

[19] *Id.*

[20] *Id.*, 501.

[21] *Id.*, 506.

[22] *Id.*, 501

steps in the right direction. Nearly 20 years later, the Vietnamese government still does not grant full religious freedoms.

The Church in the South

Whereas the Church in the North suffered significantly in the period beginning with the 1950's, this was not the case in the South. Not only did it benefit from the massive influx of Catholics in 1954, it also enjoyed twenty years of freedom (1955–75) which coincided with a period of radical renewal in the Catholic Church.[23] After the reunification of the country, when universal policies would be implanted, the South began to experience more control of religious life. Principally, the government required control over all religious organizations and also required that Christians obtain permission for many religious activities, such as the celebration of holidays, or catechism classes, etc.[24] These controls would remain in place for some time, but like in the North, some of the restrictions began to loosen in the late 1980s.

A decree issued on March 21, 1991, stated that religious activities such as prayer meetings, liturgical celebrations, preaching, and religious education that were in accord with local religious tradition and had been listed in the annual programs registered with the government no longer required permission.[25] In theory, this allowance seemed to offer much by way of religious freedom, but this was not the case. In practice, there has existed greater freedom in big

---

[23] *Id.*, 502.

[24] *Id.*

[25] *Id.*

cities, whereas in areas the government still considers unsafe, such as the western mountainous region, difficulties persist.[26] As the majority of Vietnamese population resides in these rural areas, this problem is larger than one might think. Despite the government control and restrictions, the Church in south has continued to grow in the two ecclesiastical provinces in the south, Huế and Hồ Chí Minh, although the percentage of Catholics relative to overall population has decreased.[27] Catholics in the South and in the North still face encumbering restrictions.

CULTURE AND SPIRITUALITY

Vietnamese culture has been fairly diverse when it comes to the practice of religion. The Vietnamese government recognizes six official religions: Buddhism, Catholicism, Protestantism, Islam, and two indigenous religious traditions that emerged during the colonial period, Cao Dai and Hoa Hao.[28] Of these six, Buddhism is the most pronounced, with over 70% of its population considering itself at least nominally Buddhist.[29] Christians account for a minority in Vietnam, but its history and sacrifices bear the testimony of a devout minority. Despite the differences among these religious philosophies, basically all Vietnamese share in common a worship of spirits. They believe the most important spirits are the souls of the ancestors, and

---

[26] *Id.*

[27] *Id.*

[28] Shaun Kingsley Malarney, 2426.

[29] Malarney, 2426.

as such, almost all families have altars in their homes where they perform rites for family ancestors.[30]

Vietnamese Christian life, as already established, is impaired by significant restrictions, and spiritual life is naturally affected in this way.

> Church activities are mostly limited to sacramental celebrations and pious devotions, without much impact on the socio-political and cultural order. Religious education consists mainly in teaching prayers and question-and-answer catechism class in preparation for first communion and confirmation. Instruction is most often given by the elders in the parish who, deprived of all opportunities for religious training since 1954, have not had access to the documents of the Second Vatican Council.[31]

The spirituality of the Vietnamese Church may be hindered by the challenges of resources and catechesis, but even still, it continues to grow. Phan writes, "Christian faith is nourished predominantly by the family with its practice of the daily recitation of morning and evening prayers. Prayers most often include the rosary, litanies, prayers to the patron saints (especially St. Joseph), the *Miserere* (Psalm 51) for the ancestors, and the acts of faith, hope, and

---

[30] Malarney, 2426.

[31] Peter C. Phan, "How Much Uniformity Can We Stand? How Much Unity Do We Want? Church and Worship in the Next, Millennium," *Worship* 72, no. 3 (1998), 199.

charity." [32] These popular devotions, in addition to and most especially the sacrifice of the Mass, all contribute to nourish the lives of the Vietnamese faithful. The Mass, though different than what may feel inherently Vietnamese, has been heartily embraced, even though the liturgical expressions are of foreign origin. In reference to the experience of the Mass in one of the Vietnamese tribes (Co Ho), Phan eloquently writes,

> Despite its strangeness and anomalies, the Mass achieves something unimaginable. It creates a profound unity, a union of mind and heart among the people of the Co Ho tribe that transcends time, space, race, gender, and class. It effects a union that binds them to the Vietnamese priest who celebrates the Mass with them, to the pope and the local bishop for whom they pray, to the Jews whom they have never met and probably never will but from whose Scripture they read, to the early church of the Apostles whose gospels and letters are proclaimed to them, to the present church worldwide, to the living and the dead, to the angels and saints, and to the persons of the divine Trinity themselves. [33]

In addition, the Vietnamese have also developed a strong devotion to the Blessed Virgin Mary, known to them as *Our Lady of La Vang* or *Our Lady of Vietnam.* The origin of how she came to be known as such goes back to the 18th century. The events unfolded as follows: "On Aug. 17,

---

[32] *Id.*

[33] *Id.*

1798, King Cảnh Thịnh issued an edict ordering the immediate execution of all Catholics in his realm. As persecution erupted, a group of Catholic refugees from neighboring villages escaped into the jungles of La Vang. According to the received tradition, one night, a beautiful and radiant lady with a compassionate countenance appeared to the frightened and starving refugees by a huge, old tree as they were praying for deliverance from their persecutors and protection from wild beasts. Calling herself the 'Blessed Mother' (*Đứ Mẹ*), she comforted and encouraged them to keep their faith in Jesus Christ, taught them how to collect herbs in the forest as medicine, and promised to intercede to her Son on their behalf."[34]

This site in La Vang would then become a pilgrimage site that would one day regularly draw hundreds of thousands. In the years since, buildings and edifices that have been constructed on this location have by destroyed and rebuilt throughout the years of violence; however, some structures were destroyed and never rebuilt. In 1959 La Vang was officially declared the National Shrine of Our Lady of Vietnam, marking 300 years of the Church's presence in Vietnam. [35] It is in honor of Our Lady of La Vang, that Vietnamese Catholics make the journey to this sacred site, and that also inspired for Vietnamese Americans what has now become an annual tradition in Carthage, Missouri. The annual Marian Days pilgrimage celebration every August, mirrored after the traditional Marian Days

---

[34] V.T. Pham, "La Vang, Our Lady of," *New Catholic Encyclopedia*, 2nd ed., vol. 8 (Detroit: Gale, 2003), 385–86.

[35] *Id.*

pilgrimage to La Vang, draws an estimated 50,000 Vietnamese Catholics to Carthage, Missouri each year.[36]

CHALLENGES FACED BY THE VIETNAMESE CHURCH

The country has had an atrocious human-rights record since the
end of the Vietnam War in 1975 and even as recent as the 2012 has
been listed as a Country of Particular Concern in the Annual Report
from the US Commission on International Religious Freedom. The
report cites that "individuals continue to be imprisoned or detained
for reasons related to their religious activity or religious freedom
advocacy; independent religious activity remains illegal; legal
protections for government-approved religious organizations are
both vague and subject to arbitrary or discriminatory interpretations
based on political factors"[37] and so on. When considering what
obstacles the Catholic Church in Vietnam faces today, clearly at the
forefront concerns the right to freely practice ones faith.

The stark reality for a Christian in Vietnam involves significant
sacrifice, even with recent improvements that may be rooted in
political and economic incentives. Consider this typical scenario: A
Vietnamese man becomes a Christian. He refuses to offer sacrifices
to his family ancestors any longer. His father dies, and his brothers
claim the family property, excluding the Christian because he has
essentially disowned the family. The Christian sues and demands his

---

[36] *Id.*

[37] United States Commission on International Religious Freedom,
"Vietnam," *available at* http://www.uscirf.gov/images/Annual%20Report
%20of%20USCIRF%202012(2).pdf (last accessed 7 Sept. 2015).

rights as a son. This is just a small consequence of religious freedom that the government has got to get used to.[38] The government still shows that it has a long way to go until there is social justice is upheld.

In addition to the challenges inherent in the struggle for more freedoms, the Vietnamese Church is the condition of the poor. In a backdrop of conflicting discussions between extreme communists and extreme capitalists, the principles of Catholic social teaching are being lost on society. Connected with this must be a decisive "option for the poor," which the Vietnamese hierarchy has consistently urged upon Church members in its pastoral letters.[39]

As previously discussed, catechesis is another area of concern, with materials in many places outdated or inexistent. It is, therefore, an immediate task to train or, as the case may be, re-train the clergy and religious, and through them, the laity in all aspects of theology and ministry.[40] The lack of qualified professors, however, is severe, and the level of academic preparation is far from satisfactory. In general, since 1954 in the north, and since 1975 in the south, there has been little serious intellectual formation for the clergy, as the government has permitted a few priests to go to France, Rome and the United States for advanced studies.[41] Stressing the priority of this objective is the following eloquent remark: "It is easy to be seduced

---

[38] Galli, 32.

[39] St John, 506-507; V.T. Pham, J.Y. Tan, & P.C. Phan, "Vietnam, The Catholic Church in," *New Catholic Encyclopedia*, 2nd ed, vol. 14 (Detroit: Gale, 2003), 499–507.

[40] St John, 506–07.

[41] *Id.*, 505.

by external achievements such as the building of churches and other structures. Far more important is the building of the Church by means of what a Vietnamese archbishop calls the "living bricks" of personnel."[42]

STRUCTURE

Despite a history in the country for over three hundred years, the official hierarchy of the Church in Vietnam was not established until the 20th century. On November 24, 1960 Pope John XXIII established the Vietnamese Hierarchy with Apostolic Constitution "Venerabilium Nostrorum", marking the maturity stage of the Church in Việt Nam.[43]

Before 1975 the Vietnamese Episcopal Conference, which, though called Vietnamese, in fact consisted only of the two ecclesiastical provinces of the south, (Huế and Hồ Chí Minh City) held annual meetings regularly. After national unification in 1976, the conference temporarily suspended its activities. In May 1980, the conference met officially for the first time in Hà Nội, and by September of 1994 there had been seven such meetings. Each meeting and its location

---

[42] *Id.*, 506–507.

[43] Catholic Bishops' Conference of Vietnam [CBCV], History of the Catholic Church in Vietnam, *available at* http://www.cbcvietnam.org/ History/history-of-the-catholic-church-in-vietnam.html (last accessed 7 Sept. 2015).

required permission of the government.[44]

These leaders managed the delicate task of ministering to the needs of the Vietnamese people, while toeing a careful balance with the authorities. Not only was permission needed for religious education, Masses, ordinations, etc., but property that once belonged to the Church has been confiscated by the government at different times. After 1975 all major seminaries were shut down, and the seminary property was confiscated by the government. [45] Though some of these seminaries have reopened in the time since, there is an ongoing discussion among the Vietnamese about the restoration of property once taken over by the government that still has not been returned.

In total today, according to the Conference of Vietnamese Bishops, there are eight seminaries in Vietnam, with the newest one celebrated upon its 2012 opening, throughout northern, central, and southern dioceses St. Joseph Major Seminary in Hồ Chí Minh City.[46] The seminary building was built in 1863, then rebuilt in 1963. It reopened in 1986 to train seminarians from six southern dioceses. Since 2006, it has recruited only students from Hồ Chí Minh City Archdiocese and two Dioceses of Mỹ Tho and Phú Cường. The seminary got government permission for annual recruitment in 2007. On March 19, 2012, the first stone laying ceremony of the seminary's

---

[44] St John, 503.

[45] *Id.*, 505.

[46] Online at http://www.cbcvietnam.org/Seminaries/st-joseph-major-seminary-in-ho-chi-minh-city.html

new block was celebrated.[47] The fact that this addition has been authorized is an important step for the future education of Vietnam's seminarians and is a cause for much joy and hope.

POPULAR FIGURES

The Vietnamese Church has benefitted by the example of many brave priests, religious, and laity who exemplified the Christian ideal so well, and in some instances, to the point of giving everything. Some of these witnesses to the faith have been publicly honored by the Vatican in recent decades. In 1998, Pope John Paul II solemnly canonized 117 Blessed Martyrs of Vietnam, including 8 bishops, 50 priests, 16 catechists, one seminarian, 41 laymen and one laywoman.[48] One principal saint to be included among these is St. Andrew Dung Lac, who was a popular diocesan priest. Their feast is celebrated on November 24.

Another prominent figure in Vietnamese Catholic Spirituality is Cardinal François-Xavier Nguyen Van Thuan. In 1975, when Cardinal Van Thuan was first appointed as bishop, he was sentenced to 13 years in a "re-education camp," nine years of which had been spent in solitary confinement. [49] As a testimony of the witness of the

---

[47] CBCV, St Joseph Major Seminary in Hồ Chí Minh City, *available at* http://www.cbcvietnam.org/Seminaries/st-joseph-major-seminary-in-ho-chi-minh-city.html (last accessed 7 Sept. 2015).

[48] CBCV, History of the Catholic Church in Vietnam.

[49]"Remembering Cardinal Van Thuan: The Most Important Testimony We Can Offer Is Our Forgiveness," Rome Reports (16 Sept. 2011), *available*

faith he expressed to others in all situations, while he was in prison, the government actually had to replace the guards, because one by one, they too became Catholic. On 16 September 2007, the fifth anniversary of the Cardinal Nguyễn Văn Thuận death, the Roman Catholic Church began the beatification process for him.[50] Cardinal Van Thuan remains one of the most celebrated Catholic leaders in recent history.

FUTURE OUTLOOK

Despite the reality of continued repression, there have been significant first steps in the past few years. In January 2013, the General Secretary of the Communist Party of Vietnam paid a visit to Pope Benedict XVI at the Vatican, marking an important milestone. The Vatican reported that the leaders had "cordial discussions," which touched on "topics of interest to Vietnam and the Holy See ... expressing the hope that some pending situations may be resolved and that the existing fruitful cooperation may be strengthened."[51] This encounter gives hope that the tensions that exist that date back to the rise of Vietnamese communism may finally be beginning to

---

at http://www.romereports.com/2011/09/16/remembering-cardinal-van-thuan-the-most-important-testimony-we-can-offer-is-our-forgiveness.

[50] CBCV, History of the Catholic Church in Vietnam.

[51] CBCV, Vietnamese Leader Visits Benedict XVI (25 Jan. 2013), *available at* http://www.cbcvietnam.org/Vietnam-Church-News/vietnamese-leader-visits-benedict-xvi.html.

thaw,[52] as this was the first time in decades since there have been official diplomatic relations between the two. More gradual signs have been apparent that inspire a certain hopefulness in dealing with the Vietnamese government, but this encounter is one of the more positive indicators yet of a hopeful turn for the better for the nation's Catholics and other religious minorities.

There will be many issues to work through with respect to the clergy in Vietnam, principally on the subject of the appointment of bishops. The Vatican and the communist leadership in Hanoi have long clashed over who holds the power to appoint bishops in Vietnam's 6-million-strong church, but in recent years, the two sides have settled on an agreement under which Hanoi nominates three candidates and the pope chooses one.[53] While on the surface, it might seem there is great compromise, the true freedom that is needed to fully practice the faith is still greatly impeded by these ecclesial limitations.

If the Vietnam Church is left to operate independently, some in the Vietnamese government fear it will import the Western Church and adopt its ways. The Catholic Church in Vietnam will not be the twin of the Church in the U.S. or any other nation, however. There are inherent differences in these society and culture for better and for worse. Whereas the Vietnamese, like most Asian cultures, emphasize community and stability, Westerners exalt the individual. It's hard to imagine that a culturally grounded religious freedom in Vietnam will

---

[52] "Vatican Strengthens Ties with Vietnam but Not with China," Christian Century 124, no. 4 (2007), 17.

[53] *Id.*

ever mimic the U.S. model.[54] The Vietnamese Church, left to its own devices, will share in communion with the universal Church on faith and morals, but how these are expressed will reflect a spirituality that is as unique as the religious experience of the Vietnamese has been.

The Christian Vietnamese religious experience bears undeniable testament to a willingness to whole-heartedly embrace the Church of Jesus Christ, to endure sacrifice and tribulations in the name of this Christian faith, and to peacefully and justly defend the full freedom that this faith demands. Instead of refusing to cooperate with authorities on principle because of these injustices, many in the Vietnamese clergy are urging cooperation and patience. The model that Cardinal Van Thuan offers on the way forward may perhaps be the one that will bear the most fruit. Speaking on how it is that he endured his years at the hands of the Vietnamese prison, he said:

> I just did what I could, that is, to bear witness to my faith and especially the love of Christ. I think that's the only thing that can change hearts... The most important testimony we can give is love, forgiveness and reconciliation. To forget the past and look ahead so we can build our country together and build a world that's more beautiful... the future is much more exciting than the past.[55]

---

[54] Galli, 32.

[55] "Remembering Cardinal Van Thuan."

About the Contributors

Caitlin Seadale Celella is the director of the English as a Second Language program at Holy Apostles College & Seminary in Cromwell, CT.

Fr. Allan Figueroa Deck, S.J., is currently Distinguished Scholar of Theology and Latino Studies at Loyola Marymount University and Professor of Theological Studies. He has served as the executive director of the USCCB Office of Cultural Diversity.

Dr. Robert Nyeko Obol was born in December, 1971, in Kitgum District. A priest of the archdiocese of Gulu, Dr. Obol completed his training for the Catholic priesthood in his home country of Uganda and was ordained a priest on August 18, 2001. He resides in Kansas City, Kansas, and he is a spiritual care provider to the sick.

Rev. Aniedi Okure, O.P., is the Executive Director of Africa Faith & Justice Network (AFJN: www.afjn.org) and an instructor at Loyola Marymount University Cultural Orientation Program for International Ministers (COPIM). He co-authored *International Priests in America: Challenges and Opportunities* (2006) with Dean Hoge.

Christina Price, Christina Pride is an Agapè Catholic Ministries Facilitator for Sacramental Prep, and a graduate of St. Joseph's Seminary & College. Outside of catechesis, she works with migrant and refugee communities in the US and Europe, through mentorship, resource assistance, and ESL training.

Len Sperry, M.D., Ph.D., D.Min., is a professor at Florida Atlantic University and the Medical College of Wisconsin. He is board certified in psychiatry and clinical psychology and consults for dioceses and religious communities.

Paul Turnley is an ex-Jesuit scholastic, who spent much of his business career as a Catholic Executive Director of various Protestant and interfaith organizations. He studied theology at Holy Apostles College & Seminary in Cromwell, CT.

Elizabeth Carrow Woolfolk, Ph.D. is a speech and language specialist with 50 years' experience as a clinician, professor and author of text books in language theory, assessment and intervention, and of tests for spoken and written language. She was on the faculty at Our Lady of the Lake University, Baylor College of Medicine and retired as head of the program in communication science and disorders at The University of Texas in Austin.

About the Editors

Dr. Sebastian Mahfood, OP

Professor of Interdisciplinary Studies,
Holy Apostles College & Seminary

Dr. Sebastian Mahfood, OP, is Associate Director of the Parresia Project, Vice-President of External Affairs and Professor of Interdisciplinary Studies at Holy Apostles College & Seminary in Cromwell, CT (https://holyapostles.edu). Dr. Mahfood has worked for over two decades in US seminaries and theological institutes advancing the work of missionary priests and seminarians from around the globe.

In addition to his work with missionary priests and seminarians in the U.S., Dr. Mahfood has made possible through a scholarship program in partnership with Metropolitan Archbishop Menghesteab Tesfamariam, MCCJ, the enrollment at Holy Apostles of five dozen Eritrean priests, religious sisters, and lay ministers in the pursuit of their graduate studies 100% online. He is presently assisting the Archdiocese of Tabora, Tanzania, in the development of an online educational program of studies (https://catbr.or.tz).

He serves as the senior co-chair of the Faith-Based Online Learning Directors group (distancelearningdirectors.org) and is the publisher at En Route (enroutebooksandmedia.com) and producer at WCAT Radio (wcatradio.com).

Most Rev. Richard Henning, S.T.D.

Auxiliary Bishop
Diocese of Rockville Centre, New York

The Most Reverend Richard G. Henning, STD is a native of Long Island, New York, where he was ordained to the priesthood for the Diocese of Rockville Centre in 1992. After pastoral work in English and Spanish at St. Peter of Alcantara Parish, he began graduate studies in biblical theology, earning a Licentiate at the Catholic University of America and a Doctorate at the University of St. Thomas Aquinas in Rome.

Bishop Henning served for ten years as a Professor at the Seminary of the Immaculate Conception. During those years, Bishop Henning partnered with Dr. Sebastian Mahfood to establish and oversee the Parresia Project. This multi-year project provided conferences for clergy personnel and formation leaders and promoted the incorporation of distance learning methodologies into the process of providing orientation to arriving international priests and the communities they serve.

In 2012, Bishop Henning was appointed Director of the Sacred Heart Institute for the Ongoing Formation of the Clergy. While serving as an adjunct Professor at St. Joseph's Seminary in Yonkers, he was also entrusted with the direction of a major retreat house on Long Island at the Seminary of the Immaculate Conception.

In 2018, Pope Francis appointed Bishop Henning as an auxiliary bishop. In the Diocese of Rockville Centre, Bishop Henning is a regional Vicar as well as Vicar for Pastoral Planning and Parish Evangelization. He is a trustee of St. Joseph's Seminary in Yonkers,

NY. In the USCCB, he serves on the Doctrine Committee, the Subcommittee on Translation of Scripture Text, and the Subcommittee of National Collections for the Church in Latin America.